D1279818

THE BUSINESS LIBRARY

AND HOW TO USE IT

A guide to sources and research strategies
for information on business and management.

THE BUSINESS LIBRARY

AND HOW TO USE IT

A guide to sources and research strategies
for information on business and management.

Ernest L. Maier
Anthony J. Faria
Peter Kaatrude
Elizabeth Wood

Omnigraphics, Inc.

Penobscot Building
Detroit, Michigan 48226

Ernest L. Maier, Anthony J. Faria, Peter Kaatrude, and Elizabeth Wood,
Authors
Special editorial assistance by Barry Puckett

Omnigraphics, Inc.

***

Laurie Lanzen Harris, *Vice President, Editorial Director*
Peter E. Ruffner, *Vice President, Administration*
James A. Sellgren, *Vice President, Operations and Finance*
Jane Steele, *Vice President, Research*

***

Frederick G. Ruffner, Jr., *Publisher*

The information in this publication was compiled from the sources cited and from other sources considered reliable. While every possible effort has been made to ensure reliability, the publisher will not assume liability for damages caused by inaccuracies in the data, and makes no warranty, express or implied, on the accuracy of the information contained herein.

This book is printed on acid-free paper meeting the ANSI Z39.48 Standard. The infinity symbol that appears above indicates that the paper in this book meets that standard.

Printed in the United States

Contents

Preface

The Business Library and How to Use It, first published in 1951 as *How to Use the Business Library*, has been the reliable companion of business students, librarians and practitioners for over four decades. This newest edition, the sixth, builds upon this long tradition while encompassing numerous changes that have impacted the modern business library.

The Plan of the Work

The book is divided into four sections. Section One, **Introduction to Business Research and the Library,** helps the researcher get to know the library and introduces strategies and tools for research. Section Two, **Research Strategies and General Sources of Business Information**, reviews types of research materials, including books, indexes, and databases. Section Three, **Specific Sources of Business Information,** features extensive descriptive listings focusing on traditional and non-traditional business sources, ranging from handbooks and directories to on-line library catalogs, CD-ROMS, and audiovisual programs. This section also includes a chapter on international sources and concentrated coverage of government resources. Section Four, **Using What You've Learned**, outlines how to use the research tools and strategies outlined in the book to write a business report.

Indexes

To provide access to specific areas of interest, *The Business Library and How to Use It* includes a Subject Index, Author/Title Index, and Organization and Association Index.

Although *The Business Library and How to Use It* can be used very effectively by the business student and read chapter by chapter, numerous cross-references are available for the practitioner who is searching for an explanation of a single concept or source to answer a question.

Your Comments Are Welcome

The diverse and experienced authorship team, with backgrounds in library science and business, takes pride in offering this latest edition for your needs. We welcome the comments and suggestions of readers to expand the scope and increase the usefulness of future editions.

Ernest L. Maier
Professor of Marketing
Lawrence Technological University
Southfield, Michigan 48075

Peter B. Kaatrude
Dean of Library Services
Lamar University
Port Arthur, TX 77640

Anthony J. Faria
Professor of Marketing
University of Windsor
Windsor, Ontario
Canada, N9B 3P4

Elizabeth Wood
Head, Library Information Services
Bowling Green State University
Bowling Green, OH 43403

This edition is dedicated to H. Webster Johnson, Professor Emeritus, Wayne State University, and his wife, Josephine, for their combined efforts over thirty years in developing the first five editions of this book.

SECTION ONE

INTRODUCTION TO BUSINESS RESEARCH AND THE LIBRARY

Getting to Know the Library

OBJECTIVES: This chapter will give the business researcher a brief orientation to the library.

Benefits of Library Orientation
How Things Work
- The Building Layout, Operating Hours, and Rules: a Checklist
- Classification Systems: a Checklist
- Library of Congress and Dewey Classifications

Identifying Valuable Information
- The Library Catalog: a Checklist
- Hi-Tech Versus Low-Tech Catalog Systems
  Ways to search
  Computerized catalogs
  Card catalogs
- Indexes
  Printed indexes
  Online computerized indexes
  Compact disk-based indexes
  Choosing the right index

Finding Library Material
- Finding Books
- Finding Periodicals
- Finding Other Non-Book Materials

Alternatives to the Library Collection
- Interlibrary Loan
- Library Information Brokers
- Fulltext Databases
- Other Document Delivery Options

Integrated Research Tools
Library Networks
- National
- Regional, State, and Local

The Library Staff
- Reference Assistance: a Checklist
- The Reference Desk

After completing this chapter you should be able to:

*Get your bearings in a library by asking key questions about the building, services offered, and library materials available.

*Know what functions the library catalog and indexes have in the research process.

*Plan how to get important library materials not available in your library.

BENEFITS OF LIBRARY ORGANIZATION

Doing business research is not unlike choosing a new car, new home, or new job. These endeavors represent a major investment of time and/or money and have considerable potential impact on one's future. Therefore, it is necessary to understand how and where the best information can be gathered. The payoffs for learning your way around the library include significant savings of time and sometimes money. Even more important to both the business person and the serious business student is the quality difference in the final "product" (a business plan, marketing campaign, cost/benefit analysis, class presentation, computer simulation game, or written report). When you understand the library system and you can harness the full power of its resources, the product of your research will show a mastery of key facts, ideas, and data.

Please note that timing is important. Only persons who thrive on high levels of stress will care to combine getting a sense of how the library works with completing their library research. Most will benefit from getting to know the library before starting a research project.

HOW THINGS WORK: LIBRARY BASICS

A necessary first step for the business researcher is finding out how the library works: where various parts of the collection are located (books, newspapers, computer software, etc.), where to go for services (checking out books, photocopying, asking for help, and borrowing materials from other libraries), and when the collection and services are available.

The Building: Layout, Operating Hours, and Rules

Getting to know the hours of operation and the layout of the building will save you lots of frustration and lost time. Following is a brief checklist of things to find out about library operations:

Physical Layout/Hours Checklist

1) What are regular library hours? Are there shorter or longer hours for holidays, exam times, or breaks? Are some areas and services open for shorter periods than the rest of the building?
2) How many buildings or separate areas are there? What is unique about each—subjects covered, level of difficulty (graduate, undergraduate), or something else?
3) Circulation: How long can books be kept? Can periodicals be borrowed? Are fines charged for overdue materials? Is there a reserve reading room (for supplementary material assigned to entire classes of students)?
4) Where are important services located?

a) Circulation (for checking out books, getting on a waiting list for circulating books, etc.)

b) Stack maintenance area, sometimes part of circulation (for help finding books not on the shelf)

c) Change desk or machine

d) Typing or word processing facilities, if available

e) Media production facilities (slides, transparencies, etc.),

If available:
- Lockers
- Quiet study areas
- Food and beverage vending machines
- Photocopying facilities
- Reference desk
- Business reference desk, if separate
- Business Librarian, if there is a specialist
- Interlibrary loan office (for borrowing items owned by other libraries)
- Computer searching services
- Library Director's office (to pay a compliment, lodge a complaint, ask about policy, etc.)

In addition to looking around the building and asking questions, keep an eye out for orientation materials prepared by the library. They range from booklets to walking tours, slide programs, hypercard programs, and interactive videos.

Classification Systems: a Checklist

Although libraries often seem like mazes to new users, they are more or less logically arranged. (There are, of course, arbitrary aspects of any system of organization.) The following is a list of things to discover about how different types of library materials are classified and organized:

Classification/Organization of the Collection Checklist

1) What classification systems are used for arranging books, government documents, periodicals and other types of material on library shelves? (See the section of this chapter headed **Library of Congress and Dewey Classification Systems** for a brief explanation.)

2) In what physical locations will you find the following items?
- circulating books
- reference books
- government documents
    - periodicals (bound, unbound, microform)
    - audiovisual material (slides, films, videos, audio materials)

- computer-based material (software, machine-readable data sets on floppy disk or magnetic tape)

3) Are older books and periodicals housed in a storage area? How long does retrieval take?

4) Where can you find what periodical titles the library owns as well as details about inclusive years of holdings for each title (with starting and ending dates and any gaps in coverage)?

5) How can you determine what is the latest issue of a given periodical received by the library? Where can current issues be found? Is this area self-service or is it restricted in some way?

Library of Congress and Dewey Classification Systems

Libraries have one or more classification systems, whereby materials in given subject areas are grouped together under a common system of identification letters and numbers. Such classification systems for books comprise the conceptual framework for organizing the library. (Regrettably books sometimes are found under more than one system in the *same* library, where a new classification system was adopted but staff time and money were not sufficient for converting records into a single system.) The time-honored phrase "call number" (dating from when shelving areas were closed except to library staff who would retrieve items "called for" or requested by users) is still universally used to mean book identification number.

In large academic libraries, the Library of Congress or "L.C." Classification system, beginning with a pattern of one or two letters, is common. Most business and economic topics will be assigned "H", "HA", "HB", and so on through "HG". In public libraries and smaller academic ones, the arrangement may be either L.C. or the Dewey Decimal System. Dewey starts out with a pattern of numbers (358, 650, and so on for business topics). In either classification system, after the subject classification number, there are additional code lines based on the author or editor's name and the book title. These lines are called "Cutter" numbers. Please see Chapter 2, "Strategies and Tools for Locating Materials," for the outline of both Dewey and L.C.

Writing down the complete call number as it is given is crucial to locating the needed item. Once the item has been found, browsing for more information in the same shelf location can be a good idea. But just browsing will almost never retrieve all relevant information on a topic.

SO MUCH INFORMATION, SO LITTLE TIME

The two most pressing problems you will have as a business researcher are identifying the key sources of information for your topic (timely, comprehensive, and relevant information) and getting copies of those sources.

The Library Catalog

Whenever you are exploring a new library system, the library catalog is a good place to start. Even if you are aware of a good information source (article, speech, or government hearing) you still need to locate and obtain it. If you are investigating a new topic or updating a familiar one, the library catalog will tell you what pertinent resources exist and where the resources are located. Following is a checklist of questions to ask about the catalog:

Catalog Information Checklist

1) Where is the library catalog?
2) Is the catalog computer-searchable? Are all of the library's materials entered into one database? If not, what separate databases or files must be consulted?
3) Are the titles of journals and other periodicals owned by the library included in the catalog? Is information about periodical holdings (which years or volumes the library owns) given in the catalog?
4) Are any research systems besides the library catalog accessible through the same terminals (other libraries, campus news and current events information, menu-driven online searching databases)?
5) What on-screen aids, handouts and/or instruction are available for learning to use the computerized catalog system?
6) Are there printers and/or facilities for downloading data?
7) Is there dial-up access from your dorm, apartment, office, or computer lab?
8) Is there a card catalog? Are author, title, and subject cards all filed together, or are the card drawers or cabinets separated in some way (a "divided" catalog)? Is the card catalog kept updated as new materials are bought and old ones are discarded or moved to different locations?

Hi-Tech and Low-Tech Catalog Systems

All libraries used to have a main database, the library catalog or *"card catalog"*, for locating books and most other materials distributed less than once per year (for example, yearbooks and encyclopedias). Other *physical formats*, e.g. audiovisual materials such as movies, slides, or microfilms, might have been in the main catalog or might have been in one or more separate card files. Some libraries still use cards. But larger academic institutions and some progressive smaller ones are either operating a computerized library catalog side-by-side with the card catalog or else have abandoned cards altogether.

Ways to Search

No matter what type of catalog system is available, the essentials of searching are the same. If the *author or title* of a work is known, the catalog will verify its location in the library collection. Works unfamiliar to the researcher can be identified through a *subject or topic search*.

7

Computerized Catalogs

One advantage of computerized catalogs is that they offer additional ways to find useful sources, for example:

1) keyword searches based on significant words from the title and perhaps from parts of the written description of the book;
2) author-and-title combined searching to retrieve "known items" more quickly and efficiently;
3) added search keys, such as the name of a series under which individual books may be published, possibly leading the researcher to additional titles of interest.

Availability of these features varies from one institution to another. Ask if your library has them and get some hints about how to use them.

Another benefit is that computerized catalogs frequently offer information besides call number, such as:

1) whether the item has been checked out; and,
2) whether anyone else is on the waiting list to get an item in circulation.
Some catalogs even tracks books from the moment they are ordered until they are received, processed, and placed on the shelf. In addition, most computerized catalogs offer at least some access from *offsite* locations—dorms and faculty offices, as well as from home offices of library users—in addition to terminals in library buildings.

Card Catalogs

Where card catalogs are retained *and kept up-to-date*, there can be an advantage in using them for certain problems. For very large sets of catalog information (e.g. a prolific writer or a well-established body of subject literature such as management) the card catalog may be more efficient than paging backward and forward through a forest of computer screens. The most user-friendly computerized systems, however, may have "tricks" for searching even large sets quickly and efficiently; so learn your computerized system before reverting to old technology. Beware of "closed" card catalogs, ones that have not been eliminated but *are no longer updated* as items are added to or discarded from the collection.

Indexes: The Key To Relevant Articles, Documents, and Reports

Printed Indexes

Sophisticated researchers have long been accustomed to consulting printed sources called *indexes* to locate publications such as periodical articles (magazines, journals, or newspapers). Familiar examples are the all-purpose *Reader's Guide to Periodical Literature* and the more-specialized *Business Periodicals Index.* (Please note that a few indexes such as *PAIS International In Print* and *Social Sciences Citation Index*, cover books and government documents *as well as* periodicals.)

Although occasionally you will find the perfect article for your topic by flipping through current magazines and journals, the more structured approach of using an index saves time and yields better information. (Please see Chapter 5, "Indexes to Periodical Literature and Reports," for a detailed description of some of the leading business indexes.)

Indexes available in the library are commonly included in the library catalog under their respective titles, and generally *a list of all indexes owned* by the library is available as well. You can get by with the most widely read business publications covered by general interest indexes like the *Reader's Guide* for some research topics. If your library lacks more specialized business indexes, you should plan to visit a larger library for extensive research projects.

Online Computerized Indexes

Since the late 1970s, most libraries have been offering online computer searches as an alternative to manual index searching. These typically have been "intermediated searches" performed by library staff, and they often involve a substantial fee paid by the researcher. While librarian-conducted searches are still available to researchers lacking either the time or the inclination to learn complicated searching techniques, there is a growing trend toward menu-driven online search services intended for use without a librarian's help.

Compact Disk-Based Computerized Indexes (CD's or CD-ROMs)

During the 1980s, a new technology, compact-disk-type computerized indexes (for example *Compact Disclosure* and *Infotrac*), became common. Many CD indexes as well as some online computer searching services (BRS Afterdark and DIALOG's Knowledge Index, to name just two) are designed to be operated by you, the library user.

Almost anyone can generate a list of titles from a computerized index. But pulling out a manageable list (neither too few nor too many) with precise, relevant citations is a skill that comes only with good instruction and a certain amount of experience. Because researchers ("end-users" in library jargon) are now doing so much of their own computer searching, Chapter 6 of this book, "Databases and Database Searching," is devoted to database searching techniques.

What's Right for You?

You have a choice. Most libraries maintain subscriptions to indexes in printed form, even when the titles are computer-searchable.

If you have done considerable manual searching on the topic, a computer search may not add significantly to what you've found already. In addition, consultation with a librarian may reveal that your area of research is not well-covered by computerized sources or that the complexities of your topic make it unsuitable for an easy computer search.

For most topics computerized indexes give you vastly improved access to information. Besides traditional subject and/or author access points, many computerized systems allow the user to locate useful articles by restricting to fields such as title, abstract, or publication date. What is more, various aspects of a topic can be searched simultaneously. For example, most computerized databases can select specific items, such as research studies or statistics, that deal with specific subject content. Getting such precise retrieval of information in a manual search typically takes hours if not days.

Online computer searching has been a fee-based service. Many libraries place a debit-card payment system or coin box on CD printers in order to recover part of the staggering costs of ink and paper for these systems. A few charge for search time on CD's as well as for prints. But considering the savings in time, cost may not be the deciding factor.

FINDING LIBRARY MATERIAL

Business titles are frequently, although not always, integrated with the rest of a library's holdings. If a library system is very large, or if its parent institution has a well-established business department, business titles may be in a separate section of the library from the main collection or in a separate business, economics, engineering, or technology library.

Finding Books

In libraries where materials on all subjects are integrated, the call number found in the catalog directs you to a particular shelving area. To make things more of a challenge, some materials will be in a special nook or cranny you don't know about—for reasons ranging from security to age or use-patterns. Find out if there is a storage area for older materials on another floor or in an offsite location. You can find a listing of other special storage areas on this chapter's checklist of questions about the library's physical layout.

Some catalogs indicate what floors/building areas correspond to what ranges of call numbers and special location codes. (For example, A-HF on 1st floor; Social Science/Business Reference on 2nd floor; Rare Books on 5th floor). There should be a sign, chart, or map for translating call number and location codes into shelf locations.

As mentioned earlier, the best strategy for coping with this sort of complexity is copying completely any call number and location information in the catalog and then checking a key or other search aid, to decipher the codes or symbols. Staff can be a great help as well. You should make use of their expertise.

Finding Periodicals

In certain libraries, periodicals are organized with call numbers and will be found in the same area as books. In other libraries, they are kept separate from the book collection and may be arranged in any number of ways. Alphabetical order by title is common. Another possibility is classification by subject and further subdivision into alphabetical order within a given subject section. That is, alphabetical order by title of magazine or journal within a broad academic field such as Social-Sciences-and-Business or Science or Humanities. Whether or not they are integrated with books, periodicals are likely to be kept in different locations, especially with older issues that are bound or replaced with microforms.

Ask a member of the library staff whether business titles are kept with general titles such as news magazines. Find out whether current issues in paper format are housed together with older issues bound in a hard cover. Ask which titles are retained in microform (a type of reproduction in ultra-reduced format that must be re-enlarged for viewing or printing).

Discover how long current newspapers are kept and whether they are located with magazines and journals or in a microform reading room. Inquire how to tell when periodicals are at the bindery and when they're due back. Ask if library personnel will search for missing volumes/issues.

Yet another type of system the library may have for providing copies of articles is a *self-contained microfiche collection* available with some indexes. Examples are the *Newsbank* index (available in either paper or computerized form) and *Infotrac*, a computerized index. When a citation has been located in any system with its own microfiche collection, retrieving the information is simplified, not a frustrating treasure hunt through the far reaches of the library. This can make an enormous difference in how much time must be spent in the library and how far ahead one must plan.

Another technology offering copies of the text you need involves the *image processing* capability of some the computer-driven compact disc indexes, where the complete text of an article, investment recommendation, or a company annual report is mounted on an indexing system along with the citation (publication details) for that document. *ABI/Inform, Corporate and Industry Research Reports,* and *Disclosure* all are CD systems with the option of full text access to information.

If you are confused about how to obtain copies of periodical articles, *always ask!* Many a competent man or woman has been overwhelmed by the process of accessing this type of material. Librarians know this, and they try their best to compensate for any shortcomings of these particular systems.

Finding Other Non-Book Materials

The only rule about whether non-book materials (software, audiovisual media, government documents, and so on) are kept with books is that there is little consistency from one library to another.

Some *government document collections* are integrated into regular locations within the library, (shelved with commercially produced books, maps, journals, and so on). Alternatively, a collection of federal government publications is sometimes split, with only a *few* items in the L.C. or Dewey classification and the rest classified by Superintendent of Documents or "SuDoc" numbers and housed in a separate area of the library. The document call number, usually included in indexes and bibliographies covering information from the federal government, starts with a letter or combination of letters derived from the issuing agency ("C" for Commerce, "A" for Agriculture and so on). If signs or orientation material do not make document locations clear, ask a staff member.

Other non-book items such as *computer software* and *videotapes* sometimes aren't in the same building as the library. If the library does house them, like microforms and other formats requiring special equipment, they often are in a special area of the library with technicians to maintain equipment and give instruction in its use. They may or may not be included in the main library catalog. All of these questions are worth investigating.

ALTERNATIVES TO THE LIBRARY'S COLLECTION

It is an article of faith among librarians that patrons be made aware of the whole universe of published information. Accordingly, virtually all indexes and other search aids include references to material which a given library *will not have*. In such situations, success in retrieving information will require determination and ingenuity as well as available support systems for obtaining material outside the collection.

Interlibrary Loan

A traditional option for obtaining things—from books and periodicals to musical scores—is interlibrary loan (ILL), usually a free service. ILL service may not be available to certain classes of library users. Retrieval of your requested materials may take from a few days to a couple of weeks. In addition, libraries will almost never lend reference books (for example, directories or books with facts and statistics) that must be available to patrons on a daily basis. Should you be ineligible for ILL service or need materials that do not circulate or you simply do not have time to wait, your best option may be travelling to the library that owns the item or asking a friend in that location to obtain and send copies of what is needed. Librarians usually can advise you which institution owns the book or journal you need.

Library Information Brokers

Virtually all large research libraries and even some smaller institutions have a fee-based service for patrons who require services beyond what the library can provide for free. It's worth your trouble to ask about such a service for obtaining photocopies of library materials when interlibrary loan is not your best option. There is a charge for the copies as well as a mailing and handling fee. Payment options include charging this service to a credit card or even having it billed to your address.

Fulltext

The quickest, and probably the most expensive, method of obtaining materials unavailable at your library, is an online computer search. Many newspapers, journals, and even a few encyclopedias are available via computer as fulltext online databases. In these databases you can have the text printed to paper or downloaded to disk while you wait. If you are interested, ask for a list of fulltext databases and their price per minute.

Other Document Delivery Options

Many computerized databases also offer delivery of article texts via fax transmission and/or regular mail. While slower than the almost instantaneous transmission of online fulltext retrieval, this option is also considerably less expensive and usually faster than ILL. *ABI/Inform* and *CARL Uncover* are examples of menu-driven indexes with the option of ordering article copies. Also the DIALOG and BRS online computer search companies will, for a fee, send you "hardcopy" of the text as well as the citation for many of the sources found on their respective databases.

INTEGRATED RESEARCH TOOLS

As computers have become more common in libraries, research tools have become available in different formats. Now library catalogs frequently lead you to more than just books. A growing number of libraries have mounted specific computerized indexes (for example *Business Periodicals Index On-Disk* or *CARL Uncover*) on the same computer equipment as their library catalogs, thereby creating an integrated research environment. Selecting an index from the on screen menu will give you access to relevant periodical articles to complement any books you have found. Use of an index to periodical articles via such an integrated system is usually available at no cost.

Other libraries make "gateways" available. These are computer searching services intended for *library users* instead of librarians that open up several menu-driven online databases instead of a single, specific index. *FirstSearch* and *Easynet* are examples. Libraries can choose whether to have gateways as a menu option on the same computer monitor as their catalog. But gateways often are mounted at a separate work station in the library or are accessed through your home or office computer. There commonly is a charge for using them.

Where an integrated research system is available, you should get enough instruction in its use to:
1) be able to tap its full capabilities;
2) know what kinds of references (book/periodical article/book review/ dissertation/other) are being retrieved;
3) determine accurately the availability of each item and its shelf location if your library owns a copy.

LIBRARY NETWORKS

National Networks

For decades it was easier to find out what items were in a library collection across the country than to discover what was held thirty miles up the road. This came about because of a library network called OCLC (Online Computer Library Center), created in the early 1970s for resource-sharing on a *national basis* through interlibrary loan services. Smaller and/or technological-ly "poor" libraries were not on this ground-breaking library network at first, although some joined later. A counterpart to OCLC named RLIN (Research Libraries Information Network), was subsequently formed to meet the needs of the biggest and most prestigious research libraries, some of which then ceased reporting new information about their collections to OCLC.

Such a national network can be useful for supplying missing publication information for a list of references and for locating libraries which own material your own library lacks. It is important to know whether the library allows you direct access to such networks through a public OCLC or RLIN terminal. Find out also whether users of interlibrary loan are expected to indicate the location of an item they would like to borrow. Some libraries ask the requester to supply this; others prefer to have trained personnel do it.

Regional, State, and Local Networks

In the 1990s, libraries with computerized circulation (check out) systems and computerized catalogs began forming *local, state, and regional networks*, with the expectation of increasing awareness of what resources are owned within a certain geographical area and facilitating resource sharing to maximize scarce funds. This is a logical extension of the national networks, and like the earlier networks, the local/regional/state ones are usually available to users without charge. The impact promised for such networks is quicker delivery to researchers of materials outside the scope of their "home" institution's collection.

Discover whether your library belongs to any such network. Ask if you are entitled to request materials directly from members of the network and what delivery or response time is promised. Find out whether as a remote user (via Tymnet, Telenet, or Internet), you can tap into one of these networks even if your institution *is not* a member. Please note that licensing agreements with database vendors often preclude your using a periodical index mounted on such a system. But not all systems restrict dial-up users from using indexes. And the opportunity to confirm that a larger library has books your institution lacks can help you avoid wasting both gasoline and travel time on a fruitless trip.

THE LIBRARY STAFF MEMBER: GUIDE, HELPER, OMBUDSMAN

The following are things to know about getting reference help:

Reference/Information Assistance Checklist

1) Where is the reference room or area?
2) Are business research tools incorporated into a section of the main reference collection? If not, where are they?
3) Are business specialists assigned to the reference desk? If not, are they available for consultation?
4) What general indexes does the library have? What business indexes?
5) Are any indexes computer-searchable? Is there a fee? Are they housed in the reference room or in a separate facility? How can you get instruction in their use and/or assistance in formulating a search strategy?

Reference/Information Desk

You can get assistance in learning how to get around the library and how to do research primarily at the reference desk. In addition to answering brief factual questions, advising about research, and demonstrating the use of research tools—from the library catalog or reference books to compact disk systems—librarians will help in other ways. They will occasionally refer you to a source of unpublished information (such as a trade association or government agency), send you to another area of the library (a separate technology section or a separate economics section), or offer a list of references (sometimes called a "pathfinder") tailored to a particular research topic or type of class assignment. They will also advise you of available services such as interlibrary loan, online computer searching, use of group study rooms, or extended loan privileges. They can usually explain procedures for having missing material searched or for requesting that material be purchased by the library.

Libraries have different philosophies and levels of staffing that will determine how much of the "burden" of research they will assume. In general, academic libraries expect people to be independent to a certain extent; they will teach the use of research tools, but usually spend only minimal amounts of time actually finding references, facts, and so forth for you. This does not mean, however, that you must suffer. A rule of thumb is, if you find no information and no clues to guide you in how to approach the research after 15 to 30 minutes of trying, check with a librarian. It may well be that terminology, choice of research tools, definition of the topic idea, or something else could be tripping you up. The library staff is there to help.

For many questions, *any* member of the Reference/Information Desk staff can help business researchers. When reference staff cannot clear up a problem or confusion, ask for referral to someone who knows more about business research. This specialist may have an advanced degree in business or may simply be self-taught, with a particular interest in this field of study and/or years of experience answering business questions. Whatever their backgrounds, these people will be able to help with most aspects of business research.

The first part of this chapter described how powerful and complex today's business research environment can be. You must be a good "consumer" of information, aware of the wide range of resources, and discriminating about which information is best for your purposes. While librarians and other full-time library staff are prepared to assist, it may be unwise to abrogate all responsibility to them. Like someone undergoing surgery, you have at least as much at stake as the professional involved in the enterprise, if not more. Learn how to use your library and harness its power.

2

Strategies and Tools for Locating Materials

OBJECTIVES: This chapter will discuss various access mechanisms for locating published information on a given topic.

Introduction
Library Classification Systems
- How Does a Classification System Help?
- The Dewey Decimal Classification System
- The Library of Congress Classification System
- Why Just Browsing Won't Work

Library Catalogs
- The Card Catalog
- The Computerized Library Catalog
- What to Look Under in the Catalog
- Important Differences Between Card Catalogs and Computerized Catalogs

Footnotes, Endnotes, and the Bibliography
Directories
Indexes
- Thesauri and the *Standard Industrial Classification Manual*
- Other Access Points in Indexes

Unindexed or Unpublished Information
Appendix

After completing this chapter, you should be able to:

*Identify the classification system or systems used in your library.
*List the standard three ways to look for materials in a library catalog and one or two additional ways it may be possible to search the catalog.
*Know when to use a thesaurus and/or a list of SIC codes in researching a business topic.
*Evaluate and update information found in notes or the bibliography of a published source.
*Have some idea of where you might obtain information not indexed or not available in published form.

INTRODUCTION

If libraries were not a treasure trove of information, then the FBI would never have approached librarians (unsuccessfully, as it turns out) about identifying "suspicious looking" characters and reporting what subjects they pursued. With such a wealth of resources, sometimes you will stumble on a choice bit of information. But serendipity will never come close to replacing the systematic search for pertinent, complete, and up-to-date information that will get you an "A" or a raise and promotion. To plan and follow through with a library strategy, you need to know the meaning and the function of the following elements of the library information system:

1) the classification system;
2) the library catalog;
3) indexes;
4) what's *not* indexed;
5) footnotes, end notes, and the bibliography of an article or book; and
6) serials/periodical directories.

LIBRARY CLASSIFICATION SYSTEMS

The most basic tool for finding business sources is an awareness of the classification system or systems used in your library. Early classifications systems were very simple. For example, an Assyrian one (dating from 668-626 B.C.) divided all library materials into those dealing with the heavens and those dealing with the earth; and a classification system in an early Jesuit library arranged the beautifully bound books by authors conforming to accepted church doctrine on one side of the room and books by heretics (bound in black with black edging) on the other side. The dominant characteristic shared by these early schemes and modern systems for arranging library materials is grouping materials by topic or subject.

How Does a Classification System Help?

The function of a classification system is to bring order to the library collection in three ways: first, by grouping library materials (primarily books but sometimes including other formats such as films, magazines, and/or software) on the same broad subject together in the catalog under a common subject term or heading; second, by serving as a uniform "shorthand system" or code for indicating the specific subject matter of materials; and third, by facilitating the physical organization of books and other materials in the library collection.

For example, in searching for materials about organizational behavior as it relates to corporations, you might start with the catalog heading "organizational behavior". This standard subject heading brings together materials about how members of different types of organizations interact and function. But such a broad term might turn up books from the educator's as well as the business person's point of view. If you found materials oriented more toward education than business, you might then refine and focus your search, by selecting the business-oriented sources (with the shorthand code starting with the letters "HF" rather than the education-oriented sources with the code "LB"). Also when you get to the shelf location, browsing in the general area of the items you have identified, might reveal additional books on some aspect of organizational behavior of interest to you.

Adoption of standard classification systems is beneficial for libraries because they don't have to invent their own system. Even more important, it saves you from having to learn an entirely new system for each library you use. Today there are two major classifications in use in U.S. libraries: the Dewey Decimal Classification and the Library of Congress Classification.

The Dewey Decimal Classification System

The Dewey system, most common in public and smaller academic libraries, is based on a progression of numbers from 0 to 9. Please see Appendix 1 for the general outline of this classification.

While some books on economic topics (Banks and Banking, Credit, Counterfeiting, and related topics) can be found in the 300's, the most important Dewey subject division for the economist and business person is the 600 group. It is divided as follows:

600-Useful Arts
610-Medicine
620-Engineering
630-Agriculture/Agronomy
640-Home Economics/Domestic
　　　Science

650-Communications/Business
660-Chemical Technology
670-Manufactures
680-Mechanical Trades
690-Building

The 650 group is subdivided in the following way:

650-Communications/Business
651-Office Economy
652-Writing: Materials,
　　　Typewriters, Ciphers
653-Abbreviations/Shorthand
654-Telegraph/Cables/Signals
655-Printing/Publishing/Copyright

656-Transportation/Railroading, etc.
657-Bookkeeping/Accounts
658-Business Methods/
　　　Industrial Management
659-Other Topics

The 651 subdivision is made even more specific by addition of the following decimal subdivisions:

651 -Office Economy
651.1-Office Buildings and Rooms
651.2-Equipment
651.3-Organization

651.4-Administration
651.5-Records/Files/Filing
651.6-Special Material
651.7-Correspondence/Reports, etc.

The Library of Congress Classification System

The other major classification used in the United States, the Library of Congress (LC) Classification, is found in most large academic and some large public libraries. It represents an attempt to correct some of the shortcomings of the Dewey system by increasing the number of main categories from nine to twenty-one, each beginning with a letter of the alphabet. Each letter can be used by itself or in combination with another letter. This permits more detailed analyses of subjects. It also rearranges subjects so that books in fields considered to be related (e.g. history and sociology or philology and literature) are located in adjacent sections of shelving.

Please see the Appendix for the main divisions of the Library of Congress Classification system. The social sciences, including business, are assigned the letter "H" in this system, and are further divided into separate areas by assigning an additional letter code. The following are the most important business subdivisions:

HA Statistics
HB Economics
HC Economic History
    and Conditions by Area
HD Economic History
    and Conditions

HE Transportation and
    Communications
HF Commerce
HG Finance
HJ Public Finance

Within these broad subdivisions, specific subject areas are grouped by number. For example, Accounting falls within the HF 5601-5689 range of numbers. Advertising is assigned a number between HF 5801 and HF 6182. Various aspects of Banking are found from number HG 1501 to HG 3550. Information on Investments is located from HG 4501 to HG 6051. For more detail, ask to see the H volume of the Library of Congress Classification System. It is MUCH thicker than the other volumes.

Why Just Browsing Won't Work

There are three reasons why simply browsing in areas of the business collection will not necessarily produce all of the sources important for your topic. First, LC subjects are so finely subdivided that, for example, directories covering business and law schools (in the "H" and "J" sections, respectively) will not be anywhere near the multi-subject guides to undergraduate or graduate colleges and universities located in the "L" section. Second, there may be other classification systems in use along with the Library of Congress and/or Dewey. Government documents on business subjects often are left in the classification system assigned by the Superintendent of Documents (SuDoc numbers), starting out with a letter or letters identifying the document's issuing agency. These items necessarily will be housed separately from LC and Dewey materials. And finally, an interdisciplinary topic such as the implications of the AIDS crisis for an employer, can lead you out of business classifications. You could end up with material from "hard science" areas such as medicine or technology. Or you might venture into social science areas, such as psychology or sociology. So the next tool to master is the library catalog. It provides the most complete access to books and other library materials by subject.

LIBRARY CATALOGS

Library catalogs are files listing materials available in your library. Catalog listings commonly include many other types of publications than just books: newspapers and magazines or journals; sound recordings in formats from audiotapes to compact disks; films, videotapes, or videodisks; software products such as *Value/Screen* (the floppy disk-based version of *Value Line Investment Survey*); and even large machine-readable data sets like *Citibase*, an economic time series commonly mounted on university main-frame computers.

The Card Catalog

The old fashioned card catalog is rapidly going the way of the oil lamp and the horse-drawn streetcar. But you may still encounter it in this period of technological transition. Samples of author, title, and subject cards are listed below.

Author Card

```
HD
66          Denton, D. Keith.
.D45            Horizontal management : beyond total customer
1991        satisfaction / by D. Keith Denton. -- New York :
            Lexington Books ; Toronto : Maxwell Macmillan Canada ;
            New York : Maxwell Macmillan International, c1991.
                x, 211 p. : ill. ; 25 cm.
                Includes bibliographical references and index.
                ISBN 0-669-26936-0


                1. Work groups. 2. Management -- employee participation.
            3. Customer relations.
```

Explanation of Author Card

```
Classification Number
Book Number
Author Number
Year of Publication

        Author Heading.
          Title of book...............................................................................
.........Author...........Place of U. S. Publication.......................................
U. S. Publisher...Place of Canadian Publication...Canadian Publisher..............
Place of International Publication.International Publisher.Date of Publication....
          Prelim.pages...No. of pages in text..Illustrated..Size of book in centimeters...
          Notes.........................................................................................
          International Standard Book Number.


          1. Subject entry....2. Subject entry........................................................
        3. Subject entry.
```

Title Card

```
                    Horizontal Management.
HD
66
.D45          Denton, D. Keith.
1991              Horizontal management : beyond total customer
              satisfaction / by D. Keith Denton. -- New York :
              Lexington Books ; Toronto : Maxwell Macmillan Canada ;
              New York : Maxwell Macmillan International, c1991.
                  x, 211 p. : ill. ; 25 cm.
                  Includes bibliographical references and index.
                  ISBN 0-669-26936-0


                  1. Work groups.  2. Management -- employee participation.
                3. Customer relations.
```

Subject Card

```
                    WORK GROUPS.

HD
66
.D45          Denton, D. Keith.
1991              Horizontal management : beyond total customer
              satisfaction / by D. Keith Denton. -- New York :
              Lexington Books ; Toronto : Maxwell Macmillan Canada ;
              New York : Maxwell Macmillan International, c1991.
                  x, 211 p. : ill. ; 25 cm.
                  Includes bibliographical references and index.
                  ISBN 0-669-26936-0


                  1. Work groups.  2. Management -- employee participation.
                3. Customer relations.
```

The Computerized Library Catalog

The computerized catalog has been around for the past 25 or more years and has been common in libraries of any size for at least the past decade. The formats or layouts of different computerized catalog screens are as varied as different models of automobiles or other consumer products. But the same information that you may have been accustomed to seeing on a catalog card appears somewhere on the screen or screens containing information about any item in the library. You will always find the bibliographic description of the book or other item, including author's name, title, publisher's name and location, and year of publication along with a physical description of the item including size, number of pages, whether hard or soft cover, and often price. In addition, the call number and information about the book's location within the library system will be displayed.

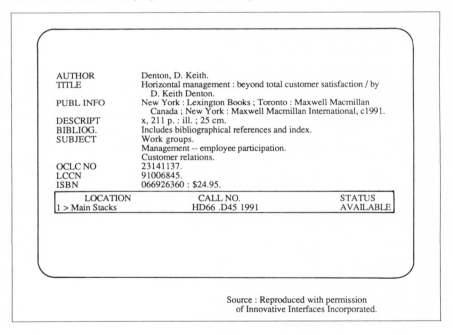

AUTHOR	Denton, D. Keith.
TITLE	Horizontal management : beyond total customer satisfaction / by D. Keith Denton.
PUBL INFO	New York : Lexington Books ; Toronto : Maxwell Macmillan Canada ; New York : Maxwell Macmillan International, c1991.
DESCRIPT	x, 211 p. : ill. ; 25 cm.
BIBLIOG.	Includes bibliographical references and index.
SUBJECT	Work groups.
	Management -- employee participation.
	Customer relations.
OCLC NO	23141137.
LCCN	91006845.
ISBN	066926360 : $24.95.

LOCATION	CALL NO.	STATUS
1 > Main Stacks	HD66 .D45 1991	AVAILABLE

Source : Reproduced with permission
of Innovative Interfaces Incorporated.

What to Look Under in the Catalog

For either the manual or the electronic form of catalog, there are three standard access points to start your search for items you already know about. You can find these items if you can remember either the author's name or the beginning words of the title accurately.

The third way to search is by subject. When you have a topic in mind but do not know of any relevant book titles or authors, you can look under the subject heading. Some card catalogs keep subject cards in one group of cabinets, and author and title cards in a separate configuration. There is a similar division among authors, titles, and subjects in most computerized catalogs, in that the "dictionaries" or lists of words the computer can retrieve are divided into groups of manageable size. So you must give the system a command (usually a short code such as "S") when you wish to search by subject.

Important Differences Between Card Catalogs and Computerized Catalogs

The most noticeable difference between electronic and traditional card catalogs is the multitude of additional ways to search for materials in the electronic format. First of all, virtually all computerized systems include a keyword or "natural language" option based on words from the title or other description of a book. This search feature is a benefit for those few times when neither you nor the librarian can figure out the appropriate standard subject heading. Card catalogs do not offer a natural language approach to subject searching, although they sometimes give you a hint in the form of a "see" or "see also" reference. Some, but not all computerized systems supply "see" and "see also" references. If you need help with standard terms for either type of catalog, librarians will be happy to show you authority books, giving the standard terminology (Library of Congress or Sears or National Library of Medicine subject headings) and help you work with these subject heading books if you desire.

In computerized library catalogs, additional access points or search "keys" (codes to type in to retrieve a particular item or list of items) are almost too numerous to mention. Your system may include any or all of the following: publisher's name; a unique standard book number assigned by the Library of Congress, the Superintendent of Documents, or some other body; publication date; location within the library system (e.g. science or fine arts branch location); physical format; and many others. When a catalog system accommodates a combination of author, title, or other search keys, you'll be able to retrieve the items you want with dizzying speed and efficiency.

Another important advantage of many computerized catalogs, is the amount of information that you can obtain quickly and easily. In addition to the standard display of bibliographic information and location information, other features include whether the item is already checked out, whether the item has been ordered but not yet received, and even what other items are on the shelf near the one you have pulled up (a kind of electronic browsing feature). This is light years beyond what you can glean from a card catalog.

Some systems allow "downloading," or the printing of the sources on paper. This represents a distinct improvement over writing out a long list by hand and avoids incomplete, inaccurate, or illegible copying.

One important disadvantage of computerized catalogs is that they are inflexible about such details as alternate spellings or the use of singular and plural words in either titles or subject headings. For example, there's labor versus labour and woman/women/wymen. Most systems can interpret either upper or lower case or a mix of both. But the use of initial articles (the, le, der, etc.) and punctuation (hyphens, colons, slashes in SuDoc numbers) are obstacles to accurate and complete retrieval of information. Be sure to use "onscreen" helps, printed instructions, and/or the help of library staff to find out the quirks and the special features of any computerized catalog you are using.

FOOTNOTES, ENDNOTES, AND BIBLIOGRAPHY

A time-honored research technique used by all but the rawest recruits in the battle to uncover information is that of branching out from one good book or article to other sources from the author's notes and bibliography (list of sources used). This familiar technique is good as far as it goes. In fact, it is the basis for the well-known *Social Sciences Citation Index* and its companion titles covering the sciences and the fine arts, all of which show relationships between the leading scholars in a given field and those who cite their published work. But sources from notes or a bibliography are apt to be old and can be either too broad or too specialized for what you want to do. The trick to intelligent use of sources from notes and bibliographies involves three steps. First, evaluate their relevance, currency, and suitability (objectivity, theoretical or applied approach, etc.) as much as possible from the title and publication facts before going to the trouble of finding them in your library or sending for them. Second, update them with current information from either the same authors or subsequent writers on the same topic. Third, if you aim for comprehensive treatment of the topic in question, glean relevant information from related fields and/or different types of publications (government documents or dissertations, etc.) via the use of the library catalog and indexes.

DIRECTORIES

To get a very broad view of a field—everything from accounting to typesetting—you might wish to get titles of magazines, newspapers, and journals from a publications directory. The *Ulrich's International Periodicals Directory* gives the current title and publisher's name and address for 140,000 publications such as popular magazines, trade journals, government documents, newspapers, and conference proceedings, along with details such as the frequency of publication and which indexes cover that publication. *Ulrich's* also provides information needed to order or submit a manuscript: editor's name, phone and fax numbers, ISSN (a standard number that follows a publication through whatever title changes it may undergo), and recent price. The *Gale Directory of Publications and Broadcast Media* gives similar information for 65,000 titles, within a geographic, rather than a subject classification arrangement. It is particularly good for tracking down less prominent newspapers in an area. The best source for audience information and advertising prices for print media is the *Standard Rate and Data* series of publications for various types of periodicals (newspapers, consumer magazines, trade magazines, and others).

INDEXES

All but the cutting-edge researcher in an exquisitely narrow field can profit from the occasional use of an index to periodical literature. Indexes provide systematic access to journal, magazine, and newspaper articles by subject terms. You have to pull article citations out of an index by the same codes used to put them in; so your idea of what to call something sometimes isn't enough. For example, in one source "organization development" will work. But a second may require you to use "organizational development", and a third may have all the things you need under "organizational change" or "organizational behavior". In the *Predicasts F & S Index: United States* "9911," an extension of the Standard Industrial Classification (SIC) codes for "industries and products," meaning Management Theory and Techniques is as close as you can get to organizational theory.

Thesauri and the *Standard Industrial Classification Manual*

The choice of subject terms is by no means standard across different indexes. So it is a good idea to use a thesaurus to get the "right" term for your topic and to pick up potentially useful related terms. Please remember, if there isn't a printed thesaurus available, your next best option is to try deducing the scheme used by article indexers. Write out a "shopping list" of possibilities and check off the ones that seem to work best in a given index.

As the most recent *Standard Industrial Classification Manual* shows, all basic industries are divided into groups based on a two-digit SIC code created by the Federal government to aggregate businesses in similar lines of work into meaningful groups for reporting and statistical analysis (01 for agriculture through 52 for retail and ending with 99 for non-classified establishments). Particular business establishments are classified by a four-digit number that indicates, for example, computer peripherals—printers and such—under the number 3577. This separates them from computer hardware manufacturers (3571, 3575, or 3845) and from computer software producers (7371 or 7372).

SIC codes are the entry point for virtually all federal publications covering business. In addition to government publications, ratio books, directories ranking companies within industry, and some indexes are arranged in SIC order. The Predicasts company has extended this number to a six-digit product, industry, or event code that will distinguish quite narrow business areas in its publications. Chief among their publications are the *Predicasts F.& S Index* series covering the United States, Europe, and non-European countries; and their sister publications including the *Predicasts Basebook* and *Predicasts Forecasts*. Check the alphabetical index in one of the preceding types of books for industry SIC's. For a specific company's SIC, check a directory. Please note that assignment of a SIC to a particular company is apparently more of an art than a science. It is not unheard of for the Standard & Poor's *Register of Corporations, Directors, and Executives* to list a different SIC than its Dun & Bradstreet rival, the *Million Dollar Directory Series* for exactly the same company.

Other Access Points in Indexes

Additional entry points (words or codes to look under) in an index can include some or all of the following: table of contents listings; author's name; subject hierarchies such as those in the table of contents or appendix of *Psychological Abstracts*, *The Index of Economic Articles* or the Commerce Clearing House publication *Accounting Articles*; company name; and individual's names. In computerized indexes, the possibilities are almost unlimited. Add to most of the preceding, the DUNS number (a unique company ID assigned by Dun & Bradstreet), publication date, product code, product name, publication name, and keywords—taken from title, abstract, and maybe even the actual text of the article itself. Please see Chapter 7 for more detailed descriptions of selected business indexes.

UNINDEXED OR UNPUBLISHED INFORMATION

Although it may not be obvious, some published business information is not covered by periodical indexes you are accustomed to using. But this information isn't necessarily lost to you; there are ways to track down some of it. The first method is to become familiar with the magazines and trade papers that regularly carry news items or features in your field of study. Compile a list of sources in your field from a directory such as *Ulrichs* or by consulting the alphabetical list of periodicals in an index that covers your field, for example the *Business Periodicals Index* in paper form or *ABI/Inform Ondisc*. Next review about six months worth of copies of these periodicals to identify which titles carry the types of items that interest you.

A quicker, if less comprehensive method would be to use the *Special Issues Index*, which tracks recurring special issues valuable for their periodic news updates, rankings, or other analyses and comparisons. A familiar example is the May special issue of *Fortune* magazine, listing the world-renowned Fortune 500 ranking of top companies.

A third way to get at material of a statistical nature not easily found in most indexes is to consult the *Statistical Reference Index (SRI)*, covering publications from state government reports to trade association statistics to familiar commercial publications like *Datamation*. Since *SRI* excludes federal government material, you will need to use its companion piece, the *American Statistics Index (ASI)*, for subject access to the vast majority of statistics buried in various periodicals and reports distributed by the United States government.

Please remember that even unpublished information may be available to the intrepid business researcher. If you can't find some information in the library, but you suspect it exists, write or call one of the organizations listed in the *National Trade and Professional Associations of the United States and Labor Unions* directory. This approach sometimes gets you a solid gold nugget of data. Alternately, interviewing a local business leader might yield good information to use in a class project. You are more apt to get cooperation in this type of questioning if you make clear that you are a student instead of a competitor and if you ask for a ballpark estimate of sales, turnover, or profit, rather than pressing for exact figures.

APPENDIX

OUTLINE OF DEWEY AND LIBRARY OF CONGRESS
CLASSIFICATION SYSTEMS

DEWEY

000-General Works   **500**-Pure Science
100-Philosophy   **600**-Useful Arts
200-Religion   **700**-Fine Arts/Recreation
300-Social Sciences/Sociology   **800**-Religion
400-Philology   **900**-History

LIBRARY OF CONGRESS
A General Works
B Philosophy/Religion/Psychology
C Auxiliary Sciences of History
D History: General/Old World
E,F History of America
G Geography/Anthropology/Lore/Manners/Customs, Sports, and Games
H Social Sciences (including Economics and Business)
J Political Science
K Law
L Education
M Music
N Fine Arts
P Language/Literature
Q Science
R Medicine
S Agriculture
T Technology
U Military Science
V Naval Science
Z Bibliography/ Library Science

SECTION TWO

RESEARCH STRATEGIES AND GENERAL SOURCES OF BUSINESS INFORMATION

3

Strategies and Types of Materials

OBJECTIVES: This chapter will give an overview of different categories of business information sources and ideas for appropriate search strategies.

Introduction to Research Materials
- Handbooks and Almanacs
- Yearbooks and Encyclopedias
- Dictionaries
- Books
- Periodical Literature
- Reports
- Directories
- Government Publications
- Audiovisual Materials

Search Strategies
- Company Information
- Information on Individuals
- Industry Information
- Product Information

After completing this chapter, you should be able to:

*Explain differences between categories of business materials.
*Think critically about the nature of business materials.
*Develop basic plans for the use of business materials.
*Be less intimidated and more confident about using materials.

INTRODUCTION TO RESEARCH MATERIALS

Business information materials vary almost as much as the application of the sources themselves. When developing a strategy to use business information, recognize that differences in materials will influence the results of your search in both quantity and quality. Chances are you will find plenty of information on any topic, but keep in mind that seeking the most relevant or precise information will allow you to be more selective and thereby reduce the overall amount of time spent on researching your topic.

Familiarity with all categories of business information materials available to you will enable you to target those sources that will systematically inform and provide you with superior research results. When using business libraries, it is extremely important to conceptualize the type of information needed and the sequence in which the information should be incorporated into your research strategy. Key questions to keep in mind are:

1) Is current information important?
2) Am I looking for textual, numeric or directory information?
3) Do I need emphasis on theory or application?

Armed with these questions, your search will be better organized, thereby saving research time and improving your research results.

Following are broad overviews of key categories of business information. More detailed descriptions and specific examples of each category are described in subsequent chapters. After the categories have been briefly described, you will find actual search strategies offering guidelines on when to use the key categories, including representative titles. The order in which you use these materials, as stated above, will depend in large measure on your answers to the preceding three questions and will determine the extent to which you will need to exhaust each category.

Handbooks and Almanacs

Handbooks and almanacs cover most business subject areas such as accounting, economics, finance, management, marketing, personnel, public relations, etc. When approaching a new subject area, handbooks and almanacs can help you develop brief topic overviews.

Handbooks and almanacs such as *IBC-Donoghue's Mutual Funds Almanac* and the *Handbook of Stock Index Futures and Options* provide concise factual as well as statistical information. Handbooks are excellent sources for well-researched articles about highly defined areas of business. Article length can vary from dictionary entry to an encyclopedia entry. You may also discover bibliographies which provide you with lists of books and articles relevant to your subject.

Almanacs provide sources of numeric data found in tables and charts, along with brief, dictionary-type entries. Many almanacs often include historical analysis in their data presentation. Almanacs are typically published annually, although this is not a hard and fast rule. It is not uncommon to find some business almanacs published, on the average, every five years.

Indexes within handbooks and almanacs are important in saving you time in pinpointing your topic and should be consulted first. In researching the 10 largest banking failures in U.S. history, for example, you would logically first think of rankings, lists, statistics, etc. You would also consider currency of information. Currency and factual information would point you in the direction of an almanac or handbook.

Such almanacs as the *World Almanac & Book of Facts* feature a table of contents found in the front of the book arranged by very broad categories. In the back of the book, you will find the subject index, which includes a very long detailed list of subjects that will more closely relate to your search category. The *Statistical Abstract of the United States*, another ready reference annual, also includes important business statistics, and is arranged in a similar format. See Chapter 8 for a more in-depth discussion of handbooks and almanacs.

Yearbooks and Encyclopedias

Like handbooks and almanacs, yearbooks and encyclopedias cover a full range of business topics. Yearbooks and encyclopedias may in some cases provide similar information. Aside from traditional encyclopedias like *Encyclopaedia Britannica* or *McGraw-Hill Encyclopedia of Science and Technology*, most business encyclopedias consist of one or two volumes. Sources such as *Encyclopedia of Advertising*, *Encyclopedia of Banking and Finance*, and *Encyclopedia of Management* provide detailed coverage of their respective fields. The scope includes histories of important events and people, definitions of theoretical and practical terms, and a subject comprehensiveness that would be difficult to replicate with any other category of business information source.

Yearbooks are more in keeping with their name, in that most are published yearly, although not always in the year that they cover. In this category you will find statistical sources, primarily governmental or trade-related, as well as overviews of important events during the year. Several good examples of each include *Yearbook of International Trade Statistics*, *Yearbook of Labor Statistics*, *Yearbook of National Accounts Statistics*, *Yearbook of Railroad Facts*, and *Merger Yearbook*. See Chapter 9 for a more in-depth discussion of yearbooks and encylopedias.

Dictionaries

Business dictionaries provide brief definitions of key terms in such fields as accounting, economics, finance, management, marketing, etc. Like handbooks and almanacs, you will find dictionaries for almost every subject area within business, from accounting through real estate. Many new dictionaries are published every year and purchased by libraries because of the ever-changing vocabulary of business. New buzzwords and jargon make some dictionaries, particularly in marketing and finance, obsolete almost overnight.

Dictionaries come into play in the research process typically in conjunction with handbooks and encyclopedias. For example, if you are doing research in marketing, it is worthwhile to keep a marketing dictionary by your side so that your understanding of the literature is in keeping with the intent of the authors and editors. See Chapter 11 for more information on Dictionaries.

Books

Literally hundreds of books are published each year focusing on many aspects of business. According to *Publisher's Weekly*, an average of 1,500 new business books are published annually in the United States. These books run the gamut from how to write a resume to foreign business etiquette. To keep up with this massive outpouring of new titles, you would have to have months of free reading time to read all that is current. Even then, you would probably fall behind.

When selecting a business book, you could concentrate on those publishers whose lists focus on business—Harvard Business School, Probus, Business One-Irwin, and AMACOM, for example. However, even with this tip, it is difficult to tell which books are worth reading in their entirety and which should be consulted selectively. Large publishing houses like Random, Macmillan, McGraw, and Wiley also have business lists that rival the more specialized presses. A good approach to take in narrowing the field of business books is to consult an established book review publication. A book review typically is written by an expert in the field and will provide an overview of the book's theme, how the book compares to similar other books, and describe the intended audience. *Publisher's Weekly* and *Library Journal's* annual "Best Business Books" column are excellent book review sources. Also, *Book Review Digest* cites and reprints excerpts of reviews of books, and *Business Periodicals Index* has a separate section citing reviews of business books.

Always consider the nature of your research when selecting business books. Are you looking for business histories or case studies? By asking yourself these questions, you are taking a first step in defining the approach to your research. Most business subjects can be approached from many different angles. For example, if you were researching the stock market and investments, you could focus on individual strategies or market movements. You could research econometric case studies or read about behind-the-scenes activities. By focusing on your research approach, you systematically organize available business literature and establish priorities.

If you choose to branch out on your own to discover lesser-known or long-forgotten gems of wisdom, then use earlier or historic editions of book review publications. There you will uncover books that made it to previous best-seller lists as well as thousands of books of equal importance that focus on narrower slices of business interest. Once you have selected your reading list from your review sources, check your library's catalog to see which ones are available for immediate use.

Periodical Literature

Over 13,000 business periodicals are published worldwide (source: *Ulrich's Periodicals Directory*). These periodicals include general titles such as *Business Week*, *Forbes*, and *Fortune*, as well as more narrowly focused titles like *Federal Reserve Bulletin*, *Global Trade*, and *Mergers & Acquisitions*. If you add to this list such general newspapers as *Wall Street Journal*, as well as trade journals like *Beverage World*, *Billboard*, and *Logger and Lumberman*, you can begin to appreciate the size of the business periodical kingdom.

When searching for periodical literature, it is critically important to begin with a subject index. The sheer number of periodicals available, both within the field of business as well as related fields, easily justifies this approach. A subject index will provide you with lists of articles arranged by both broad and narrow subject headings. Depending on which index you use, you will find from several hundred to several thousand periodicals covered.

Periodical indexes are compiled by subject indexers. They selectively assign subject heading terms to each article of every periodical that their index covers. As the researcher, you will look up a subject heading, eg. "stock markets," and you will find citations to specific articles on that subject. A citation will normally include the title of the article, author's name, title of periodical, volume, date of article, and page numbers.

As a general rule of thumb, periodicals are an important source of current information. Periodicals usually are distributed on a regular basis: weekly, monthly, quarterly, etc. Newspapers, by contrast, usually appear daily or weekly. It is possible to scan several new issues of each category every day, and to cover a diverse area of topics. As an example, for broad current business news coverage, many people read the *Wall Street Journal*, *Barron's*, or *Business Week*. For more in-depth coverage, others read *Harvard Business Review*, *Forbes*, or *Fortune*. For world news, readers might select *The Economist*, *Financial Times*, or *U.S. News & World Report*.

In the final analysis, the smart researcher will select periodicals according to subject needs. Through your business library, you can search by subject through hundreds or even thousands of journals and newspapers. You might also request access via electronic services, such as Dow-Jones News Retrieval or Nexis databases, described in Chapter 7.

Reports

Business reports are originally published for private, limited circulation and are obtainable directly from the company or from an intermediary. These information sources can include corporate annual reports, Security and Exchange Commission required filings, industry surveys, financial ratios, and proprietary documents, including market research reports. Sometimes requests must be made in person for this information, although many of the reports are available through secondary sources. Some business reports are available at your business library. This latter group includes annual reports and other corporate filings, including services published by Dun & Bradstreet, Robert Morris & Associates, Standard & Poor's, and other business research firms.

Some private reports are too expensive for a business library to purchase. These reports cover different formats such as microfiche, optical disc, or magnetic tape. Other reports, particularly market research reports, can cost thousands of dollars. These reports are published by some of the more respected market research houses such as Find/SVP and Frost & Sullivan. Such reports are prohibitively costly except to the most specialized (and well-funded) libraries.

Directories

Business directories provide entries for companies, products, and individuals. A directory entry typically includes the company name, address, telephone number, names and titles of officers, sales or revenue figures, number of employees, the date of incorporation, and product or services offered. Variations include names of directors, locations of plants, name of advertising agency, bank, accounting, or legal advisor.

Directories are considered invaluable for marketers and others who need to establish a prospect list, including names of key individuals to contact. Directories may also be useful for job-seekers, grant seekers, venture capitalists, competitive analysis, product searches—and the list goes on. The more important directories are updated frequently, for the simple reason that addresses and positions change often.

One of the best ways of keying into the world of directory information is through the multi-volume set, *Directories in Print*. This directory of directories will allow you to find directories on any given subject. Entries usually include publisher, price, and description. Most business libraries consider this directory set a key staple. See Chapter 10 for a discussion of the major business directories.

Government Publications

The United States government is one of the largest publishers of business information and its publications should be prime resources in any search. The U.S. Government Printing Office publishes thousands of different titles ranging in form from pamphlets to periodicals to reports. Subjects within the field of business include foreign trade, domestic economy data, regulations, patent descriptions, industry surveys, labor reports, and census data. Many other publications are produced by the U.S. government, but are published and distributed directly by the department or agency involved. The subject areas are just as varied as Government Printing Office publications.

The U.S. government impacts the type of business information you obtain and the way in which you access it in many different ways. For example, if you are doing research on privately held companies, you will probably have to settle for less financial information than if you were researching public companies. Government regulations dictate that more information be divulged on public companies than on their private counterparts or subsidiary operations.

The U.S. government has improved the organization of business information. The government requires that all companies, from sole proprietorships to incorporations, assign themselves a four digit industry number, within predetermined government produced classifications, when originally establishing their business. These numbers, called SIC numbers (Standard Industrial Classification) are the backbone of most business directories. SIC numbers are even used to provide arrangement for industry and marketing reports. Many companies have more than one number due to the diversified nature of their enterprises and consequently appear many times in SIC indexes or industry reports.

The Small Business Administration also publishes hundreds of helpful guides for the small business owner. These guides are typically collected by the business library and by U.S. government document depositories. These depositories are found throughout the country and are usually affiliated with public or academic libraries. (See Chapter 12 for a list of depository libraries.) The amount of information will vary from depository to depository. Every state has at least one, but no more than two, U.S. documents depositories that are considered "regional" depositories. The regional depositories contain 100% of the publications produced by the U.S. Government Printing Office.

Other popular government publications include the *Statistical Abstract of the United States*, publications of the Bureau of Economic Analysis, the Bureau of Labor Statistics, and the Bureau of the Census, as well as other agencies and offices.

Audiovisual Materials

Much business information is accessible in non-print format through audiovisual (AV) aids. Products include motion pictures, videocassettes, videodiscs, slides, filmstrips, transparencies, computer programs, multi-media, optical discs, and audiocassettes. The possibilities for incorporating AV sources into your research are broad. In the classroom, business instructors may show videos on subjects as diverse as accounting procedures or industrial plant layout. Videos of past lectures by nationally renowned business innovators are also commonly used. Audiocassettes containing audible books, such as *In Search of Excellence* and other popular business titles are also available. From videos to cassettes to computer programs, audiovisuals are an effective method of presenting material.

Most business libraries also make commercially produced videos available. Many academic libraries retain videos of important lectures that have been filmed in classes of resident or visiting faculty. Other audiovisual materials are available through catalogs either on a rental or purchase basis. Selection of this unique and important information format contiunes to grow. Additionally, specialized A-V libraries, including film archives, often make their one-of-a-kind collections available to the public through similar catalogs and other advertising means. These materials include both nationally and locally produced items. See Chapter 13 for a more in-depth discussion of audio-visual aids.

SEARCH STRATEGIES

When setting up a business information search strategy, it is important to think about the business information categories described above. By becoming familiar with, and having a working knowledge of, the type of information found in handbooks, almanacs, encyclopedias, and directories you will be able to proceed much more quickly through available materials. You will know the order in which you should consult each category of information and also how thoroughly you will need to exhaust representative sources within each category. Keeping this in mind, you will now be guided, step-by-step, through typical business information searches as they relate to company information, individual information, industry information, and product information.

Company Information

There are many reasons to search for information on companies, including employment information, investment information, marketing information, and competitive analysis. Using a fictitious name, XYZ Corporation, we will begin our search.

Directories

The first step in the search process is to verify that XYZ Corporation exists. While this may sound strange, in many cases company names do change, or are different from what is printed in a newspaper or spoken by word of mouth. To verify a company name, use a directory set containing the largest number of companies possible.

Good sources for verification of U.S. companies include *Ward's Business Directory, Dun's Business Identification Service, Dun and Bradstreet Million Dollar Directory,* and *Thomas's Register of American Manufacturers.* For verifying a foreign company name use Dun and Bradstreet's *Principal International Businesses, Kelly's Business Directory, Marconi's International Register,* or *Wenco International Trade Directory.* These directories will provide you with listings for thousands and thousands of companies involved with manufacturing and services.

Your next step will depend on the success of the company name verification. As Flowchart #1 indicates, your search will diverge into two paths, positive verification and negative verification. Positive verification indicates that you have established that XYZ Corporation exists. The directory in which you located the company will also provide additional information including address, telephone number, product or service offered, and possibly sales/revenues, SIC number, list of officers, and number of employees. Negative verification in these leading directories will indicate that you need to go back to your original source of information, verify the name again, and if at all possible, determine the state or country in which the company is located. If you are able to determine beforehand the state or country in which the company is located, you can then go back to the directories, and concentrate your search on national, regional, state, and local sources, including telephone books when necessary.

Private or Public?

Assume that you have limited information on XYZ Corporation, but that you need more. Your next time-saving step is to determine if the company is privately held or publicly held. That is to say, is XYZ Corporation traded on any stock exchange? If the answer is yes, then you can expect to find more information than if it were a private corporation. In order to determine the ownership of the company, look in the government document, *Directory of Companies Required to File Annual Reports with the Securities and Exchange Commission Under the Securities Exchange Act of 1934.* This is the definitive annual list of U.S. publicly held companies. If your company does not appear in this list, it may have gone public since publication of the most recent edition of the SEC directory, it may be a subsidiary or division of a publicly held company, or it may be privately held. Flowchart #1 indicates how to proceed under each of these scenarios.

Investment Reports

If XYZ Corporation is a publicly held company, then you will be able to consult available SEC reports, such as the 10-K and the annual report to the shareholders. Additional report services and handbooks that will provide company background, recent developments, prospects, and statistical information include *Moody's Corporate Profiles, Moody's Manuals, Standard & Poor's Corporation Descriptions*, and *Value Line Investment Survey.*

Subsidiaries and Divisions: Directories

The next step, whether XYZ Corporation is publicly or privately held, is to consult directories of subsidiaries and divisions. These tools will provide data pertaining to company affiliations and often reveal otherwise unobtainable financial data on private companies. Important directories for this research, covering both domestic and international firms, include *America's Corporate Families and International Affiliates, Directory of American Firms Operating in Foreign Countries, Directory of Corporate Affiliations, Directory of Foreign Firms Operating in the United States, International Directory of Corporate Affiliations*, and *Who Owns Whom.*

Periodicals and Indexes

Once you have completed verification of the company and obtained all available financial and managerial information from directories, the next step is to examine the company's newsworthiness. For this step, you will need to use the periodical indexes. One of the most comprehensive business index series on the market is the *Predicasts* series, which includes *Predicasts F&S Index: United States, Predicasts F&S Index: Europe*, and *Predicasts F&S Index: International.* These three indexes all contain a separate alphabetical company index section for quick research. Other important periodical indexes that can be searched by company name include *Business Periodicals Index, Business Index, ABI/Inform*, and the *National Newspaper Index.*

Library Catalog

Now that you have identified all relevant articles on XYZ Corporation, the next and final step is to plug in any gaps in your research by searching

FLOWCHART #1

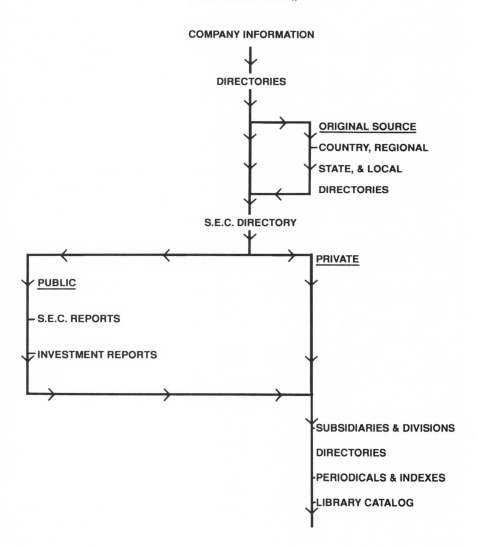

COMPANY INFORMATION

DIRECTORIES

<u>ORIGINAL SOURCE</u>

COUNTRY, REGIONAL

STATE, & LOCAL

DIRECTORIES

S.E.C. DIRECTORY

<u>PRIVATE</u>

<u>PUBLIC</u>

S.E.C. REPORTS

INVESTMENT REPORTS

SUBSIDIARIES & DIVISIONS

DIRECTORIES

PERIODICALS & INDEXES

LIBRARY CATALOG

your library's catalog. The library catalog will allow you to search by company name in both the subject field and title field through the use of authority records. Authority records are created by library catalogers and essentially provide standardization, control, and a means of access for searching proper names. The title field search will be easier to conduct if you are using an online catalog that allows for keyword searching. In searching the library catalog, you will identify books that have been written about XYZ Corporation, as well as books that XYZ Corporation may have produced internally to mark anniversaries or for other purposes.

Information on Individuals

In searching for information on business people, you will be limited by the number of information categories to be examined. As Flowchart #2 indicates, you begin by first looking in the directories that contain the largest number of individuals profiled. Also, be aware that everyone falls into two distinct groups, those living and those dead. Most of the current business biographical directories tend to profile individuals that are still living and, in most cases, still hold their respective professional position. Other categories of business information, such as older business directories and, of course, the news sources will also include profiles on deceased business people.

Directories

Several key directories with which to begin your search on business people include *Who's Who in America, Who's Who in Canada, Who's Who in European Business: Biographies of the Top 3,000 Business Leaders in Europe, Who's Who in Finance and Industry*, Standard & Poor's *Register of Corporations, Directors, and Executives*, and *Reference Book of Corporate Management*. The best of these directories list living individuals along with a brief biography, including family members, year born, schools attended, employment history, organization and club affiliations, and current address.

Periodicals and Indexes

The next step in researching information on business individuals is to search through periodicals and newspapers for articles. Here again, it is important to use your periodical indexes for speed and thoroughness. In researching individuals, keep in mind local, regional, and trade publications. This is important because the individual you are researching may be profiled at the local level or may appear in a journal pertaining to their profession or occupation. These kinds of articles may or may not provide much in the way of biographical information, but depending on the nature of the research, may serve as a springboard for initiating conversations with the individual.

FLOWCHART #2

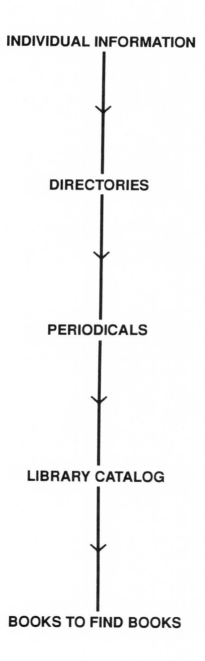

INDIVIDUAL INFORMATION

DIRECTORIES

PERIODICALS

LIBRARY CATALOG

BOOKS TO FIND BOOKS

Library Catalog

In a search for background information on individuals, never rule out the library catalog. The catalog will help you to fill in any gaps in your research. When searching for books on individuals, you probably will be successful for only the most famous business people, such as John Scully, H. Ross Perot, Armand Hammer, etc. The lesser known movers and shakers usually have not reached the status that these better-known business icons have achieved. However, use your library catalog creatively and search by industry, company, and of course individual, to determine what is readily available. As a back-up measure, look through a few of the "books to find books" such as *Books In Print* and *Book Review Digest*. These sources of book publication information will inform you about the individual being profiled. They will also provide you with leads as to what books are commercially available, either written by or about the person you are researching.

Industry Information

Information on industries is one of the more common types of queries asked in business libraries. The following search strategy, as depicted in Flowchart #3, will guide you through every facet of industry research, step by step.

Government Publications

The first step in researching industries is to define the industry itself. In order to do this, you will need to use an industry classification system. In the U.S., the system is the Standard Industrial Classification (SIC) system. The SIC is a coded, hierarchal arrangement of two- to four-digit numbers arranged by divisions, major groups, individual groups, and industries.

To locate classification numbers, use the government publication *Standard Industrial Classification Manual*. This publication includes an alphabetical list of products and services, correlated with the specific four digit number assigned to that industry. Most industry classifications will also include a brief description of the industry, along with listings of any minor industry areas covered under the four-digit number. The expanded listing can help to verify numbers for very narrow industries and to provide a context for the umbrella term under which you originally searched. Once you have verified your industry and obtained the industry classification number, you are ready to continue with your search.

Reports

The next step in the search for industry information will be to consult reports, that offer valuable textual and numeric information concerning an industry's history, performance, and prospects. One of the first places to locate textual

FLOWCHART #3

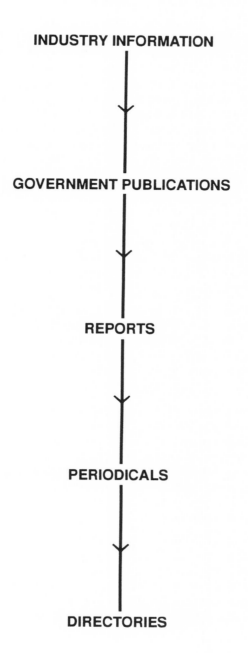

INDUSTRY INFORMATION

GOVERNMENT PUBLICATIONS

REPORTS

PERIODICALS

DIRECTORIES

industry reports is in the government publication *U.S. Industrial Outlook*. This excellent source profiles several hundred key U.S. industries each year. The SIC system is used as the classification for the book's arrangement. Each industry report covers several pages and often includes tables, graphs, and charts that visually demonstrate how an industry compares with similar industries, important component growth factors within individual industries, and other important economic measures.

Similar sources for these types of industry reports include *Standard & Poor's Industry Surveys, Standard & Poor's Analysts Handbook, Moody's Investors Service,* and *Moody's Industry Review.* Each of these publications should be consulted to obtain as much information on your industry as possible. Written from different perspectives and drawn from various information sources, each of these reports will be useful and will complement one another.

Other reports that concentrate on numeric industry performance include Robert Morris & Associates' *Annual Statement Studies, Troy's Almanac of Business and Financial Ratios,* and Dun & Bradstreet Credit Services' *Industry Norms and Key Business Ratios: Library Edition.* These numeric, financial industry performance reports cover all categories, from manufacturing of durable and non-durable goods, wholesaling, retailing, services, and contractor industries. The industries profiled are arranged by SIC numbers and contain all key profit and loss ratios for comparative analysis.

The "Business Census" produced by the U.S. Bureau of the Census is another important source of industry report information. The business census, which is released every five years, covers agriculture, construction, manufacturing, mineral industries, retail trade, service industries, transportation, and wholesale trade. In these census reports you will find numbers of establishments, sales and revenues, and employment by geographic area.

Another good source of industry reports is *Corporate and Industry Research Reports (CIRR). CIRR* is primarily a collection of industry reports that are produced by industry analysts for investment purposes. The reports are unique for their coverage and level of analysis. It is common to find reports on such topics as industry profitability, comparative company sales, market share, profits, and forecasts.

Periodicals and Indexes

Periodicals will play an important role in your search for industry information from two different angles, recency of information and detail of coverage. When researching periodicals, keep in mind that the periodical indexes are there to save you time. Most of the indexes, such as the *Predicasts F&S* series, ABI/Inform, and *Business Periodicals Index* will allow you to search by industry name, although *Predicasts* allows for more precise SIC searching.

Once you have identified articles on your industry, be prepared to evaluate the results. As mentioned, you will likely find a broad range of treatments for your industry, including trade, academic, and general accounts of activity and performance. Some periodicals, such as *Forbes*, make their industry analysis a regular feature, as in their "Annual Report on American Industry," found in the first January issue of each year. Other journals, such as *Wall Street Transcript*, a weekly newspaper, provide insider comments on specific industry performance and prospects. Remember that periodicals or newspapers that are not subscribed to by your business library may be available through their interlibrary loan service. Ask your business librarian to process the request for you.

Directories

Directories come into the picture next. Directories can be used for industry information in a number of different ways. One very important and broad method of using directories is to search for industry association information. To do this, you would need to look in the *Encyclopedia of Associations* series. In this publication, you will find a keyword index that will tie together all related terms for any existing industry association. The keyword index will then direct you to the volume of the series (local, regional, national, or international) that contains the entry for your trade group. The entry information will provide a contact name, address, telephone number, number of members, when founded, regional or local affiliates, description of activities, conference and publication information.

Other directories that will prove useful in your industry research include *Nelson's Directory of Wall Street Research*. This unique directory can prove immensely valuable in identifying individuals who are responsible for providing investor advice on publicly traded companies within industry groupings. These individuals, through their informed expertise, are instrumental in helping others make decisions regarding industry investments.

Product Information

Product research is challenging because it requires more precision than most other kinds of business research. Product names vary depending on whether you are referring to a generic name, technical name, brand name, or company name. Flowchart #4 outlines the search that you will follow in researching products.

Directories

Directories are very important in helping to define the **name** under which to begin your product research. There are several directories that you should

FLOWCHART #4

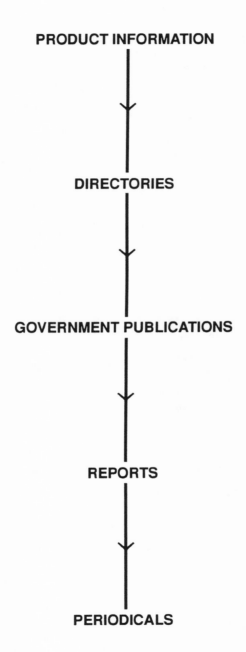

PRODUCT INFORMATION

DIRECTORIES

GOVERNMENT PUBLICATIONS

REPORTS

PERIODICALS

consult to determine which companies produce which products and which products are assigned to specific companies. The leading directories for this type of research are *Brands and Their Companies* and *Companies and Their Brands*. Each of these directories provides coverage of over 281,000 consumer products and 51,000 manufacturers, importers, marketers or distributors. The international counterparts are *International Brands and Their Companies* and *International Companies and Their Brands*. The latter directory set tracks over 80,000 consumer products and 25,000 international manufacturers, importers, and distributors.

Additional directories that are critical to product research include the *Standard Directory of Advertisers*. This valuable directory provides a "Tradename List" of over 35,000 brand names for the companies that produce the products. This directory also provides information on companies that produce and advertise these products, including annual advertising expenditures and type of media used for advertising campaigns. Another useful source of brand name information is *Thomas's Register of American Manufacturers* and *Thomas's Register Catalog File*. This directory provides extensive listings of primarily commercial brand names along with company name, address, sales rankings, and in some cases, actual advertisements.

Government Publications

Government publications can also be helpful in conducting product research. The U.S. Patent and Trademark Office publishes two key journals focusing on trademarks and patents: the *Official Gazette of the United States Patent and Trademark Office: Trademarks* and the *Official Gazette of the United States Patent and Trademark Office: Patents*. Each of these publications is updated weekly and provides the official record of newly assigned trademarks and patents. These sources are important to your product research because they provide the official record for both product descriptions and product names. Included is the name of the individual or company that developed the product or service , a description of how the product or service works, claims, and date of first use.

Reports

After idenfifying your product and who makes it the next step is to obtain background information, including competitiveness, sales, market share, and number of units sold.

Reports that are useful for product searches include *Market Share Reporter* and *Corporate and Industry Research Reports* (CIRR). *Market Share Reporter* will save you valuable time in determining the popularity of your product. Arrangement is by SIC number with over 2,000 entries providing market description, rankings of products, market share, and source publication (where the information originated). Its counterpart is the *European Market Share Reporter.*

Corporate and Industry Research Reports (CIRR), as described in the section on "Industry Information," will allow you to read actual investor analysts' reports that also contain market share segmentation. This source is unparalleled for the number of reports offered and the number of products and industries profiled.

Other avenues for obtaining product reports rest with the manufacturers and companies producing your product. By using the preceding directories you will be able to contact companies directly and request any reports available. Another approach is to use the *Encyclopedia of Associations* and contact trade and industry groups for comparative data on products pertaining to that industry.

Periodicals and Indexes

The last step in your product research is to consult the periodicals. By using a periodical index, such as *Predicasts PROMT* (Predicasts Overview of Markets and Technology) you will be focusing your search on trade journals that are likely to provide product information. The other Predicasts series, as well as more standard periodical indexes such as *ABI/Inform* and *Business Periodicals Index*, will provide coverage of articles focusing on more widely known products. For thorough coverage, it is recommended to use *PROMT* and at least one other of the more general indexes.

Books to Locate Books

OBJECTIVES: This chapter will help you to identify sources for business information found in books.

> **Introduction**
> **Why You Need Books to Find Books**
> **Historic Research**
> **Current Research**
> **Reviewing Guides**

After reading this chapter you should:

*Distinguish the best sources for locating historic books on business topics.
*Locate the best guides for current business books.
*Identify major book reviewing sources.

INTRODUCTION

Most business library collections contain thousands of books about every imaginable aspect of business. Some of these books are current, having been published within the last few years, and the rest are much older. Even with this broad coverage, most business libraries contain only a fraction of the published output, both new and old. So how do you know that the business library you are using covers your research area adequately? Really, all that you have to go on is the reputation of the library and the size of the collections. If you are looking for current research, your public business library will be helpful. For both current and more historical research, the academic libraries are unparalleled. Keep in mind that no matter what the reputation or the size of the library, no business collection has everything. All libraries, regardless of reputation and collection size, will have both collection strengths and weaknesses. This chapter will help you to identify important sources to supplement what your library owns, sources to borrow from other libraries, or even to purchase for your own use.

WHY YOU NEED BOOKS TO FIND BOOKS

If you are conducting an exhaustive search for every book written about Bretton Woods, or all of the works by the classic economist Adam Smith, what do you do to make sure that you are examining the complete publishing output? What if you just want to find out what books have been published recently on stock index futures? This chapter will guide you towards those sources that provide lists of books, both old and new, on all aspects of business. These reference guides can be considered a mega-library, if you will.

Depending on your research interest, whether you are looking for current books, classics, or getting a feel for business books published during the Great Depression, this section should be of interest to you.

When you have created a bibliography (a list of books) that you are interested in, take them to your business librarian. The librarian will first check to see if the books are in the library. For those books not in the library, you can begin to process your requests through electronic networks (such as OCLC or RLIN), as mentioned in Chapter 1, to locate and request the needed books from other libraries around the country. Which library the books are actually located in is immaterial to you. The fact that you can identify books you need that are part of the publishing record and act upon this information to obtain access to them is key. With this research knowledge you are able to transcend limitations of one library collection and delve into the complete record of the English language publishing history.

The following annotated list of "books to find books" is loosely arranged by publication date of the profiled books. Some of the sources contain records for current books as well as books published years ago. These publications will be included in the "Historic Research" section. Those publications that only profile new books, and there are more of these, will be discussed in the "Current Research" section. As you read descriptions of these entries, be aware of the level of analysis for the business books. Some of the sources are very brief in their descriptions and only contain a minimal amount of facts, such as author, title, price, and publisher information. These are commonly referred to as book catalogs. Other works, called reviewing sources, provide reviews of books which enables you to analyze whether you wish to pursue obtaining the identified books or not.

HISTORIC RESEARCH

Despite the popular belief that business research is limited to the here and now, there are many solid reasons why you might be interested in conducting historic business research. Chief among these reasons is the need to find unique, long-buried information on companies, industries, or business phenomena. Although currency of information to the business world cannot be stressed enough, oftentimes what is in vogue at the moment is a re-invention of the past. If you were doing research on a company to develop marketing campaigns, wouldn't it be useful to know something about that company that had been published years ago in the trade press? Industries have also been written about extensively over the last several hundred years. Several of the larger business research libraries in the country maintain extensive collections of corporate and industry histories. In conducting research of this nature, it is important to keep in mind that identification of a book's existence is usually all that you need to do. Thanks to interlibrary loan and other services, you do not need to be physically present at the library that owns a book you need in order to use it.

All of the following titles will be useful in conducting exhaustive searches through the published book literature of the United States. Note as you move through the list that the more recently published titles are typically the easier to find. The older the title, the more likely that you are looking for a source that was available at a handful of leading libraries many years ago. These sources for identifying books are still important, but more from a title identification basis. It is probably not likely that books assigned to a mercantile library, circa 1820, are still in that library. The library may not even be in existence anymore. The importance is that you may have discovered a title that is unique, but leave it up to your business librarian, as mentioned earlier, to track down where the book is presently held. It may be that your one-of-a-kind business history book is now located in the rare book room of a modern library that acquired the book at auction or through some similar means.

Sources

Evans, Charles. *American Bibliography: A Chronological Dictionary of all Books, Pamphlets and Periodical Publications Printed in the United States of America from the Genesis of Printing in 1639 Down to and Including the Year 1800; With Bibliographical and Biographical Notes.* (Chicago, 1903-1959, 14 volumes.)

This title is considered the leading source for identifying early publications in the U.S. Although the first volume of this set was published in 1903 by the author, Charles Evans, it was continued by other publishers up until 1959. The arrangement is chronological according to date of publication. Each volume also contains an author, title, and subject index. The entries contain author information, publisher information, and in some cases, information regarding which libraries own the book being researched.

Shipton, Clifford K. and James E. Mooney. *National Index of American Imprints Through 1800: The Short-Title Evans.* (Worchester, MA: American Antiquarian Society, 1969, 2 volumes.)

As the title implies, this is an update to the preceding work. In this index you will find an additional 10,000 entries for books not covered in Evans. Although there are other updates available, this one is considered the best. The arrangement is alphabetical by author.

Shaw, Ralph R. and Richard H. Shoemaker. *American Bibliography: A Preliminary Checklist for 1801-1819.* (New York: Scarecrow Press, 1958-1966, 22 volumes.)

This publication is important because of the time period covered. As with most of these early lists of books, the main feature is primarily to verify the existence of books and to identify where those books are located.

Shoemaker, Richard H. *Checklist of American Imprints for 1820-1829.* (New York: Scarecrow Press, 1964-1971, 10 volumes.)

Roorbach, Orville Augustus. *Bibliotheca Americana, 1820-1861.* (New York: Roorbach, 1852-1861, 4 volumes.)

Both of these titles are important because they identify books available during the period from 1820-1861. The emphasis is on providing an arranged catalog of books, rather than allowing subject access. The information provides author, title, price, and publisher.

Kelly, James. *The American Catalogue of Books.* (New York: Wiley, 1861-1871, 2 volumes.)

This title contains lists of books published between 1861 to 1871. The work is also very similar to Roorbach and Shoemaker in the amount of information provided and the method of accessing these records.

American Catalogue. (New York: Publisher's Weekly, 1880-1911, 8 volumes.)

This is the first really useful book of books that does not require a linear alphabetical title approach to finding what you are looking for. You can effectively use this book to locate books by subject. The time period covered is 1876-1910. Each entry contains brief information including author, title and publisher. This is the predecessor of many of the standard lists mentioned in the "Current Research" section.

American Book Publishing Record: Cumulative 1876-1949. (New York: Bowker, 1980, 15 volumes.)

American Book Publishing Record: Cumulative 1950-1977. (New York: Bowker, 1979, 15 volumes.)

Both of these works are major advances over their predecessors. They provide standard catalog information such as author, title, publisher and subject headings. The bulk of the volumes arrange the entries according to Dewey Decimal Classification. This is significant because it allows for more narrow and focused searches. The total number of entries between these two sources is in excess of one-and-a-half million titles.

National Union Catalog, Pre-1956 Imprints. (London: Mansell, 1968-1980, 685 volumes.)

This massive set of printed catalog cards reflects book holdings in excess of 10 million titles in over 700 libraries. The arrangement is reflective of earlier book catalogs that arranged information by author. The intent is to verify the existence and location of materials through standard catalog descriptions. This is not as effective as the preceding entry, which allows searching by subject. Because of the incredible volume of titles included, this work is considered a giant in the history of the book publishing record.

Business and Economics Books, 1876-1982. (New York: Bowker, 1983, 4 volumes.)

This work provides access to over 143,000 business books published during the time period indicated. The information for each title includes author, title, publisher and a brief physical description of the work. Reviews are not included, but the comprehensiveness of the source makes it worthwhile for identifying business publications over a broad range of time. The major part of the set is arranged by subject area. Author and title indexes are provided.

Goldsmiths' Kress Library of Economic Literature. (Woodbridge, CT: Research Publications, 1976-1983, 5 volumes.)

This set includes bound volumes which contain author, title and subject indexes. The indexes refer you to over 47,000 books that were published about business and economics before 1848. The books themselves make up the collections of the Goldsmiths' Library held at the University of London School of Economics and the Kress Library of the Harvard University Graduate School of Business. These two important research collections contain many of the world's finest economic literature. They have been reproduced on microfilm in their entirety and are available for research at selected business libraries in the U.S.

CURRENT RESEARCH

Current research sources reflect the growing scope and complexity of the modern business world. The sheer number of books published has increased exponentially. In addition, there is more awareness of other countries' economies, more global competition, and greater demand for business information from more consumers. Consequently, in doing your business research, you need to sift through the publishing record using sources that allow you to cover the most territory in the least amount of time.

The following publications are considered to be the best means of tracking the current flow of new books. Most of the sources highlighted have indexes that allow for easy access by subject, enabling you to refine your research and eliminate the superfluous. Those sources that lack subject indexing, and these are the exception, may still be of some use. For example, if you are searching for books on marketing, chances are that many of the books on that subject will have titles that begin with "market" or some variation. All of the sources in the following list that lack subject indexes allow for title and author searching.

Sources

American Book Publishing Record. (New York: Bowker, 1960-.)

This title, more readily known as *ABPR*, is a cumulation of the *Weekly Record* and is published monthly, annually, and quinquennially. The *ABPR* provides a very quick and effective way of browsing through the output of books published in English over the last 30 years.

Bibliographic Guide to Business and Economics. (Boston: G.K. Hall, 1975-.)

This publication provides identification of business books that have been added to the collections of the Library of Congress and the New York Public Library. It is updated on an annual basis. An extensive author, title, and subject index is included.

Books In Print. (New York: Bowker, 1948-.)

Subject Guide To Books In Print. (New York: Bowker, 1957-.)

These guides are a first stop for building current lists of business titles. They are considered the primary sources for libraries in their acquisitions work. Entry information includes author, title, price, and publisher. Updated on an annual basis, both publications are also available on microfiche and optical disc.

Books Out of Print. (New York: Bowker, 1980-.)

Updated annually, this source is invaluable for verifying the existence of titles. This is necessary because of the rapidity with which many books go out of print. *Books Out of Print* not only helps you to identify the existence of recently published books, but it can also help you to fill in any missing pieces such as a book's author and publisher. Arrangement is by author and title.

Business Periodicals Index. (New York: H.W. Wilson Company, 1958-.)

This is a well-established index to business periodicals and is also noted for its references to book reviews. It is updated monthly, except July, and cumulated annually. The book review section is arranged alphabetically by author and provides title, year published and includes a citation to the journal where the book review can be located.

Core Collection: An Author and Subject Guide. (Boston: Harvard Business School, 1971-.)

This annual list is a good way of keeping track of what is available in a leading business school library. Books are arranged both by author and by subject.

The list is updated monthly with the companion publication *Recent Additions to Baker Library.*

Cumulative Book Index: A World List of Books in the English Language. (New York: Wilson, 1933-.)

This title, often referred to simply as *CBI*, provides author, title, and subject access to books published since 1928. Prior to 1928, this title was known as the *United States Catalog* (published from 1899-1928). Arrangement of *CBI* is in one useful alphabet with author, title and subject entries interfiled. The records for each title include publisher, price, subject headings, and classification numbers. The coverage is not limited to American publications, but tries to encompass the publishing record of all books written in English. Included are titles published by associations, societies, university presses, and selected government publications. *CBI* is updated monthly, except August, and is cumulated on an annual basis.

Directions. (Bridgewater, NJ: Baker and Taylor, 1974-.)

This monthly publication, produced by one of the leading book vendors in the country, is an excellent guide to keeping abreast of what's new in the market. Arranged by academic subject areas, each entry provides author, title, publisher, price and subject heading information.

Forthcoming Books. (New York: Bowker, 1966-.)

Subject Guide To Forthcoming Books. (New York: Bowker, 1967-.)

These are basically advance lists of books to be published as announced by publishers. Both titles are updated on a bi-monthly basis. The subject guide arranges the titles into several hundred subject areas. Entry data includes, author, title, price, publisher, and expected publication date.

Publisher's Trade List Annual. (New York: Bowker, 1873-.)

This publication, known as *PTLA*, is basically a collection of publisher's catalogs. It is arranged alphabetically by publisher and is useful if you want to target the works produced by a specific book publisher. Large publishers as well as smaller presses are represented, but it is not a complete list.

University Research in Business and Economics. (Morgantown, WV: Association for University Business and Economic Research, 1956-.)

This is an annual publication list that concentrates on academic publications since 1956. Featured are books, working papers, bulletins and other publications of member business schools. It is also known as the *AUBER Bibliography.* Indexing is by author and arrangement is by subject and by member school. A cumulative index covering 1956-1981 has also been published.

Weekly Record. (New York: Bowker, 1974-.)

Weekly Record provides author, title, subject headings, price and publisher information on new books. Arrangement is by Library of Congress Classification number. Focus is on all books distributed in the U.S., including foreign press titles. This is one of the more exhaustive, current new book lists available. *Weekly Record* up until 1974 was a part of *Publisher's Weekly.*

REVIEWING GUIDES

Reviewing guides are important because they help you to evaluate a wide range of business books. Most reviews of books are done at the time of publication or within several months afterwards. Some book reviews are based on galleys, or pre-publication information. Unless you were working for a bookstore or library, most of your needs can be filled with "after press" reviews.

Reviews of business books are typically written by librarians, faculty, publishing staff, and business practitioners. Some reviews, particularly those featured in academic journals, are predominantly written by business school faculty. These reviews are typically quite scholarly, as would be expected, and emphasize academic titles. Reviews in library-oriented sources are generally written by librarians and include academic as well as more mainstream, popular titles. Reviews found in publisher's sources usually include a mix of reviewers including both publishing staff and librarians.

When reading reviews, pay particular attention to the recommendation of the reviewer. In library and publisher sources, recommendations usually indicate level of readership such as public library, community and junior colleges, research libraries, and practitioner. Additional points of interest, depending on the reviewers knowledge, include comparisons with similar books, critique of writing style, readability, purchase value, and so forth.

Sources

American Reference Books Annual. (Englewood, CO: Libraries Unlimited, 1970-.)

This guide is an annual review of reference books—directories, yearbooks, dictionaries, etc.—published in the U.S. and Canada. Each review provides critical evaluations and is signed by the reviewer. Reviewers are predominantly librarians, with a handful of reviewers encompassing publishing staff, faculty and practitioners. Entries include notes on whether reviews have previously been published in *Choice, Library Journal* and other library reviewing publications. Arrangement of reviewing categories is by broad Library of Congress classification and the coverage of business reference materials is unparalleled.

Book Review Digest. (New York: H.W. Wilson and Company, 1905-.)

This guide is published monthly, except February and July, with an annual cumulation. The reviews are written within 18 months of a book's publication. The reviews are sometimes written by the *Book Review Digest* staff, but more often than not are culled from the pages of *Choice, Booklist, Library Journal, New York Times Review of Books*, and over 90 other trade and news publications. *Book Review Digest* is indexed by subject and reviews are arranged alphabetically by author.

Book Review Index. (Detroit: Gale Research Company, 1965-.)

Published bi-monthly with annual and decennial cumulations, this listing service to book reviews concentrates coverage on the social sciences, humanities, and popular fiction. It features two separate author and title indexes and cites reviews from over 500 different periodicals.

Choice. (Chicago: Association for College and Research Libraries, 1964-.)

This monthly journal is devoted to academic books. The reviews are arranged by such broad categories as business, management, or labor. Each review is signed by the reviewer, typically a librarian subject specialist, and contains a purchase recommendation and the reader group for which the work is most appropriate. In May of each year *Choice* publishes its annual list of "Outstanding Academic Books and Nonprint Material."

Daniells, Lorna. *Business Information Sources*. (Berkeley: University of California, 1993.)

This is a leading source in describing outstanding business publications and is considered the business librarian's "bible." Broken down by broad subject areas, it provides a thorough treatment of the leading business reference works available and should be consulted before any large business library research project is undertaken. Reviews of books are written by the author and provide excellent evaluative material that highlights the appropriateness of the titles for business library research. This guide is typically updated every 5 to 10 years.

Key to Economic Science and Managerial Sciences. (Hague: Nijhoff, 1953-.)

Despite some publishing setbacks that have disrupted publication over the years, this is a useful tool in locating reviews of international business books. The reviews tend to be more informative than evaluative. Indexing is by subject classification with emphasis on business and economics titles.

Library Journal. New York.

Every Spring, *LJ* features an in-depth article on business books that have been published during the past year, titled "Best Business Books of . . . ."

This much-anticipated feature usually has a thematic approach revolving around whatever were the most popular or controversial issues for that year. Books selected for the article are reviewed by the column editor and purchase advice is given.

Publisher's Weekly. (New York: Bowker, 1872-.)

This is the oldest existing trade journal and announcement source for new books in the U.S. market. It is most useful for keeping up with the current flow of new books. *Publisher's Weekly* is not only a strong tool for new book selection, it is also a key source for providing reliable data on the publishing industry. This source is additionally important because it contains publisher advertisements as well as announcements of forthcoming books. The stature of forthcoming books can often be ascertained by the advertising budget and author signing information which are featured for the benefit of the book retailer.

In addition to all of the previously mentioned reviewing sources, it is important to keep up with leading journals within your subject field. Most academic business journals, and even a few popular or mainstream titles, regularly feature from one to several reviews of new business books. These journals include such titles as *Accountancy Review, California Management Review, Harvard Business Review, Journal of Economic Literature, Journal of Finance, Journal of Marketing*, and others. Ask your professor or business librarian for suggested titles within your research area.

5

Indexes to Periodical Literature and Reports

OBJECTIVES: This chapter will discuss the role of indexes in the research process and briefly explain the content and special features of selected general and specialized indexes covering business topics.

Why Use Indexes?

Four Types of Indexes
- Subject Arrangement: *Readers' Guide*
- Table of Contents Arrangement: *Current Contents: Social and Behavioral Science*
- Citation Arrangement: *Social Sciences Citation Index*
- Standard Industrial Classification Code Arrangement: *F & S Index*

Key Business Indexes Not Specialized as to Industry or Topic
- *Business Periodicals Index*
- *Wall Street Journal Index*

Specialized Business Indexes
- *Accounting and Tax Index*
- *Lodging and Restaurant Index*
- *Personnel Management Abstracts*

Interdisciplinary Indexes: Coverage of Business Topics
- *American Statistics Index*
- *Monthly Catalog*
- *PAIS*
- *Social Sciences Index*
- *Statistical Reference Index*

Specialized Non-Business Indexes: Utility to the Business Researcher

After completing this chapter you should be able to:

*Understand the different types of indexes.

*Identify a business index (one dedicated exclusively to business topics) to consult for your research.

*Identify an interdisciplinary index (one that covers business but is not dedicated strictly to business topics) that you could check for additional information.

*Explain when a specialized index should be used to supplement research done in indexes intended for a general audience.

WHY USE INDEXES?

For virtually all business research topics, having up-to-date information is of utmost importance. Exceptions to the rule would include subjects such as the history of an accounting practice, the stock market, or of a marketing phenomenon. Even with historical treatments of business topics, it is important to include current information to show what impact past events have on the present.

An index is a library source to consult for current information on topics published in magazines, journals, newspapers, or reports. However remember that the term "current" means different things in different sources. Indexing processes include a time lag ranging from about three months, in the case of printed indexes, to one or two months in the case of compact disc-based indexes, and from a few hours to a few weeks for online databases. Online databases and compact disc-based indexes will be covered in Chapter 7: "Database Vendors."

FOUR TYPES OF INDEXES

Indexes fall into four general types based on the basic arrangement of the material: 1) subject arrangement, 2) table of contents arrangement, 3) citation arrangement, and 4) Standard Industrial Classification (SIC) code arrangement.

Subject Arrangement

Nearly ever library, regardless of size will have the *Readers' Guide to Periodical Literature* (short title *Readers' Guide*) (New York: H. W. Wilson Company, 1900-) or its abridged version, covering fewer titles. Both versions are published monthly. This familiar source, recognized by virtually everyone who has done research in high school, is an example of a traditional index which groups article citations (listings that give complete publication information including author's name, article title, the name of the periodical, the volume, number, and date of the issue in which an article appears, and the page numbers) by subject. Most titles included in the *Readers' Guide* are aimed at a general audience, so there is some utility in consulting this index for non-technical information on a business topic unfamiliar to you.

The following are a few of the business-oriented journal titles covered by the *Readers' Guide*: *Black Enterprise, Business Week, Fortune, Money,* U.S. Bureau of Labor Statistics' *Monthly Labor Review,* and *Working Woman.* Since *Readers' Guide* does not cover many business periodicals, you are advised not to limit your search to this source.

Table of Contents Arrangement

An example of a table of contents index, published to facilitate current awareness in business and allied fields, is *Current Contents: Social and Behavioral Sciences* (Philadelphia: Institute for Scientific Information, 1969-). This publication (along with some electronic sources described in Chapter 9) reproduces the table of contents pages from various journals, listing the titles of articles in each issue of every journal covered. Issued on a weekly basis, it provides business people, teachers, and scholars a way to keep up with key business journals and selected books. Special features include an index of title words, an author index, and a directory of authors' addresses. Table of contents access is important where neither researchers nor their local libraries can afford key publications in a given field. Once a good article or book has been identified, generally it can be borrowed from another library. Two former *Current Contents* publications—a British one covering management and a Korean one covering foreign journals in management and economics—are listed in Chapter 14, "International Sources."

Citation Arrangement

Citation indexes are built on the "old boy" and "old girl" system. The assumption is that the most frequently cited authors in a given field are the pre-eminent thinkers in that branch of knowledge. Coverage of publications in this type of index centers on articles and books that have been cited in the bibliography (source list) by a number of subsequent writers.

Under the entry for each of the publications of a heavily cited "authority" in a given discipline (for example, Philip Kotler, a big name in marketing theory), are listed the names of later writers citing that particular article or book. Looking up any one of these later writers leads in turn to a section of the index where a full citation is given for *every source* in that writer's bibliography. Thus, citation indexes help you follow a research trail from the works of an acknowledged master in your field to work done by their disciples. In addition to this arrangement, there is a section called the PERMUTERM INDEX arranged by keywords from titles, which gives you access to cited publications by subjects. This section helps you locate key articles and books in a field that is new to you, when you don't know the names of the authorities in that field.

Social Sciences Citation Index or *SSCI* (Philadelphia: Institute for Scientific Information, 1969-) is one example of a citation index you might consult for a management or economics topic. For information about computers or a certain manufacturing technology, you could try the *Science Citation Index* or *SCI* (Philadelphia: Institute for Scientific Information, 1961-). The one drawback of using citation indexes is that some writers are interdisciplinary in their approach to a topic, citing sources that will *not* pertain to your research. The titles of cited books and articles sometimes will give you a clue to their suitability for your topic, but you cannot always determine the relevance of a cited reference without actually reading it.

Standard Industrial Classification Code Arrangement

Although it also has a section arranged alphabetically by company name, the *Predicasts F & S Index: United States* or *F & S* (Cleveland: Predicasts, 1960-) is best known for its coverage of company, product, and industry information and is arranged by Standard Industrial Classification (SIC) code number. (An alphabetical index in each issue gives the SIC number associated with different industries—a four-digit number such as 7900 for Recreation—and products—a five to seven-digit number such as 79400 for Sports Clubs and Racing.)

F & S covers over 2,000 publications, including financial sources, business-oriented newspapers, trade magazines, and special reports, as well as a considerable number of federal government documents. This breadth of coverage is one of the outstanding strengths of *F & S*.

Subjects covered range from corporate acquisitions and mergers to timely industry updates, new products, technological developments, and even some information about social and political factors affecting business (e.g. publication of a new magazine about child rearing aimed at Japanese-Americans). Foreign company operations covered in U.S. publications are in this publication.

Instead of a specific article title, *F & S* gives a short phrase or sentence summarizing the article's content. Other standard publication information is included, except that instead of inclusive pages, *F & S* gives only the starting page. Since this index includes citations to full-length articles as well as news features no longer than one or two paragraphs, the absence of an ending page can be a nuisance and can complicate requesting article copies via interlibrary loan.

KEY BUSINESS INDEXES NOT SPECIALIZED AS TO INDUSTRY OR TOPIC

The *Readers' Guide* covering all branches of knowledge and the *Social Sciences Index* devoted to a number of subfields are examples of interdisciplinary indexes you will sometimes find useful for business research. Not surprisingly, however, key business indexes—those dedicated to the field of business, economics, and management—often surpass an interdisciplinary index in the amount and quality of material found on a given business topic. This is true because, instead of a subject mix of the performing arts, business, science and so forth, key business indexes primarily cover publications written for and read by business people.

Another important characteristic of key business indexes is that they do not specialize in a particular business subdiscipline such as marketing or economics or accounting. Instead they cover the whole galaxy of business subjects. One of the important indexes dedicated to a variety of business topics, *F & S Index*, is described above. Two other print-based indexes familiar to many library users are:

Business Periodicals Index or *BPI* (Bronx, New York: H.W. Wilson Company, 1958-).

Frequency of Publication: Monthly.

Scope: Subject fields covered run the gamut of business topics from accounting to transportation as well as individual business firms, industries, trades, and even prominent business leaders. Although some of the source periodicals are published abroad (e.g. in Canada, Great Britain, and Mexico), no non-English language titles are indexed.

Arrangement: The main part of the index consists of an alphabetical subject arrangement, with appropriate subdivisions and cross references from common terminology. For example, under CLAIMS ADMINISTRATORS you may find article references under subject subdivisions for "Client relations", "Finance", and "Forecasting" along with other subdivisions for particular publications such as "Directories."

Information Given: Entries give the article title (sometimes augmented to clarify the subject as in "Free Advice [tips for the independent and creative]"), author, notes about special features such as tables, abbreviated source periodical title, volume or issue, inclusive pages, and date. Check the front of the index for the key to periodical title abbreviations. (Any time an index abbreviates, a list of titles in full form is provided somewhere in the publication.)

Special Features: Book reviews are listed in a separate section at the end of the issue under author or title.

Recommended Use: This index has information for the generalist (student or manager) on virtually every business topic. Research in *BPI* should be supplemented by consulting specialized indexes if you need more comprehensive coverage of your topic. Specialized indexes may include both more sources and publications for the specialist in the field.

Wall Street Journal Index or *WSJ Index* (Ann Arbor, MI: University Microfilms International, 1958-).

Frequency of Publication: Monthly.

Scope: Abstracting and indexing is provided for all articles in the 3-Star Eastern Edition of the *Wall Street Journal.* Included are the following: news items, columns, feature articles, editorials, letters to the editor, obituaries, selected tables, earnings reports, dividend reports, and arts reviews. Among the items excluded from indexing are most stock tables, editorial cartoons, and individual items in a column covering a potpourri of very brief topics such as CREDIT MARKETS. (From 1981-1991, indexing for the journal *Barrons'* was included in the *Wall Street Journal Index*).

Arrangement: The first section, headed CORPORATE NEWS is an alphabetical arrangement by company name. (Hint: here words starting with initials like A & W or IBM come at the beginning of their respective alphabetical sections). In any index look for a two-part company name such as "Adolph Coors" under each of its parts, i.e. "Adolph Coors" and "Coors, Adolph." The section headed GENERAL NEWS is an alphabetical arrangement of subjects based on 2,500 general subject terms such as MANAGEMENT and UNEMPLOYMENT. Current *WSJ Index* issues list the major subject headings to look under, although not all of the 2,500 subject terms are given. You will find articles under personal and non-profit organization names, place names, and product names, although in the interest of brevity the list of major subject headings excludes these.

Information Given: Article summaries from two to six lines long are given, along with the length of the article (Long, Medium, or Short), the month and day of publication (the year being listed on the front of the index), a letter designating the section of the paper, and the beginning page and column numbers.

Special Features: A user's guide explains such things as how long subject headings are subdivided. Sample entries are labelled to assist in decoding the entries, which are formatted quite differently from magazine and journal citations.

Recommended Use: An excellent source of news items about companies as well as feature articles about both companies and broader business topics, this index frequently provides background and some in-depth information on a topic. If the *Wall Street Journal Index* is not available, most other newspaper indexes, the *New York Times Index* in particular, are good alternatives.

SPECIALIZED BUSINESS INDEXES

Because there are so many specialized business indexes, only selected indexes are covered below.

Accounting and Tax Index (Formerly *Accountant's Index*, Ann Arbor, MI: University Microfilms International, 1920-).

Frequency of Publication: Quarterly.

Scope: Emphasis is on accounting and taxation, but related subjects (financial management, compensation, consulting, and the financial services industry) are included as well. Over 1,000 publications (including books, pamphlets, and journal articles) are included. Journals range from the general *Forbes* to the specialized *Rural Telecommunications* and the international *Far Eastern Economic Review.*

Arrangement: Subjects (company names, government organizations, general topics such as ROYALTIES, accounting topics such as ROYSCOTT FACTORS and S CORPORATIONS) are interfiled alphabetically with entries under authors' names. Only the largest subject sections such as the INTERNAL REVENUE CODE and LETTER RULINGS are further divided into subheadings.

Information Given: Journal entries include the article title, author's name, journal title, volume and/or issue number, publication date, and inclusive pages. Standard bibliographic information (date, publisher, etc.) is listed for other types of publications.

Special Features: A list of source publications covered by the index is provided. For users of the AICPA (American Institute of Certified Public Accountants) library, book and pamphlet entries include a classification number in parentheses, for that library. Directions are also given on how to order articles through University Microfilms International's article clearinghouse as well as about electronic access to the index (the online database and the compact disc-based version).

Recommended Use: Covering the bulk of the English-language accounting literature published worldwide, this is an excellent source for accounting. The Commerce Clearinghouse (CCH) publication, *Accounting Articles*, which overlaps somewhat with this source, is more difficult for the inexperienced researcher to use because of its arrangement. The CCH index arranges subjects under sections and paragraph numbers very similar to the complex system used for legal citations.

Lodging and Restaurant Index (West Lafayette, IN: Purdue University, 1985-).

Frequency of Publication: Quarterly.

Scope: Intended primarily for students and academicians, the index can be valuable to practitioners in the hospitality, lodging, and restaurant industries as well. Nearly fifty specialized periodicals—both trade publications and scholarly ones—are covered.

Arrangement: Articles are arranged under subject headings based on a standardized vocabulary developed by the publisher. Within each subject section, entries are alphabetized by their respective journal titles. Each article is assigned an average of 3-4 different subjects, so you have several chances to find it.

Information Given: Standard bibliographic information is given (article title, author(s), journal title, volume/issue numbers, inclusive pages, and dates). Some titles are augmented by brief article summaries.

Special Features: Key articles (those of substantial length or quality) are set off by an asterisk. The list of standardized terms is in the front of annual volumes.

Recommended Use: Covers some restaurant, hospitality, and lodging journals not in *F & S* (for example *Military Clubs and Recreation* and *Airline, Ship, & Catering Onboard Services*). If possible, you should consult *F & S*, *ASI*, and *SRI* as well as this index for comprehensive coverage of your topic.

Personnel Management Abstracts (Chelsea, MI: Personnel Management Abstracts, 1955-).

Frequency of Publication: Quarterly.

Scope: Over 100 academic and trade journals dealing with personnel management and organization development, including some published abroad are covered regularly. In addition, a small number of books are listed and abstracted (summarized) in each index.

Arrangement: Articles are listed under standardized subject headings. The same citation may appear under a broad heading such as MANAGEMENT FUNCTIONS and under more specific headings such as DECISION MAKING or PLANNING. At the back of each index issue, books are arranged in alphabetical order by title. There is a separate index section arranged by author. This section includes only periodical article authors, not book authors.

Information Given: Standard bibliographic information plus a fairly long abstract is given for both books and periodical articles. When available, a price and/or telephone number are given for books to facilitate ordering.

Special Features: See above.

Recommended Use: This is an excellent source for keeping up with what's being published in the area of personnel management and organization development. Comprehensive treatment of most topics would require also consulting *BPI*, *ABI/Inform*, *Management Contents*, *Psychological Abstracts* and perhaps a specialized index such as *Hospital Literature Index*.

INTERDISCIPLINARY INDEXES: COVERAGE OF BUSINESS TOPICS

In addition to *Readers' Guide*, *Current Contents: Social and Behavioral Sciences*, and *Social Sciences Citation Index* described earlier in this chapter, a number of other interdisciplinary indexes are worth consulting for business research. The *Vertical File Index* (*VFI*), which covers reports and pamphlets, may be useful to you if your library maintains a pamphlet file. Many no longer do. Alternatively, you can send for items mentioned in the *VFI*. Most are inexpensive, some are free. But since the publishers of titles listed in the *VFI* frequently do not maintain a large stock of them, you are advised to do so as soon as possible after finding them in the index.

American Statistics Index, or *ASI* (Bethesda, MD: Congressional Information Service, 1974-).

Frequency of Publication: Monthly.

Scope: Indexes United States Federal government publications of a statistical nature.

Arrangement: The abstract section is arranged by issuing agency, starting with Department of Agriculture. A separate index section lets you search for statistical publications under a subject or name, or under a category (eight geographic categories starting with census division; six economic categories including commodity, federal agency, income, company or institution, industry, and occupation; and six demographic categories including age, disease, education, marital status, race/ethnicity, and sex.

Information Given: Entries start with the index's unique five-digit item number which gets you from the index page to the appropriate spot in the abstract and from there to the microfiche copy of the document if your library buys the entire *ASI* collection. Next is publication information: issuing agency name, frequency of publication (annual, periodical, etc.), title and subtitle of document, physical description (number of pages, etc.), publication date, issuing agency report number, and ordering information (GPO stock number, depository item number, SuDoc number, *Monthly Catalog* entry number, Library of Congress card number, price, and which private and government entities sell the document.) Last is a general description of the publication, e.g., this "tabulations of individual income tax returns." And finally, each statistical table in the document is described in considerable detail.

Special Features: The user guide explains arrangement and entries.

Recommended Use: This is the best source for locating a specific statistic buried in a federal document or documents.

Monthly Catalog of United States Government Publications or *Monthly Catalog* (Washington, D.C.: U.S. Government Printing Office, 1895-).

Frequency of Publication: Monthly.

Scope: This source attempts to index all U.S. federal government publications, except those which are classified. It does exclude certain types of material within these broad parameters, including some agency special publications and many technical reports.

Arrangement: The main section is in order by SuDoc number (Superintendent of Documents classification number) under the issuing agency, starting with **A** for Agriculture Department and ending with **Y** for House and Senate documents.

Information Given: Entries include a wealth of information, different parts of which are used by different libraries in arranging and retrieving federal government publications. First is the entry number, the first two digits of which stand for the publication year. Next is the SuDoc classification number. Additional information can include author, document title, series statement for continuing publications, imprint (issuing agency, place of publication, etc.), notes including such details as project funding, physical description (page length, hard copy or microfiche), whether available to depository libraries, GPO stock number for ordering, price, subject headings, Dewey and Library of Congress classification numbers, Library of Congress Catalog card number, and OCLC number (the identification number for a national library cataloging and lending network).

Special Features: An extensive user guide explains how to use the *Monthly Catalog* and gives sample entries to aid in decoding the unique and complex information presented. It also explains what the Federal Depository Library program is and tells how to get copies of publications from sources as varied as online database vendors and bookstores in major metropolitan areas around the country. An order form for mailing to the GPO (Government Printing Office) is included as well. Indexes include the following access points: individual or government author; document title; subject; series/report number; contract number; GPO stock number; and keyword-in-title index.

Recommended Use: The U.S. government is one of the biggest publishers of business information in the world, and a good deal of it is available without charge. In virtually all subject areas *Monthly Catalog* is the best single source of citations for government publications regardless of format (books, pamphlets, technical reports, etc.)

PAIS International In Print or *PAIS* (New York: Public Affairs Information Service, Inc., 1991-).

Frequency of Publication: monthly.

Scope: Subjects covered include business, economic and social conditions, public administration and public policy, and international relations. The emphasis throughout is on factual and statistical information. Within the field of business, *PAIS* focuses on economic factors, industry surveys, interactions between business and society at large, and similar issues. Sources of general public interest are included, technical or highly specialized works are excluded. Types of publications indexed include books (7,000-8,000 per year), periodical articles (from a source list of 1,600 titles), selected foreign government documents; U.S. national, state, and some municipal government documents; pamphlets; microfiche (mostly U.S. government documents and publications of international organizations); and reports issued by both public and private agencies. Sources from five non-English languages are covered: French, German, Italian, Portuguese, and Spanish. Geographic coverage is not limited as long as publications are in one of these languages.

Arrangement: Citations are arranged by subject, with appropriate subdivisions and cross-references to facilitate usage.

Information Given: PAIS gives the following information: a summary of the contents of each item; author; item title and subtitle; special features such as illustrations, maps, tables, or a bibliography; appropriate bibliographic (publication) information for book, periodical, or other type of publication; and notes such as translation from another language and standard numbers useful for purchasing an item or locating it within a library (e.g. Superintendent of Documents number, International Standard Serial Number, or Library of Congress catalog card number).

Special Features: Each issue includes directories of sources (publishers/distributors) for books and periodical titles covered in that issue of *PAIS* along with the addresses of both the division of the New York Public Library that provides photocopies and a commercial document delivery service where copies can be obtained.

Recommended Use: In libraries lacking an index dedicated to international business topics, *PAIS* is an excellent place to look for information about international business or for background information about a particular country (e.g. demographics or consumer behavior). It should be used in conjunction with *Business Periodicals Index,* and if possible you should also consult the international indexes listed in Chapter 17.

Social Sciences Index (New York: H.W. Wilson Company, 1974-).

Frequency of Publication: Quarterly.

Scope: Covers ten broad social science subject areas: anthropology, community health/medicine, economics, geography, international relations, law/criminology/police science, political science, psychology/psychiatry, public administration, sociology/ social work, and related subjects). Indexes 342 English-language periodicals, some international in scope.

Arrangement: An alphabetical arrangement integrates author and subject entries, with appropriate subheadings for large subjects. For example, under SAVINGS AND INVESTMENT you might find separate sections listing references about "International Aspects", "Mathematical Models", specific countries, "Developing Countries" in the aggregate, and the history of this topic. Subject headings are derived from a number of sources, including the Library of Congress subject headings along with terms used in the field and a variety of other sources. Since not all libraries will own a thesaurus for Wilson databases, you are advised to try every term you can think of, make a list of which seem to work, and if necessary ask a librarian's help in finding information.

Information Given: Citations include article title (sometimes augmented to clarify the title or call attention to special features), author's name, notes about special features such as a bibliography or maps, the periodical title abbreviated, the volume/issue number, inclusive pages, and date.

Special Features:"Blanket references" are given for regular features of interest to researchers, (e.g. for "Scientific Expeditions" see issues of the *Geographical Magazine*.) Book reviews are listed in a section at the end of the index under author and/or book title.

Recommended Use: This index will be of interest to the business researcher for its interdisciplinary coverage of business topics as well as for its specific coverage of economics. As noted in the scope note, some international publications are included in its source list.

Statistical Reference Index. or *SRI* (Bethesda, MD: Congressional Information Service, 1980-).

Frequency of Publication: Monthly.

Scope: Indexes statistical publications from sources other than the U.S. Federal government, including commercial publishers such as those responsible for *Forbes* and *Fortune* magazines, non-profit organizations, state governments, independent research centers, and university research centers. The goal is coverage of business, economic, and social statistics of research significance on the national, state, or regional level.

Arrangement: The abstract section is arranged by type of issuing source, starting with associations and ending with universities. A separate index section lets you search for statistical publications under a subject, name, or category. Catagories include eight geographic categories starting with census division; six economic categories including commodity, federal agency, income, company or institution, industry, and occupation; and six demographic categories including age, disease, education, marital status, race/ethnicity, and sex.

Information Given: Entries start with the index's unique five-digit item number which gets you from the index page to the appropriate spot in the abstract and from there to the microfiche copy of the publication if your library buys the entire *SRI* collection. Next is publication information: issuing source name, publication type (annual, periodical, etc.), title of publication, publication frequency, physical description (number of pages, etc.), publication date, and ordering information (Library of Congress card number or International Standard Serials Number, and whether available in the *SRI* microfiche collection). Last is a general description of the publication as a whole (e.g., ''monthly report on consumer expectations''). And finally, each statistical table in the publication is described in considerable detail.

Special Features: The user guide explains arrangement and entries.

Recommended Use: This is the best single source for locating specific statistics published by entities outside the federal government.

SPECIALIZED NON-BUSINESS INDEXES: UTILITY TO THE BUSINESS RESEARCHER

Most articles and books covered in business indexes discussed earlier are written for the student, general use, or business manager, rather than a specialist such as an engineer, computer programmer, environmental scientist, or healthcare administrator. For narrower coverage of specialized fields of study, it is advisable to consult specialized non-business indexes created for those fields. This guide will not attempt a comprehensive list or review of such specialized sources. The following is a selected list: *Biological & Agricultural Index, Pollution Abstracts, Computer Abstracts, Oceanic Abstracts, Hospital Literature Index, Virology and AIDS Abstracts, Genetics Abstracts, Operations Research/Management Science, Energy Information Abstracts, Engineering Index,* and *Current Technology Index.*

In addition there are three subject-specific indexes that you might consult for business research: the ERIC (Educational Resources Information Center) indexes *Resources in Education (RIE)* and *Current Index to Journals in Education (CIJE)* for coverage of business education topics; *Applied Science and Technology Index* (which began publication with the *Business Periodicals Index* many years ago as the *Industrial Arts Index*) for technical aspects of business (such as manufacturing processes) and *Psychological Abstracts* for coverage of industrial and organizational psychology. While each of the titles listed above will duplicate some of the references found in business indexes, they should also reveal a wealth of new information.

Using an index is not always absolutely necessary. Sometimes you will find the perfect article by flipping through a dozen current magazine or newspaper issues. Other times a friend, colleague, or professor will put the perfect article into your hand. But most of the time using an index will help you generate a comprehensive, highly relevant list of sources, and it will save you time. Set a limit—say 20 minutes—for informal methods of finding articles (e.g. looking through recent issues of periodicals). If you don't find exactly what you need within this period, give up the "easy way" in favor of using an index.

6

Databases and Database Searching

OBJECTIVES: This chapter will explain what a database is and how database searching fits into a comprehensive research strategy.

> **Definitions of Database Searching Terms**
> - What Are Databases?
> **Why Are Databases Important?**
> **A Short History of Database Use**
> **Where Database Searching Fits into Your Research**
> **Getting Library Access**
> **Who Should Do the Research?**
> - End-User Searches
> - Mediated Searches
> **What Happens During a Database Search?**
> - Selecting a Database
> - Identifying the Main Ideas
> - Choosing Search Terms
> - Specifying Logical Relationships among Concepts
> - Evaluating Search Results
> **Getting Home or Office Access**
> **Tips and Pitfalls**
> - Getting Trained
> - Basic Searching Tips
> - Intermediate Search Tips
> **Database Evaluation Criteria**
> **Rationale for Using a Database Search**

After completing this chapter you should be able to:

*Decide whether you would benefit from a computerized search.

*State your research question in a form suitable for a computerized search (diagram it).

*Identify sources of information to help you choose an appropriate database for your topic.

DEFINITIONS OF DATABASE SEARCHING TERMS

What Are Databases?

The phrase "database searching" has special meaning to librarians and researchers. It is used to describe *computerized methods of searching an organized collection of information or data to retrieve selected items that you need.*

There are four principal types of databases:

Probably most familiar are the **bibliographic databases**, most of which are essentially a computerized version of a print-based index such as the *Business Periodicals Index*, enhanced by the computer's power to sort through thousands of records quickly and by the computer's power to search fields one is unable to search with print databases. They give bibliographic information—facts such as publication title, date, and so forth—that the reader needs to locate the same publication.

The second type of database is the **directory database**, again an enhanced version of the print product. Like their print counterparts, directory databases such as the *ICC British Company Directory* or Dun & Bradstreet's *Million Dollar Directory* include company names, addresses, phone and fax numbers, principal company officers, a description of the firm's business activity, and sometimes financial or sales information as well.

The third type of database is the **numeric database**. An example is Dun & Bradstreet's *Donnelley Demographics*, useful for market area analysis and site selection, containing demographic information (facts about people such as age, sex, educational level, and so forth) searchable by geographic areas. Another example is *Disclosure*, which has a wealth of financial information about companies drawn from filings with the Securities and Exchange Commission. Used primarily for accounting and finance research, this database is pertinent for company analysis.

The final type of database is the **fulltext database**. In addition to locating articles, you can choose to 1) actually read them online, 2) print out the text on paper, or 3) download to a computer disk. *American Banker*, *AP News*, and the *Harvard Business Review* are examples of full text databases. Full text articles are also often available from fully indexed databases such as ABI/Inform. Ask your librarian whether the article you are interested in is a fulltext database.

Although the online public catalog is also a "database" of sorts, most librarians do not use the phrase "database searching" to describe looking something up in the catalog. This usage may change as more and more "external" databases (meaning databases not created by the home library and not limited to the holdings of the home library) are mounted on the same computer equipment as the library's catalog.

More Definitions

Within a database there are thousands of individual entries or *"records"*. This information includes citations to publications in a bibliographic database; companies or individual information in directory databases; annual reports, economic time series, reports of demographic statistics in numeric databases; and text of articles or other publications in fulltext databases.

You usually have the option of saving time and/or money by searching, viewing, and printing parts of the record rather than the whole thing. That is, you might ask the computer to search only in certain *"fields"* of the record, such as the parts where the title and the publication date are located. See the TIPS AND PITFALLS section of this chapter for more about field searching. Also you might increase the relevance of your search in a fulltext database by requiring that several of your search terms be found in the same *paragraph* of the text. This will increase the chances that the concepts you find in the fulltext publication are related. Figure 6.1 shows a sample record from a bibliographic database and one from a fulltext database, with their respective fields and paragraphs labelled.

Figure 6.1

Sample Database Record from a Bibliographic Database

Figure 6.1a

DIALOG Accession Number

02408086
Bacterioocide makers here to face keen competition with newcomers /T1

JN = —— Japan Chemical Week January 4, 1990 P. 4 PY =
SN= —— ISSN: 0047-1766 PD =

Japan: The domestic market for new-quinolone-based bacteriocides will be almost Y100 bil/yr. Four leading companies and their products are Daiichi Pharmaceutical's Tarivid with a 37% market share and sales of Y35 Bil/yr; Kyorin Pharmaceutical-Torii's Baccidal with a 20% market share; Takeda's Cyproxan with a 19% market share; and Dainippon Pharmaceutical's Flumark with a 17% market share. New products entering the antibacterial market in spring-1990 include 2 based on lomefloxacin hydrochloride, Shionogi's Lomebact and Hokuriku Seiyaku's Bareon, and 2 based on Tosufloxacin, Toyama Chemical's Ozex and Dainabot's Tosuxacin. Shionogi's sales target for Lomebact is Y10 bil/yr. Toyama's sales target of Ozex is Y15 bil/yr. Antibacterial products have different actions than antibiotics and a broad spectrum. They are bing used more frequently against infectious diseases because bacteria do not readily develop resistance to drugs. They are frequently used in place of oral antibiotics, which may affect the overall antibiotics market. /AB
COMPANY:
Daiichi Pharmaceuticals
/CO,CO= Kyorin Pharmaceutical
Takada Chemical Ind DUNS: 69-053-8228
Dianippon Pharmaceutical

PN=
/DE EN= PRODUCT: *Quinolone Antibiotics (2834828) PC=
CN= EVENT: *Sales & Comsumption (65); Market Information (60) ED=
COUNTRY: *Japan (9JPN) CC=

/TI =	Article title	PC =	Product code
PY =	Publication year	EN =	Event name
PD =	Publication date	ED =	Event code
JN =	Journal name	/DE =	Descriptors
SN =	Standard number	CN =	Country name
/AB =	Abstract	CC =	Country code
/CO,CO =	Company name(s)	TX =	Text of article
PN =	Product name		

Source: Reproduced with permission of
©Dialog Information Services, Inc.

Figure 6.1b
Sample Database Record from a Full-text Database

Figure 6.1b

DIALOG Accession Number

└── 02503289

/TI   **Martin Marietta Builds A Big FDDI Net**

JN = ——   CommunicationsWeek   February 12, 1990   p. 4   PY =

SN= ——   ISN: 0746-8121   PD =

BY PAUL KORZENIOWSKI

ORLANDO, FLA. —One of the largest FDDI backbone networks in the country has been built by Martin Marietta Systems, which uses it to connect eight buildings at an aerospace manufacturing facility here.

The fiber distributed data interface network went into production in the fall of 1989, it connects half a dozen local area networks, about 30 computer systems, and some 1,800 users.

In May of 1989, Martin Marietta sent request for prosposal to three FDDI suppliers, whom Diamant declined to identify. In August, the company evaluated the three proposals and choice the the FX 8210 from Fibronics International Inc., Hyannis, Mass. The product is   /TX a bridge that connects Ethernet networks to a fiber optic backbone network, which operates at a speed of 100 megabits per second.

Two factors clinched the deal for Fibronics. Martin Marietta Systems was impressed with Fibronics Network Management System. And the Fibronics equipment was less expensive than competitor's gear.

To date, six different networks, including a twisted-pair Ethernet network, a Novell Inc. network, and a broadband Ethernet, are connected to the backbone network. The networks support more than 30 different computer systems including DEC VAXs, IBN mainframes, and various microcomputers, and an estimated 1,800 users, according to Diamant.

THIS IS AN EXCERPT: Copyright 1990 CMP Publications, Inc.
FULL TEXT AVAILABLE IN FORMAT 9; WORD COUNT: 563

COMPANY:

/CO,CO=   *Martin Marietta DUNS: 00-133-9217 TICKER: ML CUSIP: 573275
Bibronics Intnl

/TI =	Article title	PC =	Product code
PY =	Publication year	EN =	Event name
PD =	Publication date	ED =	Event code
JN =	Journal name	/DE =	Descriptors
SN =	Standard number	CN =	Country name
/AB =	Abstract	CC =	Country code
/CO,CO =	Company name(s)	TX =	Text of article
PN =	Product name		

Source: Reproduced with permission of
©Dialog Information Services, Inc.

The term or combination of terms you input before pressing the return button on the computer is called a "search statement." An example of a search statement is

"dogs not pitbulls"

Most search software produces a numbered line called a *set number* which shows terms used and the results retrieved for each search statement. In the following example, 1) and 2) and 3) are set numbers. The numbers showing how many items were found to match the terms in your search statement (in the example below 154, 311, and 35) may be referred to as *hits, postings, references* or *citations.*

1)	dogs not pitbulls	154
2)	cats or Siamese	311
3)	S1 or S2 and mice	35

WHY ARE DATABASES IMPORTANT?

Availability of database searching is a revolution in information technology similar to the change from hand-copied manuscripts to the use of the printing press. Both changes made information available to a wider circle of people and dissemination of knowledge faster than people had been able to imagine.

Their advantages over print-based sources are significant:

Flexibility: Search terms not limited to a subject term assigned by a third party, as is the case in many print products. You can search almost any part of the data in a database: the author's own words from the title or summary, your idea of what to call something, publication name, year of publication, a geographic area, product types, net worth in a range that you define, event codes, availability online of the text of the publication, and many other data elements stored in the computer.

Every database has different search elements. These options for searching are summarized in aid pages published by database "vendors" (companies that sell passwords for access to databases or sell databases on CD-ROM) and detailed explanations of all important technical details are given in search manuals published by either the "producers" of databases (the companies that obtain and index the publications in their respective databases) or by the database vendors.

Efficiency: In a printed index, you can only look under one aspect of your topic at a time. For example, if you are interested in the effects of international competition on the electronics industry, you start with one of three subtopics: either the electronics industry or international business or competition. You can find all three aspects of the topic eventually, but usually only after a time-consuming and frustrating search under many different subject terms.

The computer, in contrast, *searches all three ideas simultaneously*, weeding out any items that are irrelevant and picking up only those listings in which an article has been posted under more than one subject term.

Timeliness: Most database products are updated on the same schedule as their print counterparts because the database is essentially a spin-off from the computerized printing technology that has replaced manual typesetting. But database products tend to be distributed faster. And some are actually updated faster—on a weekly, daily, or even more frequent basis.

Uniqueness: Several databases do not exist in current print form. One example is the index *ABI/Inform*. Another is the Chicago Board of Trade's *Statistical Annual* covering commodities, available only in computerized form after 1986.

Other: Frequently a library chooses to provide the online version of a source rather than the print version. Where there is no charge to the researcher, the library can save money even at a high per-hour charge for online access, providing the source is seldom used. And if the patron pays for the search, then the library is out only personnel and equipment costs.

A SHORT HISTORY OF DATABASE USE

When they first appeared in libraries, database searching systems were generally available only as "online" systems. This means they were immediately and completely accessible by means of a computer work station consisting of a keyboard, an attached monitor similar to a television screen, a printer, and a telecommunications device (known as a modem) for connecting to the database vendor's much larger computer. Generally such searches were conducted exclusively by library staff after discussion with the researcher. For the most part, database searching was only available to corporate researchers and users of large academic or public libraries.

Times have changed, however. Database searching is now widely available in libraries both as online, interactive systems—many of them menu-driven to reduce the amount of training required of users—and as compact disc-based products. In fact, the late 1980's witnessed radio commercials for Information Access Corporation's compact disc-based database *Infotrac*, a real boon for homework assignments with considerable appeal to teens. (See Chapter 7 for a description of *Infotrac*.) While "intermediated" or staff-conducted searches are still available in many libraries, it is common for researchers with the time and motivation to learn about database searching to conduct their own searches.

WHERE DATABASE SEARCHING FITS INTO YOUR RESEARCH

Database searching can fill a variety of needs, from finding research studies to market data to bibliographic references and more. Selected journals can be searched for references to a given topic. Information on almost any subject can be gathered for reports, speeches, memos, or proposals. Important issues and topics concerning an organization or business can be tracked. Information about your competitors can even be sought.

Database searching can also help you avoid duplicating work that has already been done by others: compiling marketing data, forecasting economic trends, testing and evaluating products and services, or tracking legislation related to certain products. Database research can be used in almost any area of business: for example, a personnel manager might use these systems to locate articles and other documents or information related to stress, sexual harassment policies, wage and hour laws, affirmative action programs or employee benefit programs.

Because of its speed, comprehensiveness, and highly focused nature, computer searching has become obligatory in fields such as patent research, preparation of legal cases, and medical or bio-engineering research.

GETTING LIBRARY ACCESS

You should check with the various libraries in your community to see which offer database searching and what type of searching is available. You have three basic options:

First is online searching—interactive connection via telecommunication devices to a database vendor's computer at a remote site. This type of search has the potential to be the most expensive since you pay per minute of connect time. Some searches are at least partially subsidized by the library, which may include monthly subscription fees and discounts for quantity.

The second option is using a database purchased in computer tape format and mounted to run on your library's computer, on the central computer at a university, or on the computer at the central site of a network to which your library belongs. Databases in this format usually will be supplied to you inexpensively, if not absolutely free.

The third option is the compact disc-based product, sometimes called CD's or CD-ROM's. Using the same technology that delivers music to your home, compact disc-based indexes or reference texts store and retrieve information. Since they represent a fixed cost to libraries except for paper and ink supplies and you are not paying for connect or per article retrieved, CD-ROM's are often made available to you without charge.

WHO SHOULD DO THE SEARCH?

To use a database system most effectively, the user must understand the manner in which the data has been stored and how to retrieve it. Except for those database systems designed especially for use by the general public, each database requires extensive training and practice for the user to become efficient and effective.

End-User Searches

Often you have the choice of whether to perform your own search or to have a "mediated" search (one done by a librarian with your assistance). If you want to do it yourself, ask what options there are for conducting your own search. Options may include compact disc products, external databases mounted on your library's online catalog, and interactive, remote connections to a database vendor's computer as described in the preceding section. There may or may not be a fee for usage.

Most systems available to you will be "end-user" systems. That is, they are designed to be used by people with little or no formal training in database searching. Most end-user systems supply a menu of choices easily comprehended by an inexperienced person. It is a good idea to get a printed tip sheet about use and/or some orientation to the system before beginning.

Mediated Searches

Librarians call a person who conducts searches for others a "computer searcher," an "online searcher," or a "search specialist." In both public and university libraries, the computer searcher is usually a reference librarian who has been specially trained to work with database systems. Ask at the reference desk how to contact someone who will do a search for you. Some libraries provide on-demand searching—you just walk in and get what you want right away—but many academic libraries require you to make an appointment first.

WHAT HAPPENS DURING A DATABASE SEARCH?

The following are important steps in conducting a database search:

1) Selecting a database or databases.
2) Identifying the main ideas comprising your research question.
3) Choosing search terms.
4) Specifying logical relationships between concepts.
5) Evaluating precision and quantity of search results.
6) Refining/redoing the search if necessary.

When conducting your search independently, you want results that are both efficient and effective. When a library staff member assists with the search, you need to pay attention. Although the librarian is more experienced with the search process, you know what you need better than anyone else. Actively assisting when the librarian indicates a need for clarification of your ideas and terms or asks for a preliminary evaluation of search output always gets better results.

Selecting a Database

Please see Chapter 7 for information about different vendors (suppliers of databases) and for brief descriptions of specific databases. Sometimes the choice of databases is obvious because only one covers the type of information you need. More commonly, different aspects of your topic will be covered in a number of databases, and you will have to decide which point of view or orientation to the topic is best for you. For example, white collar crime, AIDS, dual career marriages and a number of other topics in which business people take an interest are covered in many databases.

Experienced searchers often know what types of information will be included in the databases they search frequently. When unsure which database to try, they go through a number of steps to select the best one. Some like to start with the *database vendor's catalog*, where databases are listed by title and indexed by broad subject (e.g. business or science or reference). The short description describes the basic content of the database and the time periods covered. For a widely covered topic, you have the choice of a database such as *ABI/Inform* that covers all aspects of business, or you might choose *Economic Literature Index*, which is focused more narrowly on economic aspects of these topics. Also you could pick a nonbusiness database, such as those that cover psychology, computers, or medicine, to get more specialized information. If your research task involves gathering data on economic cycles or stock prices instead of bibliographic citations, then you should select a "non-bibliographic" database—one described in the catalog as supplying annual report figures, economic time series or other data.

More information for your selection of a database is available in the *guides and search manuals* supplied by either the database vendor or the database producer, which usually indicate what source publications are covered. If, for example, few accounting journals are covered in a given database, it is probable that you will get little information on an accounting topic from that database. Conversely, if you have been given one very good reference by a friend or professor, and the journal is listed in the source publication list of the database you are considering, then that is a good indication that you will hit pay dirt on your topic in that database.

Another clue to the value of a given database is the *thesaurus*, a list of controlled vocabulary used in indexing and retrieving citations from a database. Controlled vocabulary is used by a database producer to group references on the same subject together in the database subject index. This list of terms sometimes is part of the search manual, but it may be a separate publication.

Often it is available as a quick look-up option on the database itself. Checking the thesaurus is a quick way of assessing database coverage.

If the specific term you want (for example, career ladders or extrinsic and intrinsic rewards) is in the thesaurus of a given database, you know the database is a good source to use. Even if your specific term is not in the thesaurus, the presence of broader terms for what you want (for example, management, personnel management, motivation and organization development) or related terms (promotion instead of career ladders or reward systems instead of intrinsic or extrinsic rewards) should encourage you to try the database you are considering. If neither the specific, nor the general, or related terms are in the thesaurus, you will want to look for a different database.

Still another factor to use in assessing the fit between your topic and a given database are the *brief documentation pages*. These are called "aid pages" by BRS, "bluesheets" by DIALOG, and "database reference cards" in the EPIC system. When you need to pull out a specific piece of information from an expensive database you are considering using, it is wise to check the aid page for details such as the following: 1) which parts of the computerized record can be searched directly to save time and money; 2) if years, language of publication, etc. can be entered as limits to restrict output to items you will be able to use. If the answer from the aid pages to these important questions is negative, you may decide not to use the database in question. Or if you use the database, you will be able to better plan the most efficient and effective way to search.

There are other considerations that show up in aid pages. Full-text retrieval is one. Usually business researchers want at least some citations to published information that can be obtained in their home libraries and photocopied. If library hours or location are inconvenient, ask if the library staff will photocopy articles and mail or fax them to you. Many libraries offer this service. If this service is unavailable, you could choose only those references with the full-text available online.

If examination of all of the above sources of information doesn't give you or the search specialist a good feel for what database to try, two of the major database vendors have a *cross-database search option*. This feature gives you an affordable sneak preview of where your topic is covered by indexing all databases handled by that vendor in one huge file. In the DIALOG file, DIALINDEX or in the BRS (Bibliographic Retrieval Service) database called CROS you can feed in key terms and check how many unique occurrences or "hits" are available for your topic in as many of the databases as you wish to query. You can run your search across all databases (a lengthy and expensive option generally reserved for the most comprehensive research). Or you can select one of the database vendor's subject categories such as BUSINESS and query all of the databases grouped in that category. A third option for deciding what databases to include in the cross-database search is to specify individual databases of your choosing (for example, you might query *Dissertation Abstracts*, *ABI/Inform*, and *Social Sciences Citation Index* as part of the literature search before writing a Master's thesis.)

Using the cross-database search option is also a good strategy if your library does not subsidize the cost of database searching and the databases you are considering are in the $75-per-hour price range (or higher), as the majority of the business, computer, and technical databases are. You may not want to pay that kind of money to search the databases themselves, when there's a good chance your topic is not covered. If using the cross-database search feature establishes that your topic *is* covered in an expensive database, it may be worthwhile to go ahead with the search. You know you will get some citations for your money. See Chapter 7 for a more detailed explanation of the cross-database searching feature.

Identifying The Main Ideas

Here's an example to help you structure your search through identifying the main idea. The question, "What effect has the adoption of the TQM (total quality management) philosophy had on company profits?" has three main concepts:

Concept 1	Concept 2	Concept 3
TQM	profits	companies or corporations

These are the concepts you must translate into terms the computer can search for. The idea of "effect" is inherent in the combination of the other three ideas, so it will not need to be stated explicitly. Since few databases include much about nonprofits, it may not be necessary to specify that you want articles to include "companies and corporations". The majority will automatically be about profit-making organizations. Having identified the main ideas, you are ready to choose appropriate terminology and to combine them into a search statement, complete with appropriate logical connectors.

Choosing Search Terms

The next step in conducting a database search is choosing terms to describe your main ideas. It is almost always advisable to identify synonyms (terms that mean the same thing) to describe each of the main ideas identified in the first example. This is because database producers—and even authors of the articles you want to find—may call a certain idea or entity by a term quite different from the one you use for it.

To return to the earlier example of the effects on company profits from using TQM, your search strategy should now have been expanded to include additional terminology such as the following:

Concept 1	Concept 2	Concept 3
TQM or	profits or	companies or
Total quality or	financial or	corporations
quality management	sales	

You have three strategies for finding search terminology: 1) looking up controlled vocabulary, 2) using a keyword or term, 3)"de-engineering" a good reference.

Controlled vocabulary. As mentioned above, if a thesaurus is available, always start there. A database thesaurus lists the "controlled vocabulary" used to index the database in question. Using any of these terms ("descriptors" in the jargon of the online searcher) that fit the concept you are researching will get you the greatest possible number of references *tailored* to your precise topic. For example, when searching the online or compact disc versions of *Psychological Abstracts* for references to women executives, it is usually best to use a combination of the descriptors "working women" AND "top level managers" shown in the American Psychological Association's thesaurus for the computerized and printed versions of *Psychological Abstracts.*

Keyword/or key term Search. When no descriptors are precise enough to fit your subject, it may be time to abandon controlled vocabulary. Virtually every computerized system can accommodate "natural language" meaning your own words along with buzzwords that specialists working in a given field use. This search option is often called a "keyword" or "key term" or "fulltext" or simply a "word" search.

For example, the phrase "glass ceiling" (meaning invisible but impenetrable barriers keeping women out of the ranks of top executives) retrieves 99 hits in the January '89 to October '93 *ABI/Inform Ondisc.* To get these same hits using controlled vocabulary, from a thesaurus for *ABI/Inform* you would have to enter a complicated search statement giving several synonyms for discrimination or remedies for discrimination (bias, sex discrimination, Americans with Disabilities Act, etc.) AND several alternatives to describe the idea of career advancement (career development planning, employee promotions, employment practices, career advancement, etc.) AND the term women. It is much easier in this example to use a keyword search.

De-engineering. Another strategy for choosing terms is to use "de-engineering"—the technique of taking apart, analyzing, and replicating—which opportunistic countries or organizations use to duplicate patented products, software, and secret weapon technology. In a database search, if other approaches have not worked, it is almost always possible to use one good citation to find additional relevant material. For example, if you could not remember the term to describe the trend toward making organizations "flatter" by getting rid of employees in the middle management ranks, in the *Business Periodicals Index* you could go from a single good reference on this topic to others tagged with the descriptor "corporate downsizing". That is why computer searchers will frequently ask you if you have already found some good sources. If they can locate the same sources in the database, they will examine the computer record for these articles to find either descriptors they haven't thought of, or keywords that may retrieve additional relevant sources.

Specifying Logical Relationships Among Concepts

The next step in designing a search strategy is specifying the logical relationships your main ideas or concepts have with each other. The computer will do your bidding quickly, but it is as literal-minded as a child and will do no more or less than what you specifically indicate that you want done. Logical relationships are specified with the words AND, OR, and NOT—called "logical operators" or "Boolean operators" by computer searchers. Note that Boolean operators can be tricky when you first encounter them.

OR is relatively unproblematical to use if you remember that it means the items joined by "OR" are all equally acceptable as search results or output. They are treated as synonyms describing one part of your search question. For example, if you type in *automotive supplies* OR *tires*, a database system will locate all references to the terms connected with "OR" and will eliminate the duplicates. As shown below, records containing both of the terms joined by "OR" will appear in your list of references once, rather than twice. This can be deduced from the fact that postings for individual sets total 529, few more than the number of postings in the final set, 524. This reduction by 5 shows that some of the 152 or 377 individual postings represent the same article posted under both terms.

1) automotive supplies	152
2) tires	377
3) automotive supplies or tires	524

NOT is probably the easiest Boolean operator to understand. It simply excludes certain aspects of a broad concept from consideration. For example, typing in *automotive supplies* NOT *tires* would focus a search on *automotive supplies* by excluding the product category *tires*.

1) automotive supplies	152
2) tires	377
3) automotive supplies not tires	147

AND is the logical operator that causes inexperienced database searchers the most confusion. Using AND to connect two concepts means asking the computer to retrieve only those sources containing *both* concepts in the same article and connecting the two concepts in some meaningful way. For example, typing in *automotive supplies* AND *tires* will bring up only sources discussing both terms in the same article. As shown below, AND restricts the total number of postings, as it makes your results more precise and more relevant.

1) automotive supplies	152
2) tires	377
3) automotive supplies and tires	5

Please see Figure 6.2 for a visual explanation of the three Boolean operators, OR, AND, and NOT.

Figure 6.2
Boolean Operators

Automotive Supplies OR Tires

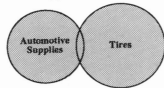

Shaded area represents information retrieved.

Automotive Supplies NOT Tires

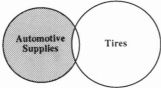

Shaded area represents information retrieved.

Automotive Supplies AND Tires

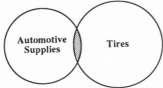

Shaded area represents information retrieved.

This difference between the Boolean "OR" AND "AND" contradicts our ordinary sense of what the words "or" and "and" mean. For example, if you asked a sales clerk to see 1) "black *AND* white ties for formal wear" or 2) "black *OR* white ties for formal wear," chances are that person would show you the whole assortment—not only solid black ties and solid white ties but also some pretty wild ones in a print, stripe, or check featuring shades of *both* black and white. Figure 6.3 contrasts the computer's interpretation of black *OR* white and its interpretation of black *AND* white with the sales person's sense of the same words.

Figure 6.3
OR versus AND: Contrast between Common Language and Boolean Logic

Salesperson's Interpretation of Black AND White Neckties

Boolean Interpretation of Black OR White Neckties

Boolean Intrepretation of Black AND White Neckties

If you ask a computer for "white AND black" ties, it would show you only the few ties featuring a mix of white and black—no solid-colored ones. Only if you asked for "black OR white" ties would it show the whole assortment —solids of either color and ties with both colors mixed. The thing to remember is that AND restricts your options while OR expands them. *Be aware of what you ask for in a database search! The computer will give it to you.*

When you first start doing your own searching, it may be helpful to diagram your strategy, as search specialists are taught to do. Some libraries provide forms and coaching in how to design a search strategy. If yours does not, the outline below may help you clarify what you are directing the computer to search for.

It is a good idea also to write in the Boolean operators you plan to use, as shown below.

Concept A	**AND**	Concept B	**NOT**	Concept C
Term A1		Term B1		Term C1
or		or		or
Term A2		Term B2		Term C2
or		or		or
Term A3		Term B3		Term C3

Evaluating Search Results

Although just about anyone can get some references via a database search, *it takes skill to get a manageable number of highly relevant citations.* Any search strategy represents a compromise between finding a small number of very precise sources on a topic and finding a large number of sources, some of which will be less relevant than others. Be ready to adjust your strategy based on the results of your search.

Not Enough Hits

Use hints from the following **TIPS AND PITFALLS** section to revise your strategy. If the revised strategy doesn't work better, seek a librarian.

Consider also whether you are in the right database. It could be that journals covering your topic are not included in the database you're using. Or for fast-breaking news, you may need to change to a newswire or current contents database that is updated more frequently than the database you're accessing.

Not Enough Good Hits

Analyze approximately what proportion of your hits are relevant and what proportion are barely relevant or worthless for your particular research topic. If you don't have many good hits, get help with your search strategy. It may be that a more experienced person can help you get better results by changing your input in one or more of the first four steps.

Too Many Hits

Evaluate the quality of what you've got. Even if some of your hits are relevant, you should not have to sort through a lot of postings to find the gems that are there. A rule of thumb is that if you end up with more than 60-100 references to sort through, you probably need help refining your search strategy.

GETTING HOME OR OFFICE ACCESS

In addition to using databases subscribed to by libraries, individuals with their own home or office computer and communications setup can connect to a wide variety of databases, offering citations to published information, supplying data (e.g. stock prices), or the full text of various publications. Chapter 7 will give more information about databases available to individual subscribers.

The process for home or office access is the same as described for library access. It cannot be said too often that the home or office database searcher should take full advantage of all training and search aids offered. Otherwise you may be spending too much time and money finding information. Or perhaps worse, because of an incomplete understanding of the complex search process, you may be missing some valuable information.

TIPS AND PITFALLS

Getting Trained

This section is not meant to substitute for formal training or for informal coaching by an experienced searcher. If you plan to do independent database searching, you will profit from having instruction in search techniques. Any powerful search system will take time to master. Even if you're not paying to use a database, get help if you are a frequent user. *Time is money* for the average business student or practitioner.

If you subscribe to one of the database services available to individuals, an instruction book, free practice time, and sometimes free training will be sent with your password. After your initial subscription period, you can refresh your skills inexpensively by using low-cost practice databases on the DIALOG, EPIC and BRS systems. (See Chapter 7 for additional vendor services that you might use.)

A final suggestion is to investigate front-end search software packages that allow you to type out your search statements in advance and upload them to the system. Ask your database vendor's customer representative for suggestions about how to do this or ask your librarian for a directory of software vendors where such a software package can be found. Uploading a "canned" search can be a great help to the slow, inaccurate typist or the person who gets too nervous to think while online.

Basic Searching Tips

1) *DO* look at any search sets with zero results. Chances are you will find an error (e.g. misspelling or wrong set number used).

1. total quality or quality management	325
2. TQM	82
3. quality management program	5
4. 1 or 2 or 3	356
5. profits or financial or sales	3841
6. companies or corporations	749
7. 3 and 5 and 6	0

The absence of hits in the final set of the preceding example could be a result of either the typo in one of the terms or the use of the wrong set number (set *3* was used instead of set 4).

2) *DO NOT* use a long phrase where a short phrase or a single term will do. The computer searches for the words you key in *exactly as you have entered them*. If the words occur, but not in the same order (e.g. "sales, industrial" rather than "industrial sales") or if they are not next to each other (e.g. "personnel management in engineering firms" rather than "management of engineering personnel") you may miss relevant hits.

3) *DO* enter variations of your term. Use acronyms (CEO, CPA), synonyms (man, male), related terms (child, adolescent, youth), different spellings (color, colour), singular and plurals (woman, women), nouns and adjectives (manager, management, managerial), simple and compound forms (online, on line, on-line).

4) *DO NOT* use words considered "stopwords" by the software you are using. These are words the computer disregards and will not search. Database documentation will identify any stopwords in addition to the following common ones: a, an, the, of, by, with, for, and to.

5) *DO NOT* use words that are contained in the name of a database (e.g. "computer" in the *Computer Database*) or words that are generic to the subject content of the entire database (e.g. "business" or "finance" in *ABI/Inform*). These words will work, but they will not add meaning or precision to your search results. And they will slow processing time to a crawl.

Intermediate Search Tips

1) You may want to combine search terms to create a more efficient search strategy. This process is known as "nesting" Boolean search terms.

DO break down you ideas into main groups. For example, if you want to search for information about automotive warranties and replacement parts, your ideas would break down into two main groups as follows:

Concept 1	Concept 2
automobiles	warranties
OR	OR
motorcycles	guarantees
OR	
trucks	

If you do not use nesting, your statement would read "trucks or motorcycles or automobiles and replacement parts or warranties". It could produce very different results, depending on whether the OR operators or the AND operator were processed first. If the OR's were processed first (as they often are) you would get relevant hits with the following subject content:

SEARCH RESULTS WHEN "OR" IS PROCESSED FIRST

truck replacement parts
truck warranties
motorcycle replacement parts
motorcycle warranties
automobile replacement parts
automobile warranties

If, however, the AND was processed first, results would be much different and most hits would *not* be satisfactory. The hits for automobiles would be restricted to items about replacement parts, not picking up anything about automobile warranties unless by coincidence a discussion of warranties occurred in an article dealing with one of the other terms specified. At the same time, many of the hits for trucks, motorcycles, and warranties would lack any mention of either replacement parts or warranties. They would be about automotive design, engineering, marketing, and a host of other subjects irrelevant to your research topic.

SEARCH RESULTS WHEN "AND" IS PROCESSED FIRST

automobile replacement parts
anything about trucks
anything about motorcycles
anything about warranties

In a case like this, the huge total number of hits in your final search set should tip you off to faulty execution of your planned search strategy. As explained in the section on Boolean logic, combining terms in an AND relationship results in a very restricted set of results and a small number of postings.

In virtually any search software, parentheses tell the computer to process everything *within the parentheses* before processing any other part of the search statement. So if you are not sure of the processing order, you would achieve the desired result by keying the search in as follows:

(trucks or motorcycles or automobiles)

AND

(replacement parts or warranties)

An alternative to using parentheses is simply to key in the parts of a search in shorter search statements as shown below, entering terms joined by OR first and using AND operators later.

1) trucks or motorcycles or automobiles
2) warranties or guarantees
3) 1 and 2

However, this startegy will take longer and cost more money.

2) *DO* use truncation to save typing. Sometimes called a "wildcard," truncation directs the computer to supply all variations on a basic word stem. In various systems a *?* or *** or *$* symbol may be used. In this way "comput*" or "comput?" or "comput$" can be keyed in to search computational, computer, computers, computing, computed, and many other variations of the word. Care must be taken not to use too short a word stem as that often produces unwanted variations. For example act* or act? or act$ will fetch actor, actors, actress, actresses, and acting. The problem is that it will also call up act and acts (as in legal matters or circus performers) along with action and other variations.

3) *DO NOT* over specify. Sometimes both inexperienced and experienced searchers will design a search statement with too many concepts or limits. This error is know as "over specification". For example, when anorexia first came to the general public's attention, a search statement asking for white AND (female or females) AND (anorexia or anorexic) would have resulted in no hits. This is because only whites and females were being diagnosed as anorexic at that time. Since all available references were categorized simply by the terms "anorexic" or "anorexia," reference to "white" and "female"—characteristics not explicitly identified in articles about anorexia—caused the search software to respond that no items answering that description were in the database.

4) *DO* nest terms and stack commands to save typing. For example, in DIALOG where descriptors are set off by ¦ **de**, you would normally key in **MIS ¦ de or computers ¦ de or computer software ¦ de**. To save key strokes, you

could simply use parentheses to nest the terms as follows: **(MIS or computers or computer software) | de**. You can also stack commands. For example, you could enter the command to select a database and at the same time enter your first search statement, by separating the two commands with a semicolon. This will save only a fraction of time for those proficient in typing; but in an expensive database, it may be worth doing.

5) **DO** take advantage of field searching to narrow search results. Field searching means restricting the search to specific parts of the record. When there are no suitable descriptors, but the number of hits from key word search is unmanageably large, restricting the search to the title or subject field is an excellent way to improve your hits.

For example, in searching for "glass ceiling," an unrestricted or fulltext search will pull up some hits where the phrase occurs only in the abstract field of the database record and, although mentioned, it is peripheral to the subject of the article. The hit may result from a statement in the abstract field to the effect that in the advertising business, women's career advancement is not much affected by the glass ceiling. But the article itself will make no more than a cursory mention of the term "glass ceiling."

Other fields to use in fine tuning your search will vary from one database to another. In the *InvesText* database, for example, it could be useful to restrict a search to investment advisory reports issued by financial centers and investment banks or brokers. This is done in DIALOG by specifying the corporate source type *sp=broker*. Another field searching option in *InvesText* is to identify substantial news items by restricting company name searches to reports about that particular company, rather than allowing a hit on any page of a report covering several companies.

6) **DO** use the limit command to refine a search with too many hits. Limits are non-subject parameters such as language of the article, publication date, or geographic area. Other limit options that you may find useful are the availability of fulltext online and major descriptors. For example, if you don't have time to find hard copies of journals, or hard copies are unavailable, limiting to fulltext saves time. Also, limiting to journal title is useful if you remember an article from a journal in a particular year, but forget the exact title. Entering subject, limiting by journal and year specifies results. Where both major and minor subject terms are assigned to every item in the database, limiting to major descriptors will fine tune results. By limiting to major descriptors, you will get only hits where your topic is the major focus of the article, not articles where it is one of several minor points mentioned.

7) **DO** use the DIALOG "expand," the BRS "root" or "stem," and the EPIC "scan" commands to see variant forms of both people's names and company

names. This is of paramount importance in any database (for example *Dissertation Abstracts International* or *Social Sciences Citation Index*) where names are not standardized but are entered in all the variant forms appearing in publications covered by that database.

DATABASE EVALUATION CRITERIA

Evaluating a database is very similar to evaluating a printed index. But since printed indexes are already paid for, many people use them without thinking about their suitability for a particular research topic. The following is a standard set of database characteristics to keep in mind when selecting the right one for your topic. The vendors have 800 numbers to call for information about database coverage and search strategies. Take advantage of them.

SCOPE: What time periods, countries, and branches of knowledge are covered? It is not uncommon for online databases to start in the 1980s or later and for compact disc databases to cover a revolving time period like "the last five years" so that as current material is added, older material falls out of the scope of the database. To do research covering earlier publication dates, sometimes printed indexes must be used. Often current information is all you need.

ITEM CONTENT: Database record content includes such factors as what items of information are included (e.g. ticker symbol, stock price, etc.) and such special features as abstracts (summaries) or charts. As databases are enhanced, often earlier records are not "grandfathered" into the enhancement, so that different parts of the same database differ. For example, abstracts or fulltext coverage will be available from a certain starting date and beyond that point into the future, but older entries are not changed to add the new feature. Similarly, databases occasionally differ in some important respect from their print counterpart. For example, the online fulltext version of *American Banker* includes a class of information not available in the print version of this paper—the complete text of speeches by notable people in the banking industry.

Occasionally a database is chosen because it contains some item of information that its competitor does not, for example, branch locations of a company as well as the headquarters location. (Remember, you'll find such details in the database's aid pages). More often the item content of databases with the same general scope (e.g. directory information about public and private companies) will be similar if not identical. What helps you choose then may be your confidence in the database producer.

SOURCE COVERAGE: No database claims to cover all periodicals or reports or publications in a given field. Any database produced by Standard & Poor's Corporation, for example, will cover a slightly different assortment of companies than a Dun & Bradstreet database. By the same token, although a business database and a computer science database will cover *some* of the same periodicals, the latter will deal with a far greater number of specialized sources covering computers. If there is a source you want to make sure to include in your search, be sure to look at the database source list to see if it's there.

SEARCH OPTIONS: If a database includes non-English sources, it is important to be able to specify by either a language code or a limit feature which languages your search results should include. Search options can also be important in a database with high connect time charges. If a ticker symbol or DUNS number (unique company ID assigned by Dun and Bradstreet) can be keyed in instead of a company's entire legal name, your search costs can sometimes be significantly reduced. In addition, search options can often help you pinpoint key information. For example, in a database including company balance sheets and/or income statements, you may want to know whether a given item or line from this portion of the database record is a searchable field. In other words, you might search only for firms having assets within certain limits for your homework assignment, marketing project, investment decision, or other research need. Refer back to the **TIPS AND PITFALLS** section of this chapter for a fuller discussion of field searching, limits, and other search options.

DEPTH OF INDEXING: All database preparers have protocols or rules for what types of items from a document (book, patent, magazine, newspaper, or journal) they do and do not index. Not all clearly state the limits of their indexing. But some do. For example, the ABI/Inform database producer, University Microfilms International, makes available a list of ''core'' sources that it indexes thoroughly and provides a list of the titles of other sources covered more selectively. Further, this company will tell search specialists the types of items (e.g. letters to the editor) they *do not* index even for the core sources. If you need this kind of information, there's no alternative but skimming key sources cover-to-cover.

UPDATING: The most important advantage online database searching has over printed indexes and CD versions of the same database, is timeliness. Online databases always are updated faster than their counterparts, and aid pages supplied to search specialists tell exactly how often each database is updated. In many databases ''updates'' are not completely current. Although a database may have indexing added monthly, every two weeks, or even daily, the information added to the database does not necessarily cover that morning's or the previous day's publication output. The indexing process builds in a certain amount of lag time (varying from one database producer to another) between receipt of source publications and production of the index.

99

PRICE: Your cost for a database search is based on three elements: a per minute charge for *connection to the database vendor's computer;* a *telecommunications* charge; and in virtually all databases, a per item charge for any *data or bibliographic citations* printed or downloaded. Some libraries factor in an estimated charge to cover staff salaries, equipment, and documentation (aid pages, manuals, thesauri, etc.) as well as staff training. Such full-cost-recovery pricing is comparatively rare even for service to researchers not affiliated with the library.

Depending on who's paying, the criterion of cost may not be too important in choosing a database. Some libraries partially or completely subsidize database searching. At some colleges and universities the business school, the graduate college, or some other entity underwrites the cost. In such cases the cost ranges from nothing to the price of a sandwich or T-shirt. But where you pay the full cost, price may play a part in deciding whether to do a database search and which of two or more overlapping databases to consult. All databases vendors supply a printed price list (usually updated more than once a year) and give up-to-the-minute price information online.

RATIONALE FOR USING A DATABASE SEARCH

Whatever the charges for a database search, it is less expensive than doing the search manually. And for the committed business researcher, budgeting for computer searches will be as automatic as budgeting for textbooks, transportation, and other necessities.

Database descriptions in Chapter 7 will make clear that it is simply impossible to search manually the multitude of databases available online and in CD format. Many of them do not exist in printed form, and those that do usually are less up to date than the online databases. When evaluated objectively, fees charged for this service by library systems are indeed a bargain.

Databases and Database Vendors

OBJECTIVES: This chapter will introduce the reader to the major business databases and database vendors and will outline the features and services they provide.

> **Introduction**
> **A Selective List of Business Databases**
> - Reference Databases
> - Industry Specific Databases
> - International Databases
>
> **The Leading Online Database Vendors: DIALOG and BRS**
> - Features and Services Offered by DIALOG and BRS
> - How DIALOG and BRS Differ
>
> **Other Online Database Vendors**
> **Other Database Formats**
> **The Internet**
> **Sources of Additional Information**

After completing this chapter, you should be able to:

*Understand the different types and databases and database vendors and choose the best source for your research needs.

INTRODUCTION

"WARNING: THIS BOOK IS OUT OF DATE"

The preceding disclaimer appears in the introduction to *Lesko's Info-Power*. What Matthew Lesko says about the short "shelf life" of his book goes double for this chapter about electronic information resources. The electronic segment of the publishing industry is made up of all computerized forms of information mentioned in Chapter 6, including the following: interactive, online computer databases, computer tapes mounted on an institution's mainframe computers, compact disc databases, and combinations of commercially-produced information with computerized library catalogs in a "multiple data access point." (This last means a single, uniform "interface" presented as a menu of database choices available via a terminal in the library and sometimes by dialing into the library system from your home, office, or other remote location). Electronic publishing of information is developing at a dizzying pace, and libraries are doing their best to keep your research environment up to date. As a result, what you read here or what you find in the library today may be different tomorrow. Please note that the costs listed in this chapter were current as of Spring 1994.

A SELECTIVE LIST OF BUSINESS DATABASES

There are four different types of databases: bibliographic (which cites author, title, and other information necessary for locating the published item), directory, numeric, and fulltext. In addition, there are hybrids, the most common being a combination of bibliographic citations and fulltext.

Given the proliferation of business databases, many precisely tailored to customer needs, it is impossible to give an exhaustive list of them. A selective list follows:

Reference Databases
(General, multi-industry focus, directory information, news, statistics, etc.)

ABI/Inform. Bibliographic with abstracts. Provider: UMI/Data Courier.

Subject coverage spans all aspects of business administration and management including the following subtopics: accounting, banking, computers, economics, engineering management, communications, finance, health care, human resources, insurance, international trends, law, management/management science, marketing, public administration, real estate, taxation, telecommunications, and transportation. Although some specific product and industry information is available, focus is on broader subject treatments useful to executives.

Record content consists of a bibliographic citation, a summary of up to 150 words, and fulltext of articles for approximately 100 of the 800 titles covered from 1991 to the present.

Sources include academic journals, professional publications, and trade magazines, some published abroad.

CENDATA. Numeric data. Some text. Provider: Bureau of the Census, U.S. Department of Commerce.

Data in this file includes key business, trade, and economic data organized in the following categories: overview of Census Bureau products and services, update on CENDATA, a brief summary of U.S. statistics, press releases, selected articles from *Census User News*, product information, user feedback, profiles and rankings, agriculture data, business data, construction and housing data, foreign trade data, government data, international data, manufacturing data, population data, genealogical and age information, 1990 census information.

Record content varies with the type of subfile. Data is presented in tables except for press releases and special reports, which contain a bibliographic citation and text.

Chase Econometrics. Formerly Econbase: Time Series and Forecasts. Numeric data. Provider: Wharton Econometric Forecasting Associates (WEFA Group).

Covers multi-year economic statistics for a broad range of subjects (some from as early as 1948) along with two-year forecasts for major economic indicators. Includes the following broad topics:

1) indicators of activity in various industry segments of the economy, agriculture, construction/housing, industrial production, manufacturers' shipments/inventories/orders, retail sales, and transportation;
2) personal income;
3) population, labor force participation, and employment/wage/salary data;
4) capital expenditures and consumer expenditures;
5) selected national accounts;
6) foreign trade, exchange rates, and balance of payments;
7) finance and government finance;
8) various cyclical indicators;
9) interest rates, consumer price indexes, and producer price indexes.

Sources range from Federal government agencies such as the Bureau of Economic Analysis to quasi-governmental bodies like the Federal Reserve Board to international bodies such as the Organization for Economic Cooperation and Development.

Corporate Affiliations. Directory information. Provider: National Register Publishing Company.

Corresponding to the print-based *Directory of Corporate Affiliations* and its companion volume for international companies, this database covers all companies traded on the New York and American Stock Exchanges or in over-the-counter transactions. Divisions and subsidiaries of these companies are also covered.

Records give name, address, phone number, description of business and four-digit SIC, executive names, and corporate structure. Parent company entries provide director names, sales, number of employees, net worth, total assets, and total liability when available.

D & B Donnelley Demographics. Numeric data. Provider: Donnelley Marketing Information Services, a division of Nielsen.

In addition to national data, subject coverage includes the following government and commercial geographic divisions: states, counties, Standard

Metropolitan Statistical Areas (SMSA), Primary Metropolitan Statistical Areas (PMSA), and Consolidated Metropolitan Statistical Areas (CMSA), city, place, zip code, Nielsen DMA's (designated marketing areas), Arbitron ADI's (areas of dominant influence), and SAMI's (Selling Area Marketing Inc).

Record content is tabular. In addition to totals within various demographic groups, figures for median and percent change are presented. Useful cross-tabulations are also available. Examples include population by age, female population by age, and black/white/hispanic/other populations, each tabulated by age and sex.

Data is from the current U.S. Census of Population and Housing enhanced by Donnelley's estimates for the current year and projections for five years into the future.

D & B Million Dollar Directory. Directory information. Provider: Dun's Marketing Services.

Both public and private companies with a net worth of at least $500,000 are covered, regardless of industry or product. Both headquarters and single-location establishments that may be partly or wholly owned by another entity are covered. Dun's Market Identifiers, a sister database, covers even more companies. Its files encompass firms with 5 or more employees and at least a million in sales, along with their affiliates.

Like the print-based *Million Dollar Directory*, online records include current address/phone/fax, a description of the firm's business both in words and in four-digit Standard Industrial Code (SIC) numbers, statistics for sales and number of employees, names of management personnel, bank and accounting firm serving the company, ticker symbol, and stock exchanges trading the company.

Data is gathered annually via questionnaires.

D & B Dun's Electronic Business Directory. Directory information. Provider: Dun's Marketing Services.

Coverage includes public and private businesses of all sizes and types in the following broad industry groups: agriculture, communications, construction, finance, insurance, manufacturing, mining, services (business and professional), public utilities, retail, transportation, and wholesale.

Records include address, phone, business description, primary and secondary SIC codes, and employee size range.

Information is drawn from Dun & Bradstreet's credit reports, telemarketing and direct mail campaigns, information filed with the government, and other sources.

DISCLOSURE Database. Directory information, numeric data and some text. Provider: Disclosure, Inc.

Coverage of public companies' official SEC filings, including the following types of filings: 10-K, 20-F, 10-Q, proxy, 8-K, registration statement, 10-C, and annual report.

The following types of data items can be searched directly:

1) directory information;
2) industry classification;
3) officers' and directors' names, titles, and ownership of company stock;
4) principal legal counsel, stock transfer agent, and auditing firm;
5) identification symbols (company name, ticker symbol, D-U-N-S number, CUSIP number, Forbes and Fortune numbers, cross-references, and subsidiaries);
6) financial data and ratios;
7) securities information (including place of incorporation), SEC reports filed, stock exchanges where traded, shareholders, types of stock issued, and shares outstanding;
8) report sections, including president's letter, management discussion, and footnotes;
9) update codes (latest quarterly report, latest annual report, etc.).

The companion database, DISCLOSURE/SPECTRUM, reports three stock ownership data items provided by Computer Directions Advisors, Inc: institutional holdings, 5% ownership holdings, and ownership by insiders.

InvesText. Numeric data and fulltext. Provider: Thomson Financial Networks.

Coverage includes reports on the following broad subject areas:

1) business planning data (forecasts and analyses of such factors as sales, operating income, earnings, and production/shipments);
2) financial analyses of companies based on data from balance sheets, income statements, and other pertinent documents;
3) analyses of industries/markets, including information from consumer spending to industry overviews and statistics;
4) various topics ranging from stock market activity and trends to updated economic perspectives, and analyses of business activity/potential by geographic area.

Data is from reports by leading U.S. and some foreign investment banks and consulting firms.

Knight-Ridder/Tribune Business News. Bibliographic with fulltext. Provider: Knight-Ridder/Tribune Business News.

Worldwide news about financial and commodity markets is covered. The following broad subject areas are included: major corporate news; regional business developments and news; agriculture, energy, insurance, and transportation industries; credit markets; and trading in commodities, manufactured goods, services, foreign exchange, securities, futures, and other financial instruments. Fulltext of newspaper and magazine articles is available the day of publication.

Sources include Knight-Ridder Financial News bureaus, wire services, and some 59 magazines and newspapers.

Legal Resource Index. Bibliographic. Provider: Information Access Company.

Covering legal literature of the English-speaking world, this database includes broad subtopics ranging from agriculture to forensic science to taxation. Access is provided by case name, by tort name, by article/commentary/review author, and by subject.

Sources include legal newspapers, law journals, legal monographs, and relevant articles from general periodicals, general newspapers, and business publications covered by other Information Access Company databases.

Management Contents. Bibliographic with abstracts. Provider: Information Access Company.

All aspects of business and management are covered, including the following broad subdivisions: accounting and auditing, advertising and sales, decision science, economics, finance, insurance, management and administration, marketing, operations research, personnel/labor relations/employee benefits, production. Since 1986 emphasis has been on banking, finance, personnel, and management issues. The database is aimed at the interests of business people, researchers, consulting organizations, law firms, educational institutions, government entities, and libraries.

Record content includes bibliographic citations and abstracts of 50-300 words.

With over 130 source publications, Management Contents (abbreviated here as MC) covers only a fraction of ABI/Inform's total number of sources. Nevertheless, because of its focus on the most widely read management journals, MC does include some sources not in its chief competitor's database. From 1974 to 1985, sources included proceedings, transactions, books, courses, and a greater number of periodicals as well as key management journals.

Media General Plus. Numeric Data. Provider: Media General Financial Services.

Focus is on stock prices, trading volume, company financial data, and industry comparisons for companies listed on the American and New York

Stock Exchanges and for those sold via the NASDAQ National Market System. Selected over-the-counter stocks are also included. Balance sheet and income statement items are available for several years. Key ratios and indexes, including S & P and Dow Jones indexes, are given.

Data comes from company reports and press releases, newswires, SEC filings, and other sources.

Moody's Corporate News - U.S. Numeric data and fulltext. Provider: Moody's Investors Service, Inc.

The database features the same range of industries covered by Moody's print-based manuals: industrial companies, banks, savings and loans, insurance, real estate and investment trusts, public utilities, and transportation. All companies (approximately 13,000) are publicly held U.S. corporations. Emphasis is given to the following types of corporate events: name changes, changes of officers or directors, acquisitions and mergers, purchase offers, expansions, bankruptcy proceedings, contracts, debt offerings (issuing bonds), new product introductions, capital expenditures, and labor developments. A companion database, Moody's Corporate News - International, provides the same information for publicly held non-U.S. companies.

Sources of information for both databases and for Moody's Corporate Profiles include the following: company quarterly and annual reports, news releases, prospectuses, proxy statements, official filings with various regulatory bodies, bulletins and lists from stock exchanges, periodicals, and newswires.

Moody's Corporate Profiles. Directory information and numeric data. Provider: Moody's Investors Service, Inc.

All publicly held U.S. corporations traded on the New York and American Stock Exchanges are covered, along with some 13,000 of the most prominent OTC companies. Besides directory information, records provide key statistics (book value, earnings, dividend record, and prices for stocks) as well as a five-year company financial history from balance sheets and income statements when available.

PAIS International. Bibliographic with abstracts. Provider: Public Affairs Information Service, Inc.

Scope includes worldwide coverage of all social science disciplines, with emphasis on public issues and formulation and evaluation of public policy. The following broad subject areas are included: banking, business, court decisions, demography, economics, finance, government, international trade and regulations, legislation, political science, public administration, public policy, and sociology. Statistical treatments of topics are featured.

Sources include books, periodical articles, pamphlets, government documents from federal, state, local, and international entities, directories, yearbooks, statistical reports, and miscellaneous publications of both public and private agencies.

PsycINFO. Bibliographic with abstracts. Provider: American Psychological Association.

The international literature of psychology and related disciplines is covered within the following broad subject areas: applied psychology (including industrial and organizational psychology), communication, developmental psychology, educational psychology, experimental human and animal psychology, personality studies, physical and psychological maladies, physiological psychology and intervention, professional issues, psychometrics, social processes and issues, sports/leisure psychology, and prevention and treatment.

Sources include journal articles, technical reports, dissertations, and books published in over 20 languages.

PTS F & S Index. Bibliographic with abstracts. Provider: Predicasts.

Coverage includes company, product, marketing, and technological news and information for all industries worldwide. Focus is on corporate changes (mergers, etc.), corporate activities from research and development to product sales, and financial data and analysis. Information about the business environment (regulations, general economic trends and conditions, demographic changes, etc.) is given as well.

Sources include periodicals and reports covered in the print-based Predicast indexes covering the U.S., Europe, and non-European countries. Coverage of trade journals is superlative.

Thomas Register Online. Directory. Provider: Thomas Publishing Company, Inc.

Over 148,000 public and private U.S. and Canadian companies are included. Suppliers of virtually every product and service available in the U.S. are included. Coverage of industrial and manufacturing companies has long been Thomas's strength. The food industry, high technology, biotechnology, and computer and electronics industries are well represented.

Sources of information include mailed questionnaires, telephone interviews, and on-site visits by Thomas Publishing representatives.

Trade & Industry Index. Bibliographic with some abstracts and some text (displayable but not searchable). Provider: Information Access Company (IAC).

Some 68 industries from advertising/marketing/public relations to library and information science to travel and hospitality are covered. News about companies, products, industries, and related issues and events are provided.

Over 300 trade and industry journals are included in the Trade & Industry source list. The database also scans general interest publications from other IAC magazine, newspaper, and newswire databases for business and trade information.

Industry Specific Databases

Accounting and Tax Database. Bibliographic with abstracts (full text of selected sources). Provider: UMI/Data Courier.

This database is aimed at accountants, tax professionals, and academic users. Subject coverage includes the following sub-fields within accounting and taxation: accounting, auditing, banking, bankruptcy, compensation, consulting, finance, government fiscal policy, and taxation.

Sources covered include prominent accounting, taxation, and financial management publications, and selective coverage of another 850 business periodicals and major news magazines. Books, dissertations, theses, and pamphlets are also covered.

Aerospace Database. Bibliographic (summary abstracts for most entries). Provider: American Institute of Aeronautics and Astronautics/Technical Information Service.

Comprehensive coverage of worldwide engineering and technology literature focusing on aerospace is provided. The following aspects of aerospace research and development and technological applications are included: chemistry/chemical engineering, aircraft design/instrumentation, aerodynamics, communications/navigation, space science, spacecraft design/ systems engineering, propellants/fuels, lasers/masers, mechanical engineering, structural mechanics, electronics/ electrical engineering, fluid mechanics/heat transfer, quality assurance/reliability, mathematics/computer science, physics, life sciences, geophysics/ earth resources, meteorology/ climatology/oceanography, environmental pollution, energy production/ conversion, social sciences.

Source literature includes journal articles, conference papers, books, theses, and both published and unpublished reports.

Health Planning and Administration. Bibliographic with abstracts (some fulltext). Provider: National Library of Medicine with American Hospital Association.

Aimed at health care professionals, students, and librarians, the database covers health care planning, financing, management, organization, and staffing. Both U.S. and international journals and publications are covered. *Hospital Literature Index* is printed from this database.

Insurance Periodicals. Bibliographic. Provider: NILS Publishing Company with Special Library Association's Insurance & Employee Benefits Division.

All branches of the insurance industry are covered: health, liability, life, property, and risk management. Within these broad areas current issues such as AIDS, alcohol and drug abuse, asbestos, pollution, self-insurance, uninsured motorists, and workers' compensation are emphasized. Perennially important topics such as advertising, marketing, and mergers and acquisitions within the industry are well-covered, as are financial planning, taxation, and other topics related to insurance.

Sources include the most respected and most widely read insurance industry journals and magazines.

Microcomputer Index. Bibliographic with abstracts (fulltext of selected book reviews). Provider: Learned Information.

Database content relates to the use of microcomputers in business, education, and the home. The following is a selected list of subject areas covered: reviews of computer hardware, software, and books; company, product, and industry news; education, business applications; electronic interfaces; electronic publishing; programming and programming languages; graphics; statistical packages; and games.

Source publications are the English-language journals covered in the print-based *Microcomputer Index* along with *Softwhere? Bargain Reports* and *Computer Book Review.*

PTS Marketing and Advertising Reference Service. Bibliographic with abstracts or fulltext. Provider: Predicasts, Inc.

Supplies multi-industry information about advertising and marketing of consumer products and services. Typical kinds of research include determining market size and share for new or existing products, tracking new product introductions, product and company news, obtaining competitive intelligence on ad agencies and public relations firms, and updates on marketing and advertising regulations.

Sources encompass advertising and marketing trade journals, trade journals from other industries (e.g. food or video rental), newsletters, academic journals covering marketing, and advertising/marketing columns from major U.S. newspapers.

Pollution Abstracts. Bibliographic with abstracts. Provider: Cambridge Scientific Abstracts.

Covers international literature on environmental science and technology, including air/land/noise/water pollution, environmental action, waste management, sewage and waste water treatment, radiation, and toxicology.

Source publications include periodicals, books, conference papers, research papers, and technical reports.

International Databases

Asia-Pacific Database. Bibliographic with abstracts. Provider: Aristarchus Knowledge Industries.

This database covers business, economics, and new industries in the Pacific Rim (North East Asia, Southeast Asia, China, India, the Middle East, Australia, and the Pacific Island nations). Subject coverage emphasizes the following business topics: acquisitions & mergers, advertising, agriculture, banking, biotechnology, general business, computers, economics, foods and beverages, government, industrial development, joint ventures, mining, natural resources, new products, OPEC, political risk, regional development, sociology, strategic planning, technology, telecommunications, terrorism, and transportation. This database is aimed at an interdisciplinary audience. (Directory information for Asian and Pacific companies is available in the Kompass Asia/Pacific database provided by Kompass International Management Corp.).

Source publications include annual reports, business journals, conference proceedings, dissertations, government documents, monographs, newsletters, Pacific Rim local newspapers, and press releases.

Canadian Business and Current Affairs. Bibliographic (abstracts from 1991 to date). Provider: Micromedia Limited.

Subject coverage includes Canadian company, product, and industry information focusing on the following topics: acquisitions & mergers, bankruptcies, business forecasts/trends, business people in the news, company activities, government activities, industry news, technological trends, crime, education, environmental issues, performing arts/literature, non-business people in the news, politics, regional/national/international news, and sports/travel/leisure/entertainment.

Source publications are drawn from those included in the following printed reference works: *Canadian Business Index, Canadian News Index, Canadian Magazine Index, Bibliography of Works on Canadian Foreign Relations,* and Ontario Securities Commission filings.

Hoppenstedt Directory of German Companies. Directory information. Provider: Hoppenstedt Wirtschaftsdatenbank GmbH.

Covers both public and private German companies with either a sales volume of at least 2,000,000 Deutschemarks or a minimum of employees (headquarter locations only). Corresponds to print-based publications published by Verlag Hoppenstedt & Co. covering major and medium-sized German companies.

THE LEADING ONLINE DATABASE VENDORS

Most academic, corporate, and large public libraries subscribe to the search services of either DIALOG Information Services or Bibliographic Retrieval Services (also known as BRS). DIALOG supplies access to over 400 databases. BRS supplies access to approximately 150, and its sister search service, Orbit (formerly owned by the Systems Development Corporation), covers another 100. Many libraries and companies have contracts with both DIALOG and BRS. Together with Orbit, DIALOG and BRS have dominated the online database searching industry for nearly twenty years.

DIALOG has consistently taken the lead in providing enhancements to search software. Examples of their innovations include the ability to scan databases for hits in the low-cost DIALINDEX file before choosing in which databases to execute a search, the ONESEARCH option that executes a search simultaneously in multiple files and includes a mechanism for removing duplicate citations from search results when there is overlapping coverage of source publications, and the award-winning COMPANY NAME FINDER file: an index of company names pinpointing in which databases the maximum amount of information on the company you are investigating will be found. Although DIALOG sets the pace, BRS never seems far behind in developing parallel software functionality.

Features and Services Offered by Both DIALOG and BRS

Documentation

- System search manuals and aid pages (free to subscribers).
- Monthly or bi-monthly newsletter communicating databases changes, training schedules, strategy tips, free practice time, and other news.
- Online news/updates.
- Price lists (print versions and online information).

Communications Network

- Toll-free telecommunication connections for accessing databases.

112

Training/Assistance

- An ongoing schedule of both free and fee-based training around the United States and developed areas of the world.
- Customer assistance via toll-free phone lines.
- Free practice time for new subscribers.
- Free practice time in selected databases each month.
- On-screen helps.
- Low-cost practice databases.

Choice of search modes

- Menu-driven or command searching.

Price breaks

- Special rates for classroom use/demonstrations and for all educational institutions including libraries.
- Non-peak pricing (chiefly evenings).
- Discounts for large volume of use.

Output Options

- Choice of record format: brief citation, full record excluding text of source publications, full record including text of source publications, user-defined format, etc.
- Choice of output process: online printing at full connect charge, online printing from captured file at reduced rates, offline printing, or downloading to disk.
- Merged output: elimination of duplicate records from search in overlapping databases.
- Selective Dissemination of Information (known as SDI): automatic updates of search results when records are added to database.

Other Services

- Search save feature: short or long-term preservation of search strategy for re-use without re-keying.
- E-mail or message switching.
- Online cost/management information.

Document Delivery

- Online ordering for text of sources.

How DIALOG and BRS Differ

The coverage of business topics in these two competing search services is markedly different. BRS lists only the following sixteen business databases:

ABI/Inform, BioBusiness, Business Software Database, Disclosure Database, Disclosure/Health (a subset of Disclosure Database), Dissertation Abstracts Online, Federal Register Abstracts, Harvard Business Review Online, Management Contents (including a backfile from 1974-1984), PATDATA (extracted from U.S. Patent & Trademark Office Records), Pharmacontacts (pharmaceutical and veterinary companies and organizations), PTS /F & S Index, PTS/ PROMT (International coverage only), Merged PTS/F&S AND PTS/PROMT file, Trade and Industry ASAP III, and Wilson Business Periodicals Index. Note that BRS has included two interdisciplinary reference databases, Dissertation Abstracts and Federal Register Abstracts, in the business category because of their utility to the business researcher.

In contrast to BRS, DIALOG has at least 130 business databases as well as many reference/multidisciplinary, news, and science databases that occasionally are useful to the business researcher. It is difficult to give a more exact figure because some databases are so large that they are split into separate files chronologically, geographically or on some other basis, and the difference between a database and a file is sometimes more a matter of semantics than substance.

In addition to the multi-subject and multi-industry databases such as the various Predicast files and ABI/Inform, DIALOG has a number of specialized business databases such as the Economic Literature Index, PTS Marketing and Advertising, and M & A Filings (mergers and acquisitions), to name just a few. It also has exceptionally good coverage of international business in databases such as Asia Pacific, Euromonitor Market Research, Delphes European Business, Hoppenstedt Directory of German Companies, the ICC databases covering international business and the United Kingdom, and the Kompass databases covering Asia and the Pacific, along with Canada, Europe, and the United Kingdom. For years you could only get better international coverage than DIALOG's by paying a premium for Easynet access or subscribing to the services of several database vendors such as Radio-Suisse and Infomart. Since DIALOG's parent company, Knight-Ridder, Inc., acquired DataStar from Radio-Suisse in March of 1993, DIALOG users can probably anticipate further enhancement of access to international data and information.

The depth and breadth of DIALOG's newspaper database list is another major strength in its coverage. DIALOG's online access to the full text of over 250 newspapers, newswires and current event sources, supplemented by thorough indexing of both business and general news, is a resource of unparalleled value to business researchers.

OTHER ONLINE DATABASE VENDORS

America Online

This database service is much like CompuServe in both its content and presentation.

America Online (AOL) provides all of its services at once and does not divide them into basic and premium services. As such pricing is different than those services that are divided. AOL charges a basic per-month fee that includes a certain amount of connect time. After the included connect time is used, a per-hour usage fee applies.

Information is organized into the following categories: News and Finance, Entertainment, Travel and Shopping, People Connections, Computing and Software, Lifestyles and Interests, Learning and Reference, and Online Support. You can also access stock quotes, top news stories for the day, "What's New," and e-mail with the click of a mouse.

The business portion of this database is excellent. Like CompuServe, it offers access to stock quotes, bond and mutual fund information. There is extensive analysis of the information presented. Exchange rates, interest rates, home financing facts, and other financial details are available.

Most useful is the Business News section, which includes Company Actions, Company Changes, and Company Finance Information, all accessed by keyword. The actual news coverage provided by AOL is superior to that provided by its competitors. The full text of *Time* magazine is available weekly. The international coverage is excellent and accesses several overseas news sources. At present, the *San Jose Mercury News*, *Chicago Tribune* and *New York Times* are available in full text form.

Internet access is available through the AOL Internet Center. For more details, see the Internet section later in this chapter.

The major difference between America Online and systems such as DIALOG and BRS is its ease of use. The screens are easy to interpret and pleasant to view. Icons, or pictures with a descriptive word, create a main menu. For example, a profile of a man with the words "People Connection" below it constitutes the icon for accessing information about people. No aid pages are included in light of the user-friendly format. AOL does provide online help as well as a toll-free telephone number to obtain immediate assistance with specific problems.

Attis North America

This vendor's online information system, called Attisnet, gives access to information about Mexico. Information sources include a great many Mexican entities from periodicals (*El Universal*, *El Financiero*, and *El Economista* to name three) to banks to Chambers of Commerce to national government bodies. In addition information from the World Bank and Price Waterhouse goes into the database.

The Attis main menu has the following ten options:

1) General information: Mexico's history, geography, economy, states and main cities, population, transportation and communications systems, political/ administrative system, professional associations, Mexican embassies and consulates, foreign embassies and consulates in Mexico, and Mexican physicians recommended by foreign embassies.

2) Legal information: foreign investment and trade regulations, the Mexican trade system, North American Free Trade Agreement (NAFTA), bi-lateral conventions with European countries, European Community (E.C.) general system of preferences, E.C. investment partners, import/export facilities, labor regulations, and Mexican law governing the promotion and protection of industrial property (patents and other types of licensing).

3) Tourism: tips and information for tourists.

4) News: news about changes in currency values, metals prices, and interest rates along with stock exchange developments and updates to NAFTA.

5) Economic information: data on Mexican imports and exports, balance of trade, main trading partners, and main domestic economic indicators.

6) Financial information: Mexican accounting principles and practices, monetary policy, taxation and capital transfers, exchange control regulations, features of Mexico's financial system, information on banking and securities instruments, and public financial indicators.

7) Attis circle: news items about personalities, business opportunities, and service and industrial companies.

8) Companies handbook: directory information on Mexican companies.

9) Agenda: dates of Mexican fairs and public and bank holidays.

10) Info System: news and searching tips for Attis system.

The Bibliographic Citation File (BIBL)

This is an index of selected English language publications about U.S. public policy and current events from 1976 to the present. Publications include periodical articles, government publications, United Nations documents, and pamphlets. The database may be searched by date, author, article, book, journal title, or individual words. It is updated daily.

Canadian Centre for Occupational Health and Safety (CCOHS)

Through CCINFOline, researchers have access to over 50 online databases covering a wide range of occupational health and safety topics. Examples include safe handling of hazardous chemicals, pest management and safe use of pesticides, AIDS, measurement of workplace noise and radiation levels, occupational health and safety legislation, and people and organizations who give advice and/or help with occupational health and safety problems. Information from U.S. and international sources supplements that from Canadian entities.

CompuServe

According to the *Information Industry Directory*, the Source (owned by the Reader's Digest Association) was acquired by CompuServe Inc., which had been founded in 1979, and the services of the two database vendors were merged. Small wonder then that CompuServe now enjoys name recognition even among people who are not frequent library users.

Basic membership benefits from CompuServe include unlimited connect time to access databases in the following categories: News, Sports, Weather, Electronic Mail, a Reference Library consisting of *Grolier's Academic American Encyclopedia* (updated quarterly), Peterson's College Database, and a practical medical reference source called HealthNet, Shopping, Financial Information, Travel & Leisure, Entertainment & Games, and Membership Support Services including a directory of CompuServe members, a practice forum, support forums for learning to use CompuServe software, and online customer assistance. The New Member Guide index offers an alphabetical list of databases. And its directory gives one to two paragraph descriptions of individual databases as well as the acronyms needed to access them directly.

For a one-time charge of around $40 and a small monthly fee, you get communications software, a pamphlet-sized user's guide, and a subscription to a monthly news and tips magazine. Payment options include the $8.95 flat monthly rate for unlimited connect-time to these basic services or the Alternative Pricing Plan, a pay-as-you-go option with a membership fee of $2 per month plus connect charges for only those services that you use. CompuServe compares their basic services to a basic cable television subscription and extended or premium services to getting premium-priced cable TV access. However, an important difference is that on CompuServe you have instant access to extended and premium services anytime you want, merely by choosing them from a menu and paying the fee differential. And after that search session you are not obligated for any premium fees until and unless you again choose to go beyond basic access.

The business portion of basic membership includes access to current stock prices, options prices, and market indexes, including the following types of changes: trading volume, high price, low price, latest price, amount of change, and time of last trade or quote. In addition you can get exchange rates for major foreign currencies (updated twice daily) and current values for mutual funds and money market funds. You even get a mortgage payment calculator. For a fee beyond the basic monthly membership, scores of other highly respected databases can be accessed via CompuServe. These include among others, Business Dateline, Compustat, Disclosure II, Dun's Market Identifiers, Investext, Mediamark Research Database (produced from annual national marketing survey data), S & P MarketScope, and Thomas Register.

CompuServe also offers access to the Internet as part of its basic service. Via CompuServe the user can access the World Wide Webb, e-mail, FTP, and all other Internet functions (see the Internet section of this chapter).

Cruising Online: Larry Majid's Guide to New Digital Highways, by Lawrence J. Majid is an excellent source for comparing CompuServe and its major competitors, America Online and Prodigy. Majid compares the three vendors in terms of database content, currency of information, scope of coverage, and ease of use. Majid also discusses content unique to each service.

As with any online system, CompuServe exposes the uninitiated user to a few pitfalls. The introductory membership booklet and the new member guide published in *CompuServe Magazine* are never as current as the online database lists. As a result, an attempt to get financial information from a database listed variously as Valueline Financial Statements & Forecasts or Value Line database II (go VLINE) results in a message that this source is no longer available online. (Since catalogs never get updated as often as online changes occur, this type of problem can happen in a search system from *any* database vendor.)

Because company names frequently are not standardized across CompuServe databases, it is a good idea to search by ticker symbol. If you don't know the ticker symbol, you can get it at no cost by entering the company name after the command "go basic money."

As in any other online system there are additional tricks to learn about deciding which database to use, how to move around in the system, and how to plan search strategies. The main difference between CompuServe and search systems designed for librarians (DIALOG, BRS, EPIC, or DataStar, for example) is that CompuServe publishes no aid pages. Instead you are invited either to learn by experimentation or to consult online helps.

One final thing to be aware of is that while databases costing a premium advise you of your charges as you exit, the "go billing" command to get your cumulated charges operates with approximately a 48 hour time lag. If you are concerned about costs accrued in premium or extended databases, you may prefer to add your total changes for each database manually at the end of each day's searching.

DataStar

The DataStar search system, set up in 1981 to provide information for and about Europe, now provides access to over 250 databases with worldwide coverage. This system is owned by Knight-Ridder, the parent company of DIALOG. Long-term plans may include complete assimilation of DataStar into the DIALOG family of databases, but for an initial period, at least, DataStar is still accessed separately from the DIALOG system. DataStar offers a command-driven mode of searching for librarians and other experienced database searchers. Many DataStar databases such as Investext Broker Research, Predicasts PROMT, and Trade and Industry Database are available via DIALOG, BRS, and other American database vendors. But DataStar's European coverage is unparalleled. (A contractual agreement for direct DataStar access is not necessary for the infrequent user, since Easynet offers an alternative source of access via either BRS or Telebase.)

In addition to an alphabetical list of databases, the DataStar catalog supplies the customary list of databases by topic. And unlike other vendors, this publication has the category "Business" broken into a number of useful subheadings. Besides the industry headings (Aerospace, Automobiles, Banking, etc.) there are geographic groupings (Austrian Companies, EC Companies, EC Legislation, Pacific Rim, etc.) and also subheadings for broad business topics such as Management, Market Research, and Trade— Imports/Exports.

Data Times

This information network provides access to over 2,000 business, financial, and news sources, including over 100 newspapers, 1,000 magazines, business journals, and industry publications; over 300 international sources, newswire services, company and industry reports, and historical stock, bond, and mutual fund prices.

Dow Jones News Retrieval (DJNR)

This vendor's current brochure proudly cites the company's record for supplying business information in various formats for over one hundred years,

119

an impressive credential. Although designed for professionals in business, finance and for individual investors, DJNR also offers academic rates to qualifying institutions including primary and secondary schools and degree-granting, non-proprietary institutions of higher education. Not all databases are made available to academic users. The following databases are excluded: Tradeline, Duns Financial Records Plus, Dow Jones Real Time Quotes, Investex, CLIP, and Dow Quest. Securities dealers pay higher rates than other users.

DJNR offers several of the same services available from DIALOG and BRS including the following:

1) free connect time for new subscribers
2) a user guide available in both print and online format
3) hands-on classroom training sessions in 30 different cities or at the subscriber's corporate headquarters
4) selective dissemination of information via the Dow Jones Clipping Service covering over 1,000 publications or the Dow Jones Tracking Service, which gathers news items and price quotes on up to 125 companies
5) fulltext coverage of more than 1,300 sources
6) a choice of command searching or menu-driven searching, customer service via phone (*not* toll free)
7) electronic mail
8) online cost and usage information.

Additionally, DJNR has several of the same features available from CompuServe such as the capacity for online buying/selling of stocks, making airline reservations, and shopping in an "electronic mall." Like other vendors DJNR also sells communications software and other information-retrieval and database-management software geared to its databases.

There is considerable overlap of databases between DJNR, DIALOG, BRS, CompuServe and other databases vendors as well. But DJNR can claim exclusive coverage in some areas. In addition to four newswires available elsewhere, DJNR has the following five exclusive newswires:

1) Dow Jones News (coverage from *Barron's* and the *Wall Street Journal* as well as Dow Jones News Service)
2) Dow Jones International News (coverage of the domestic, Asian, and European editions of the *Wall Street Journal* along with Dow Jones International newswires)
3) Professional Investor Report (reports of unusual intra-day trading of some 5,000 stocks)

4) Dow Jones Capital Markets Reports (international coverage of fixed-income and financial-futures markets)

5) Federal Filings (notice and analyses of significant SEC filings, bankruptcy, and other key federal filings).

DJNR has exclusive fulltext coverage of the *Wall Street Journal* and *Barron's*. It also has exclusive online access to transcripts of the Public Broadcasting Service program "Wall $treet Week" and to career advice and employment opportunities (the "talent for hire" section) from the *National Business Employment Weekly*.

Subscriber options include either prime time pricing at rates determined by baud rate or non-prime time pricing in three different tiers of flat-fees. The three flat-fee categories—News & Quotes, Forecasts & Analyses, and General Interest—are available at monthly fees of approximately $25, $25, and $13 respectively. Tiers can also be merged into four different combinations at monthly fees of $35, $35, $45 or $50 respectively. The DJNR searcher will also need to note surcharges ranging from $.50 to $102 per information unit in certain databases. The top of the scale is for a Dun and Bradstreet report on the company profile, history, operations, and financial status of a company. This information would cost a lot in any database, whether print or electronic format.

Dow Jones has reached an agreement with West that would allow its subscribers to access the WESTLAW database.

Legislative Information Files

These files give details about federal legislation proposed from the 93rd Congress (1973) to the present. Entries include the following information: bill contents, status, amendments, sponsorship/co-sponsorship, committee of referral, companion bills, bill number, public law number, and in some cases the full text of the proposed legislation. The database may be searched by subject, keywords, sponsor/co-sponsor, short title, bill and public law numbers, bill type, committees, and date of introduction. Since it is updated daily, this file is probably the best single source of information for tracking the progress of a bill through the legislative process.

Inquiries should be directed to the following address:

> Science and Technology Division
> Library of Congress
> Washington, DC 20540
> Telephone: (202) 707-5639

LEXIS/NEXIS

LEXIS

The LEXIS online fulltext database of legal materials has revolutionized the process of legal research. The general body of legal literature comprised of case law, statutes, and other significant legal texts from state, U.S. Federal, United Kingdom, and international jurisdictions is included. In addition virtually all legal specialties from admiralty law to tax law are covered.

Arrangement is by libraries drawn from the jurisdiction or the type of law and by subdivisions within each library. The General Federal Library has some 90 subfiles, including the *Federal Register*, the *Congressional Record*, the *Code of Federal Regulations*, and *Presidential Documents* among others. The specialized law files include the following topics: banking, bankruptcy, labor, environment and energy, federal and state tax, trade (domestic and international), insurance, intellectual property (including copyright, patents and trademarks), corporation law, law governing mergers and acquisitions, health, ethics, immigration, military law, utilities, real estate, accounting, securities, and pensions. Many of these topics are treated in multiple files.

Searching is based on any significant word in the text of a LEXIS document and can be limited by date, jurisdiction, court, or judge. As with other database search systems, LEXIS offers various options for output from the citation to the full text. Also the system has the capacity to save and re-execute searches. Selective dissemination of information is available as well.

NAARS

The National Automated Accounting Research System (NAARS) is a joint offering of LEXIS/NEXIS and the American Institute of Certified Public Accountants (AICPA). It features fulltext information from annual reports and other types of financial statements, as well as authoritative and semi-authoritative accounting literature. It is an invaluable resource for researching theory and practice in the fields of accounting and finance. Access can be made directly through the LEXIS system or indirectly through the AICPA's Total Online Tax and Accounting Library gateway to LEXIS.

NEXIS

This fulltext online search service covers magazines, newsletters, newspapers, government documents, wire services, and other sources of information important to business researchers. Like its sister service LEXIS, it is divided into libraries. The following is a list of them:

1) BACKGR

Covers hot news topics such as crime, health and medical issues, natural disasters, and environmental problems.

2) BANKS

Covers banking news and issues as reported in both general and industry publications.

3) CMPCOM

Covers communications and computer industries news and issues as reported in industry periodicals.

4) CMPGN

Covers political campaigns including information on campaign issues, office holders, candidates, contributors, contributions, and other news.

5) ENRGY

Covers energy-related news and issues from periodicals, wire services, and government documents.

6) EXEC

Covers activities and actions of government agencies including public laws, regulations, and proposed treasury regulations as reported in periodicals, government documents, and wire services.

7) INFOBK

Covers news from the *Miami Herald*, the *Philadelphia Inquirer*, the *New York Times*, the Asian and domestic editions of the *Wall Street Journal*, and the *Journal of Commerce*.

8) INSURE

Covers news and issues related to the insurance industry as reported in periodicals and industry reports.

9) LEGNEW

Covers news and issues related to the legal profession and the U.S. legal industry as reported in industry periodicals and documents.

10) LEXPAT

Covers patents registered with the U.S. Patent and Trademark Office.

11) MARKET

Covers news and issues pertinent to the marketing industry and its subfields (advertising, public relations, and sales) as reported in industry periodicals.

12) NEXIS General News and Business

Covers general news in all business fields as reported in periodicals, government documents, news wires, and other sources.

13) PEOPLE

Covers news items and biographical information on government officials and other public figures as reported in periodicals and news wires.

14) SPORTS

Covers sports news and issues as reported in industry periodicals and newspapers.

15) TRAN

Covers news and issues related to the transportation industry as reported in general periodicals, industry periodicals, government documents, and other sources.

Library of Congress (LC)

With the caveat that members of Congress receive first consideration for reference requests and that government agencies are given second priority, the Science and Technology Division of LC does undertake to help other researchers. Access to LC databases is available either through state libraries or through on-site usage. The following is a list of LC databases:

Library of Congress Information System (LCCC/MUMS)

This is essentially a record of books cataloged by the Library of Congress, which attempts to collect a copy of every book copyrighted in this country. LCCC or Library of Congress Computerized Catalog file has records for books cataloged from 1968 onward and a few dating from before that time. It can be searched by author, title of book, or subject. In addition to books, MUMS files include catalog records for computer files, sheet music, maps, serials, and sound recordings and other audiovisual materials. They can be searched by author, title, subject, keyword, genre/format and several other access points.

MAGS/MAGB

This database contains bibliographic citations to magazine and journal articles from 1980 to the present. The listings have been extracted from the Magazine Index, which is produced by Information Access Corporation.

National Referral Center Master File (NRCM)

This database is a historical one, since the National Referral Center was abolished in 1986 in a round of budget cuts. Although no new data is available, old records indicate the names of organizations that supplied information about topics in the fields of science, technology, and the social sciences.

Online Computer Library Center (OCLC)

OCLC, a relative newcomer to the database search service market, has begun to take business away from firms (DIALOG, BRS, and Orbit) who were pioneers and acknowledged leaders of this market for close to two decades. Starting its EPIC search service for librarians in the late 1980's with a handful of high-use databases, OCLC carved out a profitable niche by charging considerably lower connect fees than other database vendors. The list of EPIC databases has risen to over 30, among them the following business databases: ABI/Inform, Business Dateline, Business Organizations, Agencies, and Publications, Business Periodicals Index, Compendex Plus, Consumers Index, PNI (Pharmaceutical News Index), PsycINFO, and Wilson Business Abstracts.

This vendor soon developed a menu-driven search service called FirstSearch, intended for researchers with little or no search training. FirstSearch also offers over 20 databases including ERIC, Social Sciences Index, PAIS, Article First, and Wilson Abstracts. Indexed fields are limited to author, title, subject and keyword. It has fewer business databases than EPIC, and many of its files cover a shorter time period than EPIC databases of the same name. This difference reinforces the Chapter 6 recommendation in that you pay attention to the coverage dates when evaluating a database. Also you should use a search service offering access to the full spectrum of bibliographic, numeric, and fulltext databases if your research question requires a comprehensive approach. Restricting yourself to the least expensive databases and database vendors is poor economy if it gets you limited results and adversely affects your grade or your chances of winning a contract.

Orbit

Owned by Questel-Orbit, Orbit Search Service offers access to about 100 online databases. Orbit is known primarily for its exceptional coverage of science, technology, and patents, as well as energy, engineering and other subject areas. In addition, it offers access to the following twelve business and industry databases: ABI/Inform, ACCOUNTANTS (online version of *Accountant's Index*), API Energy Business News Index (online version of *Petroleum/Energy Business news Index*), Chemical Economics Handbook, Chemical Industry Notes (same title as print version), CorpTech (online version of *Corporate Technology Directory, Regional Sales Guide to High-Tech Companies*), ENERGYLINE (online version of energy information from *Environmental*

Abstracts and all materials from *Energy Information Abstracts*), LABOR-DOC (online version of *International Labour Documentation*), Materials Business File (online version of *Polymers/Ceramics/Composites Alert*, *Steels Alert*, and *Nonferrous Alert*), PIRA (online version of *International Packaging Abstracts*, *Paper and Board Abstracts*, *Printing Abstracts*, *Nonwovens Abstracts*, and *World Publishing Monitor*), RAPRA Abstracts (online version of *Adhesives Abstracts*, *RAPRA Abstracts* covering the rubber/plastics/polymer industry, and *Advanced Materials Abstracts*), and World Surface Coatings Abstracts (same title as print version).

In addition to database searching, Orbit offers through its ORBDOC service online ordering of the fulltext of sources cited. Its suppliers include both database-specific suppliers (e.g. the Society of Automotive Engineers) and "comprehensive" suppliers, who supply the text of a broad spectrum of publications.

PREMARC

This database contains LC records dating from 1898 that are excluded from the LCCC/MUMS file.

Radio-Suisse Services

Like DIALOG and BRS, Radio-Suisse offers other valuable services in addition to its command mode database search service. For those who search infrequently, there is the FOCUS menu-driven search mode. Other useful services include e-mail, bulletin boards, gateways to other databases such as FIZ Technik (a German online service specializing in engineering and industrial management information) and the *Official Airline Guide*. Radio-Suisse claims in its catalog that its TRADSTAT World Trade Statistics service is "the most comprehensive online source of the world's official government import and export figures." (TRADSTAT statistics are gathered from the U.S., Canada, ten European Community members, five European Free Trade Association members, two South American countries, and three Far Eastern nations). Radio-Suisse gives discounts for using the service at stated off-peak times.

Southam Electronic Publishing

In a recent subscriber guide Southam claims that Infomart Online is "the most comprehensive source of Canadian news and business information." The centerpiece of the service is its more than 60 Canadian databases, but for Canadian subscribers its gateway access to the DataTimes/Dow Jones News Retrieval Service also provides vital access to U.S. general and business news.

Following are highlights of Informart's coverage:

1) Canadian news (full text of over 18 Canadian newspapers)
2) news wires (full text of 8)
3) broadcast coverage (transcripts of current affairs shows)
4) industry publications (full text of Canadian publications on energy, forestry, insurance, mining, and other key industries)
5) company information (both financial and directory/ownership information)
6) directory information encompassing manufacturing companies, municipalities, and national and international trade, and product and trademark information for Canada and the U.S.
7) current and historical quotes from all four Canadian stock exchanges.

Telebase

Telebase Systems, Inc., the granddaddy of all database vendors with respect to size, connects users via its Easynet system to over 850 online databases covering virtually all fields of knowledge. The following information providers are included in Easynet: BRS, DataStar, DIALOG, FT Information Online, Ltd., G. Cam-L'Europeenne De Donnes, H.W. Wilson, Newsnet, Pergammon Financial Data Services, Questel-Orbit, Telescan, and Vu/Text. Easynet features a common command language so that the experienced searcher can do the same things in any Easynet database that he or she is used to doing in more familiar search services. There's no need to spend a lot of time training or reading documentation. For researchers with less experience in online searching or less experience in searching particular databases, Easynet provides a step-by-step, menu-driven mode of searching.

The main Easynet menu offers five searching options. With the first menu option, Easynet chooses the database for you after leading you through a menu of questions similar to those a librarian might ask in preparation for an intermediated search. In this method of Easynet searching, you first pick a field of knowledge (e.g., "Business") and from the menu pick a specialty within that field (e.g. Banking & Finance). After choosing what type of publications you want to cover (professional journals, trade journals, investment newsletters, or books on banking or investment), you input your subject and let Easynet do the rest. With the second menu option, Easynet scans a number of databases for hits on your topic and then lets you choose one to search. Again you are led through a search interview, selecting first a database category to scan (e.g., finance/insurance/real estate). Next you enter a topic. And finally, after reviewing the number of hits in each of the databases in the category, you choose a database (e.g. Magazine ASAP) to search. When the search has been executed, you may view, print, or download as many citations as you want.

The third and fourth options from the main menu permit you to choose a database and to search it in either the command-driven or the menu-driven mode. You would select option three or four if you know of a good database for your topic but did not have direct access to it.

The fifth Easynet menu option, the Investment Analy$t database, is geared specifically to the investor's need for news items, reports, and stock price quotes about specific companies. Produced by Telescan Stock Evaluation Service in Houston, Texas, this database represents a scaled-down version of the wealth of information on stocks and mutual funds Telescan gathers and makes available to direct subscribers. Unless you have hours of time and lots of money to spend, Investment Analy$t will satisfy your needs for online investment information.

Information and data in the Investment Analy$t database comes from standard and highly respected sources. Historical stock and mutual fund price information in this database comes from Standard & Poor's *MarketScope*. Official company filing information (10-K's, 10-Q's, etc.) comes from a firm called Market Guide, Inc. Soon a direct online connection to the SEC (Securities and Exchange Commission) will furnish an additional source for this type of information. Brokerage reports are obtained from Thomson Financial Network's *Investext* database. Earnings estimates are supplied by Zacks Investment Research, Inc.

Two things may be somewhat daunting to the first-time Easynet user. The first stems from Easynet's function as a transparent "gateway," or computer hookup into other database vendors' systems. If you need to disconnect, you are well advised to learn Easynet's commands. Otherwise you will not get out of the second vendor's system for some time and could be charged for connect time without research results. Also, you should be aware that you cannot rely on Easynet's database catalog descriptions. The catalog is not supplemented by monthly updates nor re-issued annually as are those of DIALOG and BRS. Before experimenting with unfamiliar databases that seem promising, you will save time and avoid frustration by checking the up-to-date online database descriptions.

West Publishing Company

A giant among publishers of print-based legal material, West was slow to get into electronic publishing. Its WESTLAW service was introduced some four years after the LEXIS Service was established. WESTLAW provides access to the following five types of databases: Federal case law, state case law, topical specialties from admiralty law to workers' compensation, a periodical database of selected articles from law reviews and bar journals, and a database of specialized material, including publications from the Bureau of National Affairs, the American Bar Association, Commerce Clearinghouse, and other highly-respected sources.

OTHER DATABASE FORMATS:
COMPACT DISC AND MAGNETIC TAPE OR CARTRIDGE

The appeal of CD's over online access is a predictable one-time cost per year. Instead of paying a membership fee and having variable expenses, depending on how much searching is done, organizations buying CD's and other machine-readable database formats can readily calculate how much to budget. They can offer unlimited use without building into the budget a "fudge factor" to cover phone charges, per-minute connect charge, and charges for output (viewing, printing, or downloading of citations, text or data). Another appeal of CD's is their availability from the user's location. Many libraries, both academic and public, have dial-in access to their LAN's (Local Area Networks) on which the CD's run. From the comfort of home or office, users can have access to these databases or CD's at any time, for free.

Since alternatives to online searching are usually provided to you free of charge, you will undoubtedly find CD's, diskettes, and magnetic tape formats attractive and useful. Please be aware of two caveats. First, even the largest and best-funded libraries are unlikely to provide the entire galaxy of different database choices available from online database vendors in CD, diskette, or magnetic tape. Typically they will buy a few for which they anticipate high use. For some topics, CD's and other fixed-cost formats will suffice. For comprehensive treatment of a topic you may need either a greater variety of sources or an online search. In such cases, consider what it costs to gain access. Your grade, if you are a student, or the continued success of your firm, if you are in business, may well be worth the money.

The second warning concerning relying on compact discs and other alternatives to online searching is that your library may have a subscription with less than frequent updating. Even though monthly updating is available, your library may have opted for the less- expensive quarterly or twice-yearly updates. While the library is reluctant to charge for CD use, its budget may not support monthly updates for all of its CD's. The frequency of updates is usually included in the description of the database, found by using the "Help" screens. If you don't see this information ask the librarian.

Virtually every publisher whose printing processes have been computerized offers CD and/or magnetic tape formats as alternatives to the print-based and online products that dominated the information industry for decades. Knight-Ridder Financial Publishing and DRI/McGraw Hill each offer a dazzling assortment of formats including CD's, diskettes, and magnetic tape. Knight-Ridder bills its CRBInfo Tech CD as the "largest database of fundamental commodity information," augmented by the "most extensive database of daily historical prices available on over 315 futures, cash, index, and options markets." DRI, which proudly points to 60% of the top U.S.

financial institutions among its clients, claims to have "the largest private collection of financial and economic information worldwide." The major areas of coverage of its millions of data series include the following: global financial instruments, global commodities, U.S. and Canadian equities, U.S. bonds, industries, and historical data and forecast for the U.S. and international economies. An example of a non-commercial provider of CD's, magnetic tapes, and online access is the Canadian Centre for Occupational Health and Safety (CCOHS). The CCOHS offers indexing and fulltext of its 50 databases in CD as well as online format. Its Material Safety Data Sheet, a numeric database, is available on magnetic tape.

Another interesting phenomenon in electronic publishing concerns the business professor or other researcher who grows impatient with the multi-industry focus of commercial products and decides to produce and market an electronic database. One example is the ComIndex. Business researchers delving into the historical aspects of journalism and other forms of mass communication might well appreciate this CD's coverage of 37 communication journals from 1970. Annual updates (when they become available) may focus on the same topics. Another example is the Database of Marketing Research, covering 21 academic marketing journals from January 1970.

Two commercial CD database vendors—SilverPlatter and DIALOG—each provide access to dozens of databases. SilverPlatter supplies the following business databases on CD: Banker's Almanac, COMLINE, Gale Global Access: Associations, Predicast F & S Index plus Text, RSWB (German construction, engineering, and municipal planning /development), SEC Online on SilverPlatter, SEC ONLINE-10K, and UK Corporations.

DIALOG Ondisc provides the following business databases on CD: DIALOG OnDisc Aerospace, DIALOG OnDisc American Banker, DIALOG OnDisc Canadian Business and Current Affairs, DIALOG OnDisc COMPEN-DEX*Plus, DIALOG OnDisc Corporate Affiliations, DIALOG OnDisc Directory of U.S. Importers and Exporters, DIALOG OnDisc IDD M&A Transactions, DIALOG OnDisc Standard & Poor's Corporations, DIALOG OnDisc Thomas Register, DIALOG OnDisc TRADEMARKSCAN-FEDERAL, and DIALOG OnDisc TRADEMARKSCAN-STATE. Its chemical, engineering, medical, health, and Federal Register CD's frequently are useful for business research as well.

The Bowker Publishing Company supplies the vast majority of its time-honored general reference books in CD format, for example:

> **SciTech Reference Plus** is a combination of bibliographic information from *Books in Print* and the Bowker International Serials

database, together with directory information about scientists, engineers, R & D labs, and technology firms from other Bowker publications.

Library Reference Plus combines information from *American Library Directory, American Book Trade Directory, Publishers, Distributors, and Wholesalers*, and *Bowker Annual Library and Book Trade Almanac*.

Enviro/Energyline Abstracts Plus, with information from the print-based *Environmental Abstracts* and *Energy Information Abstracts*, covers topics of potential interest to business researchers from global warming to gasoline prices.

Some CD databases are available from their publishers. One example is Newsbank, an index to regional business publications and covers over 100 newspapers from all across the United States and Canada. Also included are selected articles from American and international newswires, which make this source very timely. This database is updated monthly. Additional examples of CD's available exclusively from their publishers are *ABI/Inform Ondisc* (University Microfilms International, UMI) and the *Academic Index* (Information Access Company, IAC).

The *Academic Index* provides bibliographic references to more than 400 scholarly and general interest publications. Covered subject areas include business, humanities, social sciences and current events.

IAC also sells the *Expanded Academic Index*, which provides both bibliographic references to and abstracts from more than 960 scholarly and general-interest publications. Both Academic Indexes are updated monthly.

All IAC databases have the capacity for Boolean Logic. In addition using the function known as PowerTrac, the user can employ limiters such as date, journal name, author words in the title. This function makes finding specific articles easier. For example, if a user remembers seeing an article about corporate mergers in the *Wall Street Journal* in a given year, the article can be easily located by using PowerTrac to eliminate all articles about corporate mergers that are in other journals or years.

There are several business-related CD's that are available from a variety of providers. A few are listed below:

American Business Directory. Directory information. Provider: American Business Information, Inc.

This directory indexes over 10 million businesses. Records can be searched by name. SIC code, yellow page heading, geographical location, address, state, city, zip code, or area code. Records include current address, telephone and fax numbers, and a description of the business.

Company Profile. Numeric data. Directory information. Provider: Information Access Company.

Data includes current public and private financial information for more than 150,000 companies. Emphasis is on hard-to-find company information.

Corporate and Industry Research Reports. Numeric data. Provider: Bowker Electronic Publishing or Silver Platter.

This database provides reports from securities and investment banking firms.

Government Publications Index. Bibliographic. Provider: Information Access Company.

This database provides bibliographic references to documents in the U.S. Government Printing Office's Monthly catalog. Listings include subjects, authors, and issuing agencies for these documents. The information goes from 1976 to the present and is updated monthly.

InvesText. Text. Provider: Information Access Company.

Covering forecasts and reports prepared by top Wall Street and international brokerage firms, this database provides investment data about more than 11,000 U.S. and international companies spanning over 53 industries.

Canadian Business and Current Affairs. Bibliographic. Dictionary information. Some text abstracts. Provider: Micromedia Limited.

Corresponding to the online database (see International Databases Section), this database provides information about Canadian companies products and industries. The CD version also includes Ontario Securities Commission filings.

General Business File. Bibliographic. Some text. Provider: Information Access Company.

Database content reflects all aspects of business and management including company and industry information. It provides bibliographic references to and abstracts from 800 business, economic, management, trade, and industry publications. Also included are directory listing and descriptions of more than 150,000 companies. There is also a backfile that covers 1982-1991.

National Technical Information Service. Text. Provider: DIALOG or Silver Platter.

Updated quarterly, this CD product provides summaries of completed government sponsored studies in a variety of topics, including those related to business.

Legal Trac. Bibliographic. Some text. Provider: Information Access Company.

Corresponding to the Legal Research Index, this database provides access to citations about all aspects of the law. In a single listing, subjects, titles, authors, cases, and statutes are alphabetized, and articles cover more law reviews, bar association journals, and newspapers.

Please note that all Information Access Company (IAC) CD databases listed here are part of the Infotrac family of databases, as mentioned in chapter 6.

THE INTERNET

According to a report in *The New York Times* on May 14, 1995, there are an estimated 30 million Internet users. The Internet originally appealed to academic and research professionals. In recent years, however, the Internet has become increasingly interesting to people using PC's at home.

The Internet was created about 20 years ago by the U.S. Defense Department. Its purpose was to connect a computer network to other radio and satellite networks. Researchers in computer science, government employees and government contractors were the only people who used it until 1987. At this time, the network was upgraded, and everyone was allowed access to the Internet.

There are two main ways of accessing information on the Internet: Gopher and the World Wide Web.

Gophers

Gopher software originated at the University of Minnesota, home of the Golden Gophers, hence the name. The name is appropriate, however, since the software is designed to offer information, the "go fer" it. The information is structured in hierarchical menus, and you go for directories to subdirectories to files. Some files are text files and others allow you to key search or TELNET to other sites.

There are five advantages to gopher software:

1. It's easy to use. There are no complicated functions, and it's easy to learn.

2. It has "bookmarks." The user can flag files and put them into "bookmarks" for easy access later.

3. Keyword searches are available. VERONICA allows the user to employ keyword searches on specific sites.

4. Easy access to other resources. The gopher user can connect to other types of resources such as TELNET without requiring an address, as is necessary with the World Wide Web.

5. Simple and rapid retrieval. The user can send, download, and save files quickly and easily.

The disadvantage to gopher software is its disorganization. There is no standard terminology used. For example, topics classified under "Sports" in one gopher may appear under "Leisure and Recreation" in another. Also, users often forget where they are in the gopher.

The World Wide Web

The World Wide Web (WWW) is just that—a web of information. It uses "hypertext" to link the user to other documents. The user accesses the web through a "browser" such as Lynx, Mosaic, and Cello.

The advantages to the Web are too numerous to list. Here are three of the major benefits just to indicate the capabilities of this resource:

1. It provides links. Hypertext allows the user to move easily between topics of interest in separate servers. The simple commands, "follow a link" and "perform a search" are the only two commands needed to conduct a search among a variety of servers, and both are done with the "point-and-click" of a mouse.

2. The sites provide multimedia resources. Gophers only provide text. Web sites often have color illustrations, sounds, and music.

3. The Web is organized. The user's location is always clearly displayed, and exiting from the site is simple.

Key word searching on the Web is available using "search engines." Examples of search engines are Yahoo, Web Crawler, Lycos, and EINet Galaxy. Addresses for these sites are available in Internet Directories. If these directories are difficult to locate, ask the librarian for help. Site addresses change, so be persistent until you find the right one.

Access to the Internet

"Surfing the 'net" can be done using commercial services, three of which were mentioned earlier in this chapter: America Online, CompuServe, and Prodigy. The "For Dummies" series of books (i.e. *America Online for Dummies, Prodigy for Dummies,* etc.) is an excellent source of information about how to sign up for one of these services.

Libraries often provide free access to the Internent. Some have dial-in access so users can avail themselves of the service at home even when the library is closed. Be sure to ask what "browser" the library is using to ensure that it fits your needs. Be aware that some browsers, such as Lynx, do not support images or sounds in the World Wide Web.

In addition, software vendors such as IBM and Microsoft plan to include Internet access using software that also provides spreadsheets, word processing and other functions.

IBM's OS/2 and Micorsoft's Windows '95 are the most prominent examples of such access.

For general information on the Internet the user should consult the following resources:

The Online Users Encyclopedia: Bulletin Boards and Beyond, by Bernard Aboba (Reading, MA: Addison-Wesley Publishing Company, 1994). This comprehensive guide provides a host of basic information about how to get online and what to expect once there. As Aboba puts it, "This guide is balanced between the itsy bitsy details and THE BIG PICTURE."

The Whole Internet: Users Guide and Catalog, by Ed Krol (Sebastopol, CA: O'Riley and Associates, Inc., 1994). This is *the* definitive user guide to the Internet. It covers all the pertinent topics including what the Internet is, how it works, ethical aspects of its use, TELNET, FTP, gophers, e-mail, WWW, newsgroups, WAIS, troublshooting, and how to get connected.

The following resources will be particularly helpful to the business researcher interested in the Internet:

Doing Business on the Internet: How the Electronic Highway is Transforming American Companies, by Mary J. Cronin (New York: Van Nostrand Reinhold, 1994).

The Internet Business Book, by Jill H. Ellsworth (New York: John Wiley and Sons, 1995).

Internet for Dummies, by John R. Levine (San Mateo, CA: IDG Books, 1993).

Internet World. This magazine is an excellent source of current information about the Internet in general and about web sites specifically.

The Internet Yellow Pages, by Harley Hahn (Berkley, CA: Osborne McGraw-Hill, 1994).

SOURCES OF ADDITIONAL INFORMATION

CD-ROMS In Print. (Detroit: Gale Research, published annually.) This guide to CD-ROM products claims comprehensive international coverage of some 8,000 titles. Each entry has up to 25 items of information, including many of the following: producer of the database, coverage dates of information/data on CD, frequency of updating, computer hardware requirements (e.g. amount of memory, compatibility of the CD with different types of computers and computer peripherals), description of search software and operating system, print and/or online equivalents, availability from U.S. and non-U.S.

distributors, and networking or site license fees and stipulations. Eight indexes include the following options for looking up individual CD products: alphabetical arrangement by the title of the CD product, subject index including such topics as Bibliographies & Indexes, computer tools such as Clip-art, industries from Agriculture & Animal Husbandry to Travel & Tourism, and branches of knowledge such as Biology and Women's Studies, U.S. distributor index, non-U.S. distributor index, database provider index (meaning the entity producing the database), software provider index, publisher index, and a separate Macintosh index. Special features include essays on topics such as the growth of the CD publishing industry and trends in the Japanese segment of the industry.

Directory of Online Databases. (Detroit: Cuadra/Gale: 1979-.) Claiming comprehensive, international coverage of databases offered in an online, interactive mode (providing they are publicly available), this twice yearly publication covers over 5,300 databases and sub-files. Product descriptions consist of up to 15 items of information. They include the following: database name and acronym, including former names and alternate names more commonly used than the "official" database name, type of information (e.g. directory, citations to printed literature and graphic images), subjects covered, description of data items included in a database record, languages, geographic areas covered, time span covered, updating frequency, the producer (the entity gathering and organizing the content of the database), the vendor selling access, terms and conditions for use of the database including costs, and alternate formats such as compact disc or magnetic tape. The publication has three main sections: product descriptions, database producers, and database vendors offering access. In addition there are three indexes: subject index, geographic index, and master index.

Information Industry Directory. (*IID.*) (Detroit: Gale, published annually.) The two volumes, with supplement, were formerly called the *Encyclopedia of Information Systems and Services.* It covers the following 23 functional and service breakdowns: abstracting and indexing organizations, associations interested in the provision of information, electronic publishing, library automation, and related fields, community information and referral agencies (including both private and government organizations), organizations providing retrieval from computerized databases, consultants, database producers (who create computer-readable data files) and database publishers, entities whose purpose is collection, analysis, and dissemination of raw data, document delivery organizations, vendors supplying electronic mail facilities along with information systems and services, fee-based information brokers, both library and non-library organizations, information and resource sharing networks, consortia, and systems, software and systems for management of library functions such as circulation, magnetic/diskette information publishers, mailing list services, vendors of computerized information storage and retrieval who also supply texts in micrographic formats (microfilm or microfiche, whose greatly reduced size requires high magnification to read), online host services (vendors of multiple databases searchable through proprietary retrieval software from remote locations), optical publishers (including CD-ROM and optical disc publishers along with entities offering conversion services for publishers), entities conducting regular, continuing research focused on the information field, selective dissemination of information or current awareness services, software producers, providers of electronic transaction services (e.g. shopping or ordering documents), and videotext and telex services.

Entries have some or all of the following types of information:

1) organizational information including name/address/phone, year established, name and title of chief administrator, number of staff and breakdown by position;
2) related organizations;
3) description of the entity's purpose and scope of activity;
4) sources of input for the organization's information activities;
5) description of stored information, including time periods covered and quantity of information stored in machine-readable, micrographic, and other published or unpublished formats;
6) description of any information-related printed, microform, or computer-based publications issued by the organization, other major services provided by the organization, identification of the organization's clientele along with conditions of database use, including any restrictions;
7) projected publications and services;
8) remarks and addenda;
9) contact name and phone/fax/telex number.

There are seven separate options for finding information: a master index by name or keyword (including inverted word order), subject index based on a modification of the Library of Congress list of subject headings, a databases index, a print and microform publications index, a software index, a personal name index, and a geographic index.

The *Information Industry Directory* is far and away the most comprehensive single source of information for the electronic publishing industry, and most of the time it is also very complete. There is, however, the rare exception. Comparing entries from the DRI Commodities database, you will see that *IID* covers the basics of what is included in this time series, but for some entries the *Directory of Online Databases* includes more details. One notable difference is the latter's list of commodity exchanges that submit data about price and trading volume for the DRI Commodities database and the mention of two additional data sources. Another example of *IID*'s rare incompleteness is that it doesn't mention Roger Ebert's Movie Reviews, one of the basic (free) CompuServe databases. In most cases, however, *IID* lists CompuServe databases and gives more information about them than the CompuServe pamphlet/catalog provides. The conclusion that you can draw is, "If multiple sources of information about electronic products are available, check more than one source."

Lesko's Info-Power by Matthew Lesko, 2nd ed. (Detroit: VIP/Gale Research, 1994.) This book is subtitled "Over 45,000 Free and Low Cost Sources of Information for Investors, Job Seekers, Teachers, Students, Businesses, Consumers, Homeowners, Techies, Artists, Travellers, Communities and MORE!" A throw-back to the 1960's power to the people ideal, the introduction starts by thanking the reader for "buying, borrowing, or stealing" the book. The arrangement corresponds roughly to the audiences enumerated in the subtitle.

The book starts with an essay about how possessing information will empower you. The 31 subject-specific chapters go on to give details about specific state and federal sources of information for virtually every need from financial help for the poor, elderly, and unemployed to current awareness of developments in international relations and defense. Examples are given of how people would use the specific types of information covered— such as how an insurance company could find out what rates its competitors charge or in what areas of service its competitors receive the most complaints. Many but not all listings describe information available in computerized form (for example magnetic tape) or as a computer print out. As mentioned in this chapter's introduction, *Lesko's Info-Power* is updated online through CompuServe.

Manual of Online Search Strategies (New York: G.K. Hall, 1992.) This book has a chapter about database evaluation and selection as well as a chapter about databases particularly useful for retrieving specific facts or data. It also covers fields of knowledge from agriculture to social and behavioral sciences. Several chapters treat topics potentially useful to the business researcher, such as legal databases. Without a doubt the chapter about United States business and economics databases and United Kingdom business and economics databases are the most useful to the business researcher. Only if you intend to do a lot of your own searching would the amount of detail in this book be useful to you. But its logical arrangement and clear, non-technical language make it easy to read if you *do* need it.

Optical Publishing Directory. (*OPD.*) (Medford, NJ: Learned Information, Inc., 1986-.) This book originally was called *Optical/Electronic Purchasing Directory.* Like *CD-Roms in Print*, in a recent edition it has a brief essay about trends in the CD-ROM marketplace. And like *Lesko's Info-Power*, it warns about how fast a printed directory becomes outdated. Covering a modest 700 sources selected for their appeal to a fairly general audience, the *OPD* covers a good many electronic information sources of interest to business researchers.

Entries, only two per page, are brief and easy on the eyes. Three types of information are included for each CD title. First is product data including the following: publisher's name, alternate title for the CD, current search software version, type of contents (e.g. fulltext or images or bibliographic or statistical/numerical information), area of interest (meaning subject area such as Business, Education, or General Reference), languages, geographical coverage, data source, and product description. Second comes complete details about what kind of personal computer hardware and software are needed to run the product. And third are "market data" including when the product first was shipped (brought onto the market), availability of demo copies and back editions, names of distributors if different than the database publisher, and price including some discounts and network or consortium pricing information.

There is an "applications" index categorized by areas of interest. General areas with some databases useful for business research include General Reference (e.g. *GPO Monthly Catalog*) and Social Science (e.g. *Econlit*). 146 databases are listed under Business. Some are two versions of the same database distributed by different vendors. Other applications with specialized databases useful for some business research include the following: Agriculture, Computer Science, Education, Engineering, Law, Medicine/Life Science, Military, and Physical Science.

A product type index gives access to CD's by type of content as described above. In addition to the type of contents that might be expected (bibliographic citations or graphic images, for example) are headings for Music/Sound Effects.

A very useful feature of this directory is the company directory (misnamed "index") which lists some 325 publishers, search software providers, and distributors of CD products.

Research Guide to Corporate Acquisitions, Mergers, and Other Restructuring by Michael Halperin and Stephen J. Bell. (Westport, CT: Greenwood Press, 1992.) The book is an example of what researchers deserve to see more of—research guides that include a discussion of electronic resources. The authors present a section called "Information Checklist," providing the following categories of business information: company background, company financials, industry information, marketing information, legal information, and strategic information. For each category of information needed, they give a list of typical questions for the researcher to pose, a selected list of online and/or CD-ROM databases, and some strategy suggestions as to how the various databases can be used.

After the Information Checklist there is an appendix showing where you can obtain access to databases recommended by the authors. The familiar database ABI/Inform, for example, is available via at least four database vendors: DIALOG, BRS, DataStar, and NEXIS. If your library subscribes to any of these online search services, you can get access.

The chart of online databases and vendors is not exhaustive. At least five databases in the CompuServe catalog (AP News, Businesswire, Disclosure, InvesText, and UPI News) are not credited to CompuServe in Halperin and Bell's book. But theirs is still a very good list, since it covers not only the vendors with which nearly all librarians are familiar (DIALOG and BRS) but also search services less well known to many librarians. These include ADP Data Services, DataStar, Dow Jones News/Retrieval, LEXIS/NEXIS, M.A.I.D. (Market Analysis and Information Database), Newsnet, and Securities Data Corporation.

Ulrich's International Periodicals Directory. (New Providence, NJ: 1932- New York: Bowker.) *Ulrich's* is as one of two old standards for finding information on print-based publications ranging from popular magazines to trade journals to government documents to conference proceedings. In recognition of the boom in electronic publishing the most recent edition features an 18-page section entitled Vendor Listing/Serials Online that is a directory of many important players in the electronic segment of the publishing industry. It includes companies described earlier in this chapter who supply access to a large number of databases (in many cases hundreds of different choices) both fulltext and numeric or bibliographic (BRS, CompuServe, DIALOG, DataStar, Orbit, others). Sometimes the publication has its own database name and/or file number (e.g. *American Banker*, DIALOG file 625). More commonly, however, hundreds of source publications are indexed in a single database (e.g. ABI/Inform) and the text of their articles is offered as one of a handful of different formats for viewing, printing, or downloading the results of a search in that database. In such cases, *Ulrich's* lists the fulltext publication and tells which database(s) gives access to it. For example, in the BRS search system the text of *Aerospace Daily* is in the database with the name TSAP, whereas in the DIALOG system the text of articles from the same publication is found in file 624. Another little twist to using fulltext online is that the publication may be available in more than one database on the same search system. For example, on DIALOG *Applied Genetics News* is in both file 16 and file 636. So the "remove duplicates" feature described in DIALOG training materials can be a real help in ensuring that you do not pay twice for the same piece of information.

In addition to big players in electronic publishing, the Vendor Listing includes a small number of organizations with as few as one electronic product listed (e.g. National Data Corp, publisher of *International Financial Statistics* and Research Libraries Group Network, publisher of *Avery Index to Architectural Periodicals*).

Inclusion of foreign entities is a strength in *Ulrich's* coverage of electronic publications. Examples are BELINDIS (a subsidiary of the Belgian Ministry of Economic Affairs) with six electronic titles listed and QL Systems, Ltd., the Canadian publisher of at least 25 electronic titles, including among others the *Canadian Business Index*, the economics section of *International Bibliography of the Social Sciences*, and *Investor's Digest of Canada*.

Since *Ulrich's* is found even in libraries of quite modest size, it may be more readily available to you than the more comprehensive, but considerably more expensive *Information Industry Directory (IID)*. Please bear in mind that the latest catalog of any vendor generally will be much more complete and more current than the listing for the same vendor in any directory like *Ulrich's* or *IID*.

SECTION THREE

SPECIFIC SOURCES OF BUSINESS INFORMATION

8

Handbooks and Almanacs

OBJECTIVES: This chapter will provide you with an overview of specific handbooks and almanacs that are key to business research.

> **Introduction**
> **Handbooks**
> - Administration and Management
> - Auditing and Accounting
> - Computers
> - Credit and Finance
> - Health and Nonprofit Organizations
> - Human Resources
> - Marketing and Public Relations
> - Production
> - Real Estate
> **Almanacs**

After reading this chapter you should be able to:

*Identify the major business handbooks and almanacs.
*Be aware of key features in many important business handbooks and almanacs.

INTRODUCTION

Webster's International Dictionary defines a handbook as "a concise reference book covering a particular subject or field of knowledge." The American Library Association's *ALA Glossary of Library and Information Science* defines a handbook as "a compendium, covering one or more subjects, arranged for the quick location of facts and capable of being conveniently carried." Business handbooks are among the best examples of general survey books. For example, a marketing handbook might contain abridged "textbooks" of marketing principles, advertising, marketing research, sales management, and industrial marketing. Such treatment of the field makes the handbook valuable to those who need a quick refresher in a particular area or an overview of basic information on a business subject.

While handbooks contain general discussion material, almanacs normally present information in a statistical format. According to *Webster's*, an almanac is "a publication containing a collection of useful or otherwise interesting facts or statistics usually in the form of tables and often covering the period of one year." The *ALA Glossary of Library and Information Science* describes an almanac as "a compendium, usually an annual, of statistics and facts, both current and retrospective. May be broad in geographical and subject coverage, or limited to a particular country or state or to a particular subject."

HANDBOOKS

Handbooks will be covered first and, because of the large number, will be categorized by subject area.

Administration and Management

The following handbooks in administration and management will be of interest to the researcher:

AMA Management Handbook. (New York: American Management Association, 1994.) This handbook contains a great deal of information useful to the student who wants a general reference book on business. The contents include data on marketing, production management, personnel management, office management, financial management, and general management.

Basics of Successful Business Planning. (Saranac, NY: AMACOM Book Division, 1982.) This book presents several examples of planning in an effort to acquaint the reader with the theory and practice of business planning. A practical step-by-step approach is given to assist readers in developing their own business plans.

Business Researcher's Handbook. (Washington, D.C.: Washington Researchers, Ltd., 1983.) This guide shows the reader how to define information needs, organize research projects, manage your research time and resources, and effectively present your findings.

Handbook for Business Writing. (Lincolnwood, IL: NTC Publishing Group, 1993.) Describes how to write business letters, memos, press releases, business reports, proposals, and dictation.

Handbook for Memo Writing. (Lincolnwood, IL: NTC Publishing Group, 1991.) Discusses how to prepare, write and review effective memos, how to avoid common memo mistakes, and how to send memos by electronic mail. Over seventy examples of good memos are included.

Handbook for Professional Managers. (New York: McGraw-Hill, 1985.) This handbook of over 1,000 pages covers management topics ranging from accounting and cost control to zero base budgeting.

Handbook of Business Problem Solving. (New York: McGraw-Hill, 1980.) This handbook deals with problems in organization, staffing and development, marketing, strategy planning and control, new products, information systems, and data processing.

Handbook of Business Strategy. (Boston: Warren, Gorham & Lamont, Inc., 1991.) Provides an overview and analysis of business unit strategy, corporate strategy, tools for strategy development and analysis, formal strategy methods, and how to best organize for strategic management.

Handbook of Industrial Organization. (New York: Elsevier Science Publishing Co., 1989.) Overviews determinants of organizational format, empirical analysis methods for organizational review, international issues, government relations, and the marketplace and its affect on the organization.

Handbook of Managerial Tactics. (Boston: CBI Publishing Co., Inc., 1976.) This book presents steps designed to carry out a plan of action for management strategy.

Hoover's Handbook of American Business. (Austin, TX: Reference Press, Inc., 1993.) Included are complete details on 500 businesses in the U.S. that dominate the industries in which they operate.

How to Prepare an Effective Company Operations Manual. (Chicago, IL: Dartnell Corp., 1979.) This guide outlines methods for creating a system for communicating company operational procedures and philosophies. It explains techniques for obtaining and organizing input; analyzing forms, systems, and files; using word processing equipment; and choosing charts, graphs, and illustrations.

How to Select a Business Site: The Executive's Location Guide. (New York: McGraw-Hill, 1980.) This reference provides a checklist of factors affecting the selection of a suitable business site. Also explored are key considerations in site selection, including transportation systems, the availability of labor and executive talent, the availability of financing and tax abatement incentives, accessibility to markets, and the availability of fuel, energy, and raw materials. The human factor is stressed, and procedures for transferring personnel and their families are described.

Improving Productivity Through Advanced Office Controls. (Saranac Lake, NY: AMACOM Book Division, 1991. Reprint Krieger Publishing Co.) This reference describes techniques designed to cut costs by 20 to 40 percent and improve individual and departmental performance. It discusses performance standards, work management programs, and wage incentives and includes sample charts, tables, reports, and inter-office memos.

Management Development and Training Handbook. (New York: McGraw-Hill, 1983.) This handbook is designed as a standard reference work in management development and training. Directed to senior managers, administrators, personnel managers, and management development specialists, this volume includes articles from recognized world authorities. There are over forty contributors from a dozen countries in North America, Europe, and the developing world. The handbook is in five parts: (1) Management Development, (2) Management Training Methods, (3) Management Training Programs, (4) Organization Development, and (5) Planning and Organization.

Management Information Systems. (New York: McGraw-Hill, 1993.) This handbook presents the systems engineering and management views of the organization, guidance, and evaluation of integrated systems. It provides information system aids in achieving the organization's strategies, goals, and managerial and operational control requirements.

Managing People at Work: A Manager's Guide to Behavior in Organizations. (New York: McGraw-Hill, 1992.) This publication explains discoveries in the behavioral sciences during the last thirty years that are of particular value to managers. It concentrates on practical, usable methods and provides information for analyzing dimensions of the behavioral sciences that pertain to problems in the business world encountered by managers.

Office Administration Handbook. (Chicago: Dartnell Corporation, 1984.) This handbook covers all aspects of office administration.

The Standard Handbook of Business Communication. (New York: The Free Press, 1984.) Discusses written, verbal, and organizational communication, as well as nonsexist and intercultural communication, and communication theory.

The Strategic Management Handbook. (New York: McGraw-Hill, 1983.) This is a comprehensive guide to business strategy including sections by industry leaders on topics such as strategy formulation, corporate planning, the strategic audit, pricing, human resources, and the use of outside consultants.

Subcontract Management Handbook. (Saranac Lake, NY: AMACOM Book Division, 1981.) This book provides guidance for those who manage major subcontracts or who wish to become acquainted with the basic practices and procedures required to administer a subcontract.

Successful Management of Large Clerical Operations. (New York: McGraw-Hill, 1981.) This book discusses how to improve the cost effectiveness of clerical service operations and increase customer satisfaction. It provides plans, checklists, strategies, and tools applicable to a variety of situations and stresses management decision-making techniques.

Supervisor's Standard Reference Handbook. (Englewood Cliffs, NJ: Prentice-Hall, 1988.) Covers a wide range of topics of interest to first level supervisors including lack of cooperation, failure to follow orders, poor work, absenteeism, ignoring safety rules, opposition to change, spreading of rumors, prejudice, and resentment of other employees.

Warren's Forms of Agreements. (New York: Matthew Bender & Co., Inc., 1975.) The desk edition of *Warren's Forms of Agreement* is abridged from *Warren's Forms of Agreements Business Forms*, Vols. 1-3. This edition, suited to the busy practitioner, is based on considerations of practicality, wide-spread usage, and statutory compliance. It is an overview of the major fields covered in *Warren's Forms of Agreement.* For greater detail than that provided by this volume it may be necessary to check statutory and case law of the particular jurisdiction. Many legal and business implications may require further research.

Auditing and Accounting

Researchers interested in auditing and accounting may wish to check these references:

Accountants' Cost Handbook. (New York: Ronald Press Co., 1983.) This handbook explains fundamental cost concepts and principles, presents major cost systems and the methods and techniques derived from them, and describes and analyzes proven cost practices, standards, forms, records, and reports.

Accounting Handbook for Nonaccountants. (Boston: CBI Publishing Co., Inc., 1985.) Today many nonfinancial executives and managers are interested in learning about accounting. This handbook provides the necessary background in both the basic concepts and eccentricities of accounting.

Attorney's Handbook of Accounting. (New York: Matthew Bender & Co., Inc., 1979; updates available.) This handbook does not make accountants out of attorneys; rather it enables attorneys to help clients interpret accounting statements, working papers, and accounting procedures. It helps attorneys understand and present financial data and legal problems to the business-person.

Cashin's Handbook for Auditors. (New York: McGraw-Hill, 1986.) This handbook covers the entire field of auditing, including accounting principles, auditing standards, professional ethics, legal liability, the SEC, independent auditing, internal auditing, government auditing, and special investigations.

Handbook of Accounting and Auditing. (Boston: Warren, Gorham & Lamont, Inc., 1988; annual supplement.) Provides an overview of financial accounting, auditing, special accounting reports, accounting for specialized types of businesses, and research in accounting.

Handbook of Applied Accounting Mathematics. (Englewood Cliffs, NJ: Prentice-Hall, 1982.) Covers accounting mathematics for leases, implied interest, depreciation, monetary debt, LIFO and FIFO inventory procedures, inflation accounting, monetary and non-monetary exchanges, algebraic concepts, and algebraic formulas.

Handbook of Model Accounting Reports and Formats. (Englewood Cliffs, NJ: Prentice-Hall, 1987.) This handbook covers general purpose financial statements, responsibility reporting, sales operations reports, sales activity reports, marketing reports, manufacturing cost reports, inventory reports, and cash reporting.

Handbook of Modern Accounting. (New York: McGraw-Hill, 1983.) This handbook provides in-depth coverage of accounting from traditional methods and procedures to developments in electronic data processing (EDP) and computerized systems.

Portfolio of Accounting Systems for Small and Medium-Sized Businesses. (Englewood Cliffs, NJ: Prentice-Hall, 1977.) This portfolio contains contributions and reviews by members of the National Society of Public Accountants. This volume lists a series of accounting systems for 68 types of small businesses. It covers such diverse areas as advertising agencies, beauty shops, churches, florists, auto supply shops, landscape businesses, travel agencies, and variety stores.

Computers

There are many handbooks dealing with computers. Selected examples that are of interest to businesspeople include the following:

The Dow Jones-Irwin Handbook of Microcomputer Applications in Law. (Homewood, IL: Dow Jones-Irwin, 1987.) A non-technical guide to microcomputer use in the legal office. Covers litigation support, time accounting and billing, communications, networking, and word processing.

The Laser Printer Handbook. (Burr Ridge, IL: Irwin Professional Publishing, 1989.) Includes how to plan, purchase, and operate a wide range of printers and related software for business use.

MRP II - A Handbook for Software Survival. (Falls Church, VA: Oliver Wight Publications, Inc., 1988.) Covered are software for manufacturing resource planning, sales and operations planning, master production scheduling, and MRP subsystems.

Networking: An Electronic Mail Handbook. (Glenview, IL: Harper Collins, 1986.) Basic guide to electronic mail that reviews the technology, explains how to set up an in-house system, discusses necessary hardware and software, and covers local area networks and teleconferencing.

Credit and Finance

Credit and finance researchers can find useful information in these publications:

Bank Officer's Handbook of Commercial Banking Law. (Boston: Warren, Gorham & Lamont, Inc., 1989.) Material covered includes all aspects of banking regulation and legislation, an overview of the U.S. banking system, the Federal Reserve System, national banks, bank holding companies, branch banking, bank examinations, and all forms of financial transactions.

The Banker's Handbook. (Burr Ridge, IL: Professional Publishing, 1988.) Major sections of this handbook cover the banking industry, bank segments, geographic banking differences, industry competition, foreign banks, banking management, accounting and controls, investments, credit, retail banking, wholesale banking, trust services, and bank marketing.

Bankruptcy Law Handbook. (Los Angeles, CA: Lega-Books, 1985.) Presents thorough review of bankruptcy law, who may file and under what conditions, circumstances generally leading to filing, exempt properties, administration of the bankruptcy, handling claims, and reorganization.

Credit Manual of Commercial Laws. (New York: National Association of Credit Management, 1993.) This updated edition is geared to credit executives, accountants, lawyers, business managers, and corporate leaders engaged in the extension of credit from one firm to another. It covers the Bankruptcy Reform Act, procedures to follow under the code for liquidations and reorganization proceedings, consumer protection, bad check laws, antitrust laws, credit cards, assumed names, leasing of personal property, legislative changes, and recent court cases of relevance. It also contains sample contracts and forms, as well as a glossary of legal terms.

Dow Jones Investor's Handbook. (New York: Dow Jones & Co., 1990.) This handbook provides a summary of the most widely quoted stock market averages. Included are daily closings, monthly closings, quarterly earnings, dividend records, price/earnings ratios, and stock highs and lows.

Financial Analyst's Handbook. (Burr Ridge, IL: Professional Publishing, 1988.) Examines the ins and outs of economics, equity, and company and industry analysis; portfolio theory and practice; quantitative aids; information sources; and legal and ethical standards.

Financial Handbook. (New York: Ronald Press Co., 1981.) This is a concentrated reference work on corporation finance, money, and banking. The

151

contents include corporate stock; bond financing and borrowing; commodity trading; financial planning; banking procedure; government financing agencies; international banking, money, and credit; financial reports and analysis; pensions and profit-sharing plans; savings institutions; and working capital.

The Foreign Exchange Handbook. (New York: John Wiley & Sons, 1983.) Covered are institutions involved with foreign exchange, exchange controls and legislation, spot dealing, dealing calculations, the gold market, financial futures, and payment systems.

Handbook for Banking Strategy. (New York: John Wiley & Sons, 1985.) A complete overview of how to manage financial institutions and develop business strategies.

Handbook for No-Load Fund Investors. (Burr Ridge, IL: Irwin Professional Publishing, 1993.) A very complete reference on no-load and low-load mutual funds. It provides the latest performance information on over 1,000 funds and includes a directory.

Handbook of Budgeting. (New York: John Wiley & Sons, 1993.) Provides a short overview of all aspects of the budgeting process.

Handbook of Business and Financial Ratios. (Englewood Cliffs, NJ: Prentice-Hall Inc., 1986.) This guide provides ratios for financial analysis and planning, ratios for measuring operational effectiveness and control, ratios for controlling direct costs, ratios for monitoring overhead, ratios for assessing income objectives, ratios for industry comparisons, ratios for analyzing financial position, ratios for cash flow planning, and ratios for evaluating investments.

Handbook of Business Planning and Budgeting for Executives with Profit Responsibility. (New York: Van Nostrand Reinhold Co., Inc., 1983.) Provides guidance on new product planning, strategic planning, controlling inventories, assuring product quality, and pricing.

Handbook of Corporate Finance. (New York: John Wiley & Sons, 1986.) This handbook covers financial planning, financial forecasting, financial strategy analysis, ROI measurement, options, small business finance, cash management, accounts receivable management, capital budgeting, mergers and acquisitions, leasing, dividend policy, and pensions.

The Handbook of Economic and Financial Measures. (Homewood, IL: Dow Jones-Irwin, 1984.) Major issues covered are GNP, corporate profits, capital spending, capacity utilization, construction activity, unemployment, leading indicators, government policy, the balance of payments, the money supply, inflation, and economic forecasting.

Handbook of Fixed Income Securities. (Burr Ridge, IL: Irwin Professional Publishing, 1990.) Covers all major fixed income markets including money market instruments, corporate bonds, mortgage-pass throughs, bond swaps, and "Fedwatching."

Handbook of International Financial Management. (Burr Ridge, IL: Irwin Professional Publishing, 1989.) Contains valuable topical information on currency exchange, transfers of funds, and a variety of skills necessary for managers engaged in international finance.

Handbook of Investor Relations. (Burr Ridge, IL: Irwin Professional Publishing, 1988.) Among the topics covered are creating practical and effective investor relations policies and strategies, the crucial role of investor relations in mergers and acquisitions, and professional requirements and training.

Handbook of the Bond and Money Markets. (New York: McGraw-Hill, 1981.) This volume gives an analysis of the bond and money markets. It gives practical information on the size, growth rate, and breakdown of these markets. It also presents the role and psychology of participants in the bond market and discusses effects of high interest rates and high inflation.

Handbook of Stock Index Futures and Options. (Burr Ridge, IL: Irwin Professional Publishing, 1988.) Explains how to use contracts for investing, hedging, arbitraging and covers regulatory, accounting, and tax considerations.

International Finance Handbook. (New York: John Wiley & Sons, 1983.) Wide coverage includes international financial markets, international financial systems, exchange rates, foreign exchange controls, foreign trade practices, foreign exchange futures market, Eurocurrency market, foreign interest rates and loans, and money markets by country.

Health and Nonprofit Organizations

Researchers in the areas of health and nonprofit organizations may use these resources:

A Communications Manual for Nonprofit Organizations. (Saranac Lake, NY: AMACOM Book Division, 1981.) This guidebook offers ways to evaluate, implement, and update a nonprofit organization's communication processes. It focuses on image building; recruiting volunteers; communications applications, management, and organizational development techniques; marketing; and the clarification of goals.

Health Care Marketing: Issues and Trends. (Rockville, MD: Aspen Systems Corp., 1985.) This work is a compilation of original, revised, and reprinted works offering frameworks for, viewpoints on, and definitions of health care marketing. It deals with the unique problems and strategies of marketing a hospital or health care facility and includes sections on local political conflicts and the cost of vital marketing research.

Marketing for Hospitals in Hard Times. (Chicago: Teach'em, Inc., 1981.) This anthology probes marketing approaches for hospitals and health care facilities. The topics include "Relating Planning and Marketing," "Marketing Research to Keep You Competitive," "How to Change the Patient Mix," "How to Market Specialized Services," and "Promotional Do's and Don'ts." The book contains case histories; examples of questionnaires and opinion polls; sampling information and Techniquest; and explanations of marketing formulas, patterns, and tools.

Marketing for Non-Profit Organizations. (Boston: Auburn House Publishing Co., 1981.) This volume discusses marketing and fund-raising problems and basic marketing concepts such as cost analysis, behavior, segmentation, and marketing research.

Planning for Survival: A Handbook for Hospital Trustees. (Chicago: American Hospital Publishing Co., 1985.) This is a guide to long-range planning for hospital administration.

Human Resources

Labor and personnel topics may be found in the following references:

Handbook of Employee Benefits. (Burr Ridge, IL: Irwin Professional Publishing, 1988.) Covers such areas as dependent care, employee assistance programs, retirement plan investment objectives, taxation of benefit plans, and executive retirement packages.

The Handbook of Human Resource Development. (New York: John Wiley & Sons, 1990.) Covers all major topics in human relations including financial aspects, design of learning systems, evaluation of programs, service industries, health services, and future trends.

IFM Standard Manual of Employee Compensation and Fringe Benefit Programs. (Old Saybrook, CT: Institute for Management, 1981.) This looseleaf volume is divided into sections covering wage and salary development, standards and job evaluation, incentive systems, fringe benefits, expense accounts and executive salaries, wage guidelines, and tax information on costs of doing business.

Marketing and Public Relations

Marketing covers many topic areas. Some good references in this area are the following:

Advertising Handbook for Health Care Services. (New York: The Haworth Press, 1986.) Gives advice on using an ad agency, dealing with the media, performing the legal review of ads, and using graphics standards.

Advertising Manager's Handbook. (Chicago: Dartnell Corp., 1995.) The *Advertising Manager's Handbook* treats almost every aspect of modern advertising, including campaign planning, agency selection, prospect identification, copy writing, headlines, media research, surveys, source material, corporate image, and bidding.

Cable Advertiser's Handbook. (Lincolnwood, IL: NTC Publishing Group, 1985.) A thorough review of cable advertising and how to blend a cable campaign into a firm's marketing mix.

Complete Handbook of Profitable Marketing Research Techniques. (Englewood Cliffs, NJ: Prentice-Hall, Inc., 1982.) A marketing research guide covering data collection, research design, attitude measurement, sampling procedures, data analysis, and computer uses in marketing research.

The Complete Travel Marketing Handbook. (Lincolnwood, IL: NTC Publishing Group, 1989.) A complete guide on how to promote and operate a travel business with advice from many industry leaders.

Consumer Market Developments (Fact File Series). (New York: Fairchild Books, 1992.) This book includes general trends in the U.S. economy, income and purchasing power statistics, consumer expenditures, retail prices, housing, employment, population changes, marriage and divorce, and educational attainment.

The Direct Marketing Handbook. (New York: McGraw-Hill, 1992.) Provides information on planning, management, research, media, the creative process, production, and applications, and includes checklists, glossaries, and computer terms, for use in direct marketing.

The Distribution Handbook. (Falls Church, VA: APICS, 1984.) Included are checklists, tables, and graphs, as well as a bibliographic guide to more in-depth treatment of critical subjects.

Drop Shipping as a Marketing Function: A Handbook of Methods and Policies. (Westport, CT: Quorum Books, 1990.) A complete overview of drop shipping and how to use drop shipments in your business.

The Effective Use of Advertising Media: A Practical Handbook. (Brookfield, VT: Brookfield Publishing Co., 1985.) A down-to-earth reference book that explores the complete range of advertising media.

The Executive's Handbook of Trade and Business Associations. (Westport, CT: Quorum Books, 1991.) Identifies major trade associations, discusses how to optimize their services, discusses association resources, and describes how they work.

Fact Book: An Overview of Direct Marketing and Direct Response Marketing. (New York: Direct Marketing Association, Inc., 1986.) This compilation of broadscale statistics and general background data offers direct marketing information and experts' evaluations of future trends. It features mail order techniques, planning and analysis, and postal and delivery requirements. Included are a history of mail orders and a definition of direct marketing. This volume also provides data on markets, media, credit and collections, international marketing, government regulations, education, self-regulation, and ethics.

Franchise Annual Handbook and Directory. (Lewiston, NY: Info Press, Inc., published annually.) Complete details are provided on over 5,300 franchise organizations operating anywhere in the world.

Franchise Handbook. (Milwaukee, WI: Enterprise Magazines, 1985.) Information is included on over 1,700 franchise organizations.

Handbook for Public Relations Writing. (Chicago: American Marketing Association, 1988.) Includes media relations, brochures and press kits, newsletters, house magazines and trade journals, writing for television and radio, print media, and computers in public relations.

Handbook of Advocacy Advertising (Business and Public Policy Series). (New York: Harper Business, 1987.) Examines corporate use of advertising to speak out on social, political, and economic issues. Includes numerous case studies.

Handbook of Demographics for Marketing and Advertising. (Lexington, MA: Lexington Books, 1987.) Designed to assist in marketing and strategic planning, this handbook provides valuable information on the changing consumer marketplace, spending habits, demographics, and lifestyles.

Handbook of Modern Marketing. (New York: McGraw-Hill, 1986.) Includes short pieces by 120 marketing scholars on all aspects of marketing and marketing strategy planning.

Handbook of Product Design for Manufacturing. (New York: McGraw-Hill, 1986.) Provides guidance on the designs of parts made by metal forming, machining of metals, metal castings, plastic parts, assemblies, and surface finishes.

Handbook of Sales Promotion. (New York: McGraw-Hill, 1985.) A good resource book that covers couponing, sampling, premiums, rebates, sports promotions, point-of-purchase, specialties, executive gifts, and promotion law.

How to Get and Keep Good Industrial Customers Through Effective Direct Mail. (New York: Lavin Associates, 1990.) This guidebook will help the small industrial manufacturer, distributor, and independent manufacturers' representative by offering basic techniques of marketing, budgeting, scheduling, and planning. Included is information on buying lists, selecting advertising themes and presentations, writing business letters and direct mail copy, and saving money on printing and art services. This guidebook also provides an explanation of postal classes and procedures.

Lesly's Handbook of Public Relations & Communication. (New York: AMACOM, 1991.) Topics covered include how to work with federal and state governments, how specific organizations can best utilize public relations, international PR, effective communication techniques, the corporate PR department, and legal considerations.

The Management of International Advertising: A Handbook and Guide for Professionals. (Westport, CT: Quorum Books, 1989.) A comprehensive overview and guide for advertising in international markets.

Marketing Economics Guide. (New York: Marketing Economics Institute Ltd., 1985.) This is an updated annual detailing every significant retailing area in the U.S. Statistical information is given on population, income, and retail sales for 1,500 retailing centers throughout the country.

Marketing Guidebook. (New York: Trade Dimensions, 1992.) This volume gives comprehensive information about the grocery industry. Information is broken down into 79 major U.S. market areas, with profiles of each wholesaler and chain, showing names and numbers of stores served, financial summary, buying committee, product lines, private labels, listing of key personnel, population, color-coded market area maps, food brokers, rack jobbers, specialty food distributors, magazine distributors, and candy and tobacco distributors.

Marketing Handbook. (New York: Ashgate, 1988.) The *Marketing Handbook* is a useful reference for the person concerned with planning and executing marketing functions. The various writers take functional approaches in their discussion of the marketing process from the planning of the product, through channels of distribution, to the ultimate user. Advertising, sales promotion, research, and other functions are treated in terms familiar to the businessperson.

Marketing Manager's Handbook. (Chicago: Dartnell Corporation, 1983.) Explains how to develop a profitable marketing plan with a step-by-step guide to the planning process.

The New Products Handbook. (Burr Ridge, IL: Irwin Professional Publishing, 1985.) Discusses new product development from idea generation to test marketing; includes contributions from 23 new product professionals.

The New Venture Handbook. (New York: AMACOM, 1992.) Managerial guide to planning, developing, and running your own business.

Planning for Out-of-Home Media. (New York: Traffic Audit Bureau Publications, 1987.) This reference describes how to plan, buy, and measure out-of-home media (billboards, transit ads, etc.). In addition to listing creative ideas, the publication includes growth and trend data, size and production information, and research availabilities.

The Practical Handbook and Guide to Focus Group Research. (Lexington, MA: Lexington Books, 1988.) Provides step-by-step guidelines on planning, carrying out, and interpreting focus group research.

Profitable Purchasing: An Implementation Handbook. (Falls Church, VA: APICS, 1990.) Discusses legal aspects of purchasing, the Robinson-Patman Act, blanket orders, and purchasing capital equipment.

The Public Affairs Handbook. (New York: AMACOM, 1982.) Covers public affairs management, public policy, government relations, relations with the local community, communications, and the education and training of employees in this area.

Public Relations Handbook. (Englewood Cliffs, NJ: Prentice-Hall, Inc.) Includes topics on relations with the public, stockholders, industry, employees, community, dealers, customers, and governments. Specific fields are considered, such as public relations for labor organizations, financial institutions, trade associations, newspapers, radio, television, and entertainment. Other sections focus on how to secure information from the public and how to organize a public relations department.

Public Relations Handbook for Law Firms. (New York: Blackwell, 1992.) Topics include: building a high profile, increasing referrals from other professionals, serving clients better, and attracting the best recruits.

The Publicity and Promotion Handbook: A Complete Guide for Small Business. (Boston: CBI Publishing Co., 1982.) A step-by-step approach to public relations for the small business. Discusses such topics as news stories, feature articles, press releases, photography and photo filing, awards programs, advertising, using the office as a marketing tool, preparing presentations, and effective use of print media.

The Publicity Handbook. (Chicago: NTC, 1991.) Explains the job of the publicist, basics of good media relations, keys to newsworthy publicity, writing for the press, effectively accessing print and broadcast media, getting pictures published, preparing material for broadcast, and complaints and solutions.

The Publisher's Direct Mail Handbook. (Philadelphia: ISI Press, 1987.) Outlines how to approach specific markets; select and use mailing lists and card decks; and plan, design, and produce catalogues.

Running Conventions, Conferences, and Meetings. (Saranac Lake, NY: AMACOM, 1981.) Over 30,000 conventions are held in the U.S. each year. This volume provides essential information for conference, convention, and meeting organizers.

The Sales Manager's Handbook. (Chicago: Dow Jones-Irwin, 1983.) This handbook presents current information, practices, and procedures for managing the sales force. The areas covered include: selection, training, supervision, and compensation of the sales force; fringe benefits; contests; territories; quotas; sales agents evaluation; sales analysis; sales budgets; and many related topics.

That's a Great Idea: The New Product Handbook. (Oakland, CA: Gravity Publishing, 1986.) Complete guide for generating, evaluating, developing, and protecting your ideas for new products and services.

Production and Productivity

The reader may find the following publications valuable for research in production and productivity:

Handbook of Industrial Engineering. (New York: John Wiley & Sons, 1991.) The 107 chapters of this book cover specific approaches to enhancing productivity and human resources in the workplace, systematic guidance in the techniques and benefits of job design, methods engineering, ergonomics, manufacturing resources, quality control, and facilities design.

Handbook of Manufacturing and Production Management Formulas, Charts and Tables. (Englewood Cliffs, NJ: Prentice-Hall, 1987.) This handbook supplies many formulas, charts, and tables needed to maximize machine output, match machine capabilities to production requirements, improve worker performance, keep inventory costs to a minimum, and monitor and improve quality.

Juran's Quality Control Handbook. (New York: McGraw-Hill, 1988.) Includes statistical quality control measures, upper management quality, companywide planning for quality, quality and income, managing human performance, supplier relations, and customer service.

The Prentice-Hall Illustrated Handbook of Advanced Manufacturing Methods. (Englewood Cliffs, NJ: Prentice-Hall, 1988.) Discusses many techniques in factory automation, TIME (total integration of all manufacturing elements), and manufacturing automation strategy.

Production Handbook. (New York: Ronald Press Co., 1987.) This illustrated handbook provides information on engineering and industrial management. Specific topics discussed include: production control, materials handling, plant layout, time study and operation analysis, inspection, tools and jigs, job evaluation, job estimating, and factory budgets.

Production and Inventory Control Handbook. (New York: McGraw-Hill, 1986.) Written by nearly 100 expert contributors, this book discusses the production process, requirements preparation, tactical shop floor control, and distribution planning.

The Warehouse Management Handbook. (New York: McGraw-Hill, 1988.) Explores all aspects of warehouse operations and provides suggestions for the most efficient approaches.

Real Estate

Real estate investors and researchers can find useful information in these publications:

Marketing Industrial Buildings and Sites. (Atlanta: Conway Publications Inc., 1980.) This book is devoted to marketing enterprises that are both industrial and consumer oriented. It addresses common causes of failure among construction activities such as inadequate marketing, poor locations, or lack of demand.

Marketing Professional Services in Real Estate. (Chicago: Realtors National Marketing Institute, 1981.) Directed toward real estate brokers, this book provides information on advertising, promotion, and public relations. It presents marketing tools for developing objectives, and for researching and identifying a market. Included are 200 examples and a color portfolio. The differences between marketing a product and marketing a service are also discussed.

Modern Real Estate and Mortgage Forms: Modern Condominium Forms. (New York: Warren, Gorham, & Lamont, Inc., 1986.) This volume is useful to those involved in condominium projects, such as the attorney, developer, builder, title company, escrow company, lenders, insurance companies, savings and loan associations, mortgage brokers, property management agents, architects and engineers, regulatory agencies, and others.

The Real Estate Handbook. (Homewood, IL: Dow Jones-Irwin, 1990.) Answers questions asked about real estate by those in business or related fields. The first section of this five-part publication focuses on decisions necessary when buying/selling or borrowing/lending. The second part deals with appraisals, feasibility, and other analyses. The third part is on marketing. The fourth part discusses both traditional and new financing sources and an orientation about the mortgage market for borrowers and mortgage investors. The fifth part portrays about 10 different types of real estate investments in terms of use and has a chapter on condominiums and joint ventures/ syndicates.

ALMANACS

While there are hundreds of almanacs, the following represent examples that would be of interest to businesspeople:

The Almanac of Business and Industrial Financial Ratios. (Englewood Cliffs, NJ: Prentice-Hall, 1993.) Provides financial ratios representative of U.S. businesses and an analytical profile of corporate performance.

The Almanac of Consumer Markets. (Ithaca, NY: American Demographics Press, 1989.) Contains data on population, the labor force, state-by-state information, school enrollments, deaths, households, income, expenditures, age, race, religion, ethnic origin, and other facts.

Automotive News Market Data Book. (Detroit: Crain Communications, published annually.) Provides information on over 2,000 automotive and automotive parts manufacturers with a list of key executives.

The Business One Irwin and Investment Almanac. (Burr Ridge, IL: Irwin Professional Publishing, 1993.) This almanac features business trends, landmark developments, basic data and statistics, major business information sources, aggregate data on major industries and companies, executive compensation, real estate, stock and bond markets, money markets and taxes, and other investment opportunities.

The Canadian Almanac and Directory. (Toronto: CAD Publishing Co., published annually.) Includes the addresses, names, and titles of government officials; customs, tariffs and banking information; and transportation information.

Computer Industry Almanac. (Dallas: Computer Industry Almanac Press, 1993.) Provided are an overview of the computer industry, computer manufacturers, products, prominent people in the industry, the international marketplace, advertising and marketing, education, employment, financial facts, forecasts, industry history, news items and events, organizations, and publications.

IBC-Donoghue's Mutual Funds Almanac. (Ashland, MA: The Donoghue Organization, published annally.) Covers over 2,000 open-end and closed-end mutual funds including money market and municipal bond funds.

Information Please Almanac. (Boston: Houghton Mifflin Company, 1947-.) An annual compilation of lists of current facts, statistics, and information in many subject areas, including government activity, current events, world affairs, science, geography, business and economics, entertainment and culture, religion, sports, travel, and nutrition and health.

Insurance Almanac. (Englewood, NJ: Underwriter Printing and Publishing Company, published annually.) Covers over 3,000 insurance companies which write fire, casualty, accident and health, life, and Lloyd's policies; also lists mutual and reciprocal companies.

The International Television & Video Almanac. (New York: Quigley Publications, published annually.) Covers producers and distributors of pictures, television service companies, stations and programs, television codes, and related information for all major countries.

The World Almanac and Book of Facts. (New York: Pharos Books, published annually.) A compilation of facts on economic, social, educational, and political activities for major countries of the world.

9

Yearbooks and Encyclopedias

OBJECTIVES: This chapter will provide you with an overview of business-related yearbooks and encyclopedias.

> **Introduction**
> **Yearbooks**
> - Accounting
> - Computers
> - Finance and Investments
> - Government
> - Management and Human Resources
> - Marketing
> - Mining and Minerals
>
> **Encyclopedias**
> - Accounting
> - Banking, Credit, and Finance
> - Computers
> - General Business Information
> - Government, Legal, and Real Estate
> - Management and Human Resources
> - Marketing
> - Mining and Minerals

After completing this chapter you should be able to:

*Select the best yearbooks and encyclopedias for your research needs.

INTRODUCTION

Yearbooks and encyclopedias are somewhat similar to handbooks, almanacs, and directories. All contain information on a selected topic, or range of topics, and all cover a certain period of time. The American Library Association's *ALA Glossary of Library and Information Science* defines a yearbook as "an annual compendium of facts and statistics of the preceding year, frequently limited to a special subject" while an encyclopedia is defined as "a book or set of books containing informational articles on subjects in every field of knowledge, usually arranged in alphabetical order, or a similar work limited to a special field or subject". *Webster's Third International Dictionary* expands the definition of encyclopedias to "a work that treats comprehensively all the various branches of knowledge and that is *usually* composed of individual articles arranged alphabetically."

As the above definitions show, yearbooks are generally more limited in subject matter as compared to encyclopedias, generally present only facts as compared to the more complete discussions of subject matter found in encyclopedias, and are generally limited to a one year period whereas encyclopedias may cover a much longer time span. These guidelines were used to divide the references shown on the following pages into the categories of yearbooks and encyclopedias.

YEARBOOKS

All good libraries contain many yearbooks covering a wide range of topics. The following listing is limited to yearbooks that are of particular interest to business people and business students. Keep in mind that yearbooks are generally quite specific in the subject matter covered, generally contain only facts or statistics, and generally cover only a one-year time period. These sources are published annually:

Accounting

Accounting Trends and Techniques Annual. (New York: American Institute of Certified Public Accountants.) This is an accounting review of the financial statistics released annually by several hundred major corporations in their corporate reports.

Annual Statement Studies. (Philadelphia: Robert Morris and Associates.) In publication since 1923, this annual has an excellent reputation for providing financial ratios and rankings of company performance by three quartiles (upper quartile, median, lower quartile) within approximately 350 industry sectors. Information for the reports is drawn from banking institutions.

Industry Norms and Key Business Ratios: Library Edition. (New York: Dun & Bradstreet.) Known for its extensive listings of over 800 industries, this publication has been produced annually since 1982. Statistics are taken from D&B's credit reporting service.

National Society of Public Accountants-Yearbook. (Alexandria, VA: National Society of Public Accountants.) This yearbook covers association members and committees of the NSPA as well as affiliated state organizations. Included are member names, addresses, telephone numbers and type of membership.

Computers

Computer Publishers and Publications Yearbook. (New Rochelle, NY: Communications Trends, Inc.) The publisher name, address, telephone number, key personnel, year founded, brief description, and other information is provided for over 275 computer book publishers and 1,400 periodicals in the computer field. Included are companies in the U.S., the United Kingdom, Canada, and Australia.

Information Management Yearbook. (Kent, England: Institute of Data Processing Management.) Lists over 10,000 people and organizations in the field of data processing.

Finance and Investments

Business Statistics. (Washington, D.C.: Government Printing Office.) This is compiled annually by the U.S. Department of Commerce Bureau of Economic Analysis, and promoted as a supplement to the monthly *Survey of Current Business.* Contents feature historical data and methodological notes for approximately 2,100 series covering 20 general business, labor force, domestic and international trade, transportation, commodities, and manufacturing topics.

Jobson's Yearbook of Public Companies. (Parsippany, NJ: Dun & Bradstreet.) This annual contains financial details for all publicly held companies. Companies are indexed by country and by type of business.

Knight-Ridder CRB Commodity Yearbook. (New York: Commodity Research Bureau.) An excellent source covering production, consumption, and trading data for over 100 specific commodities in the areas of industrials, precious metals, livestock, grains and oilseeds, and imported goods.

Securities Industry Yearbook. (New York: Security Industry Association.) This yearbook ranks all publicly held companies by financial performance in the preceding year, provides a directory of Security Industry Association members, general financial information, and other information that would be of interest to people in financial professions.

Statistical Annual: Grains, Options on Agricultural Futures. (Chicago: Chicago Board of Trade.) Annual data on wheat, corn, oats, soybean options, and futures.

Statistical Annual: Interest Rates, Metals, Stock Indices, Options on Financial Futures, Options on Metals Futures. (Chicago: Chicago Board of Trade.) Annual data on government securities, market index, municipal bonds, silver and gold, options, and futures.

Statistical Annual: Supplement. (Chicago: Chicago Board of Trade.) Annual data on futures contracts, receipts, shipments, cash prices, and crop production.

Thorndike Encyclopedia of Banking and Financial Tables. (Boston: Warren, Gorham & Lamont.) Contains current data on interest rates and investment yields, foreign exchange rates, state interest rate ceilings, bad-check laws, and taxation.

World Currency Yearbook. (Brooklyn, NY: International Currency Analysis, Inc.) This is the definitive source for specific currency history, transferability, developments, varieties, administration, and statistical information.

Government

Municipal Yearbook. (Washington, D.C.: International City Management Association). This yearbook contains six chapters covering municipal profiles, legislative and judicial data, salaries, expenditures on services, local profiles, and profiles of those in elective offices.

Management and Human Resources

Hofstra University Yearbook of Business. (Hempstead, NY: Hofstra University Press.) This is a multivolume yearbook that covers all aspects of business management, business operations, administration, marketing, finance, production, and other important business areas.

Marketing

Advertising Age Yearbook. (Chicago: Crain Books). This annual reference contains the leading events, facts, figures, and personalities of the past year in the advertising field. It is a compendium of statistics and features illuminating the past year in advertising.

Broadcasting & Cable Marketplace. (New Providence, NJ: R.R. Bowker). Annual covers all television stations, radio stations, and cable systems in the U.S. and Canada. Also included is information on television and radio networks and personnel, satellite networks and services, film companies and advertising agencies, government agencies, trade associations, schools with broadcast programs, and suppliers of professional and technical services to the broadcast industry.

Demographic Yearbook. (New York: United Nations). Contains comprehensive and detailed international demographic statistics on the size, distribution and trends in population, natality, fetal mortality, infant and maternal mortality, general mortality, marriage, and divorce.

Electronic Market Data Book. (Washington, D.C.: Electronic Industries Association.) This annual data book provides elaborate statistics on consumer electronics, communications equipment and services, computers and industrial electronics, electronics components, government electronics, electronic-related products and services, and electronics in the world economy.

The Lifestyle Market Analyst. (Wilmette, IL: Standard Rate & Data Service.) This annual publication provides detailed demographic, lifestyle, media, and other population characteristics for all U.S. Standard Metropolitan Statistical Areas (SMSAs).

Mass Communications Review Yearbook. (Thousand Oaks, CA: Sage Publications.) Covers the effects of viewing TV, viewer misconceptions and retention, women as portrayed in the media, media and culture, mass communications, new technologies, and data on the American telecommunications industry.

Statistical Yearbook. (New York: United Nations, 1993.) This heavily used source of global information presents data compiled by the UN Statistical Division in the fields of demographic statistics, national accounts, industry, energy, and international trade.

Ward's Automotive Yearbook. (Detroit: Ward's Communications.) A leading industry publication, this reference covers industry trends, retail sales, vehicle and truck production, and registrations. International in scope.

Mining and Minerals

American Bureau of Metal Statistics Yearbook. (New York: American Bureau of Metal Statistics.) This yearbook provides worldwide data on copper, lead, zinc, and other nonferrous metals. It contains over 180 statistical tables dealing with mines, smelters, and refinery information. Also included are inventories, imports, exports, consumption, and prices.

Energy Statistics Yearbook. (New York: United Nations.) This publication provides a comprehensive collection of international production, consumption and trade statistics covering solid fuels, gaseous fuels, liquid fuels, electrical energy, and nuclear fuels.

Jobson's Mining Yearbook. (New York: International Publications Service.) Pertinent statistics, including names, addresses, products, key personnel, and size are provided for mining companies around the world.

Metal Statistics Yearbook. (New York: Fairchild Publications.) In publication for over 80 years, this guide lists production, consumption, prices, and shipments for over two dozen specific metals.

Minerals Yearbook. (Washington, D.C.: Bureau of Mines, Department of the Interior.) Includes company names, addresses, type of activity, location, production levels, and other data for all principal producers of iron ore, cement, lime, gypsum, clays, sand and gravel, phosphate rock and other non-fuel minerals.

Oil and Gas Journal Databook. (Tulsa: PennWell Publishing Co.) Includes rankings of the top 300 companies as well as surveys, forecasts, and reports covering production, processing, drilling, construction, and refining.

ENCYCLOPEDIAS

The following references, of general or specific interest to business people, typically contain more qualitative information, cover a wider subject area, and a longer period of time than do yearbooks.

Accounting

The Accountant's Desk Handbook. (Englewood Cliffs, NJ: Prentice-Hall.) This is an overall accounting reference guide for accountants, lawyers, engineers, company treasurers, controllers, and business people of all types. It covers all areas of financial accounting, cost accounting, cost information for management, planning for profit, accounting systems and procedures, auditing, special fields of accounting, and administering accounting practices.

Encyclopedia of Accounting Systems. (Englewood Cliffs, NJ: Prentice-Hall.) Covers all aspects of accounting with particular reference to computerized applications.

Banking, Credit, and Finance

The Desktop Encyclopedia of Banking. (Chicago: Probus Publishing Co.) This is a complete and handy reference guide to banking terms and practices.

The Encyclopedia of Banking and Finance. (Boston, MA: Bankers Publishing Company.) In its 67th year, this standard source contains approximately 4,200 entries alphabetically arranged. In addition to definitions of thousands of basic banking, business, and finance terms, in-depth articles cover historical background, analysis of recent trends, illustrative examples, statistical data, and citations to applicable laws and regulations.

Encyclopedia of Investments. (New York: Warren Gorham & Lamont, Inc.) Complete reference guide to all forms of investing.

Encyclopedia of Technical Market Indicators. (Burr Ridge, IL: Irwin Professional Publishing.) A unique work that provides authoritative descriptions and analyses of over 100 market performance indicators.

Mutual Fund Encyclopedia. (Chicago: Dearborn Financial Publishing, Inc.) This comprehensive guide profiles nearly 1,300 load, no-load, and low-load funds with the best five-year performance records industry wide. Included are money market funds, aggressive growth, asset allocation, income, international, precious metals, sector and government bond funds.

Palgrave Dictionary of Money and Finance. (London: Macmillan Press Ltd.) This 3-volume set is a companion work to *The New Palgrave: A Dictionary of Economics.* Contains over 1,000 essays on such topics as institutional analyses and descriptions, monetary history, and problems of financial regulation.

Thorndike Encyclopedia of Banking and Financial Tables. (Boston: Warren, Gorham & Lamont.) The leader in financial tables, this book is divided into six sections: 1) real estate, mortgage, and depreciation; 2) compound interest and annuity; 3) interest; 4) savings; 5) installment loans, leasing, and rebate; and 6) investment. Within each section there are tables to show an amount, rate, term, payment, or yield.

Computers

Encyclopedia Macintosh. (San Francisco: Sybex.) Arranged into five sections: 1) system software and utilities, 2) applications, 3) hardware, 4) resources, and 5) glossary. This title is touted as the most comprehensive collection of information about the Macintosh ever assembled.

Encyclopedia of Artificial Intelligence. (New York: John Wiley & Sons.) This important reference provides in-depth articles on all aspects of artificial intelligence (AI). The articles are written primarily for professionals from other disciplines who seek an understanding of AI, and secondarily for the lay reader who wants an overview of the entire field or information on one specific aspect.

Encyclopedia of Computer Science. (New York: Van Nostrand Reinhold.) A comprehensive, authoritative reference containing over 600 articles. Historical and survey information, graphs, tables, and other illustrations make this one-volume work easily understood by the layperson.

Information Industry Directory. (Detroit: Gale Research.) This comprehensive annual two volume set with its supplement formerly was called the *Encyclopedia of Information Systems and Services.* It covers over 5,000 information services worldwide (over 2,200 in the U.S.).

McGraw-Hill Personal Computer Programming Encyclopedia: Language and Operating Systems. (New York: McGraw-Hill.) An excellent basic source for background information, this desktop reference covers the major personal computer implementations of high-level programming language interpreters and compilers, command language, applications software, and operating systems.

PC-SIG Encyclopedia of Shareware. (Blueridge Summit, PA: Tab Books.) Providing comprehensive coverage of low-cost IBM-PC software; this

169

compendium of information offers detailed program descriptions and product reviews arranged by categories.

The Software Encyclopedia: A Guide for Personal, Professional and Business Users. (New Providence, NJ: R.R. Bowker.) Contained in two volumes, this source describes over 16,000 microcomputer software packages from over 4,000 publishers.

General Business Information

ALA World Encyclopedia of Library Information. (Chicago: American Library Association.) Contains information on such topics as world history, biographies of famous people, world libraries, education, research, and international statistics.

Collier's Encyclopedia. (New York: Macmillan Publishing Co.) Over 2,000 distinguished writers have contributed to this general reference encyclopedia.

The Columbia Encyclopedia. (New York: Columbia University Press.) Similar to *Collier's* in scope, this encyclopedia is compiled by distinguished scholars and covers a wide range of subject areas.

The Encyclopaedia Britannica. (Skokie, IL: Encyclopaedia Britannica, Inc.) This reference comes in 24 volumes and is considered the oldest and one of the finest in the English language. Contains information on all areas of human knowledge.

The Encyclopedia Americana. (Danbury, CT: Grolier Publishing Co.) This encyclopedia comes in 30 volumes with emphasis on science and biography.

The Encyclopedia of Associations. (Detroit: Gale Research.) Containing entries for over 89,000 associations and organizations. Categories of groups covered include: 1) national, nonprofit membership associations, 2) international associations, 3) local and regional associations, 4) nonmembership organizations, 5) for-profit organizations, 6) informal organizations, 7) defunct organizations, and 8) untraceable associations. Entries consist of association names, addresses, telephones, purpose, publications, meetings, year founded, number of members, number of staff, annual budget and who to contact for further information.

Encyclopedia of Business Information Sources. (Detroit: Gale Research.) This comprehensive reference directs you to sources of business information arranged under 1,140 subject areas. Each entry provides listings of where to find information on a given subject in print and electronic formats. Names, addresses, telephone and fax numbers are listed when relevant.

McGraw-Hill Encyclopedia of Science & Technology. (New York: McGraw-Hill.) This international reference work of 20 volumes contains over 7,500 excellent articles in all disciplines of science and engineering. Written for the layperson, these articles provide excellent background material for understanding scientific applications within the business field.

The New Palgrave: A Dictionary of Economics. (London: Macmillan Press Ltd.) Although titled a "dictionary," this excellent reference sets a standard for other business-related encyclopedias. Arranged into four volumes, this set provides over 2,000 lengthy signed articles and 700 biographical essays written by experts in the field covering economic theory and doctrine.

Van Nostrand's Scientific Encyclopedia. (New York: Van Nostrand Reinhold.) This encyclopedia features approximately 7,000 entries covering animal life, biosciences, chemistry, earth, atmospheric sciences, mathematics, information science, medicine, anatomy, physiology, physics, plant science, space, and planetary science. A useful resource for supplemental business decision information.

Government, Legal and Real Estate

The Arnold Encyclopedia of Real Estate. (New York: John Wiley & Sons, Inc.) This volume, arranged alphabetically, consists of definitions and explanations of words and terms commonly used in real estate. Also included are real estate statistics by geographic area.

Encyclopedia of Geographic Information Sources. (Detroit: Gale Research.) Useful for real estate decisions, this guide lists sources of business, economic and financial information on 75 countries, 81 major cities, and 333 U.S. metro areas.

Encyclopedia of Government Advisory Organizations. (Detroit: Gale Research.) Nearly 6,000 boards, panels, commissions, committees and other groups that advise the President and various departments and agencies of the Federal government are highlighted. Included are organization names, addresses, principal executives, legal basis of the organization, purpose, reports and publications and descriptions of activities.

Encyclopedia of Legal Information Sources. (Detroit: Gale Research.) Covers over 19,000 books, periodicals, newsletters, reviews and digests, newspapers, audiovisual materials, research centers and institutes, clearinghouses, professional associations and societies, databases and other organizations and sources of information on the legal profession.

Encyclopedia of Real Estate Leases. (Englewood Cliffs, NJ: Prentice-Hall.) Essential reference for lease information and forms pertaining to apartments, condos, billboards, businesses, farms, ground, industrial, oil, gas, and minerals, shopping centers, and timber.

Management and Human Resources

The Crafts Business Encyclopedia: Marketing and Management. (New York: Harcourt Brace & Company.) Provides a wide range of marketing, management, production, and purchasing information for people involved in the crafts trade.

Encyclopedia of Careers and Vocational Guidance. (Chicago: J. G. Ferguson Publishing Co.) Included in the four volumes is valuable information on career development which would be useful to students, teachers, administrators, and anyone involved in career development.

Encyclopedia of Corporate Meetings, Minutes and Resolutions. (Englewood Cliffs, NJ: Prentice-Hall.) This two-volume set includes text and forms covering all areas of corporate practice including meetings, management, compensation, securities, charters, and by-laws and reorganization.

Encyclopedia of Management Techniques. (New York: Crane, Russak & Co., Inc.) Covers all aspects of business management and administration including techniques for improving management efficiency.

Marketing

Encyclopedia of Franchises and Franchising. (New York: Facts on File.) A good source for historical and current information on franchises and terms related to this business activity.

Working Press of The Nation. (New Providence, NJ: Reed Reference Publishing Co.) This is a comprehensive guide to over 22,000 communication outlets and 120,000 people involved with the media. Information is provided on major daily and weekly newspapers, magazines, television, radio, photographers, and other media in the U.S.

Mining and Minerals

Chemcyclopedia. (Washington, D.C.: American Chemical Society.) Includes over 800 chemical manufacturers and suppliers to the chemical industry in the U.S. and Canada. Each listing contains the company name, address, telephone, and pertinent company information.

Encyclopedia of Minerals. (New York: Van Nostrand Rhinehold Co.) Provides detailed geological information on iron ore, cement, gypsum, clays, sand and gravel, phosphate rock, and other non-fuel minerals.

Encyclopedia of Physical Sciences and Engineering Sources. (Detroit: Gale Research.) A useful guide to supplement the area of mining and minerals. This guide lists over 16,000 citations including directories, associations, databases, periodicals and research institutes. Arrangement is alphabetical covering over 400 subjects.

International Petroleum Encyclopedia. (Tulsa: PennWell Books.) This reference provides a solid overview of world developments, country by country. Analysis is detailed and includes company activity, government involvement and maps.

Modern Plastics Encyclopedia. (New York: McGraw-Hill.) Over 5,000 suppliers of more than 350 plastic products are listed by company name, address, telephone, product offerings, and services. The listing includes companies in the U.S. and Canada.

Petroleum Terminal Encyclopedia. (Houston: Stalsby, Wilson Press.) Over 2,000 corporate and independently owned oil terminals capable of storing refined and crude oil products, natural gas, petrochemicals, asphalt, or lube oil in the U.S., Canada, and Europe are indexed. Each listing includes company name, address, telephone, name and title of contact person, terminal location, hours, method of supply for outloading, description of facilities including high and low water levels, storage capacities for each product, and types of products handled.

10

Directories

OBJECTIVES: This chapter will provide you with an understanding of the importance of researching business information directories.

> **Introduction**
> **Directories**
> - Directories of Directories
> - Business - General
> - Computers
> - Education
> - Environment
> - Financial
> - Food and Drugs
> - Industrial
> - Insurance
> - Marketing
> - Minerals
> - States
> - Travel

After reading this chapter you should be able to:

*Have a better understanding of the wide range of business directories that are available.
*Know about specific directories that will enable you to begin your research.

INTRODUCTION

A directory, not to be confused with a catalog, handbook, or encyclopedia, is a source book that provides information on a variety of subject matter. *Webster's* defines a directory as "an alphabetical or classified list containing names and addresses." The American Library Association's *ALA Glossary of Library and Information Science* describes a directory as "a list of persons or organizations, systematically arranged, usually in alphabetical or classed order, giving addresses, affiliations, etc., for individuals, and address, officers, functions, and similar data for organizations." This chapter includes directories that provide listings of names and addresses as long as the listing is, in some fashion, of a business nature. There are hundreds of non-business directories that are not included here.

While all directories present facts such as names and addresses, many provide more detailed information. This information might include goods produced by companies, location of plants and offices, size of work force, detailed stock and financial information, supply sources, and other classifications. Directories attempt to serve as a ready, serviceable guide for those requiring specific facts on a particular subject or in a particular field. Business directories are commonly known as trade directories. They serve as sources of information for each particular type of enterprise, industry, or allied field covered by the directory.

There is little uniformity of size or presentation among directories. Many directories are small enough to slip easily into a pocket; some are of normal book size or slightly larger; and others are bulky and large, often coming in several volumes. There are several major directories which attempt to identify all known directories in print. These will be briefly described before moving on to a listing of major business directories.

DIRECTORIES

Directories of Directories

Directories in Print: An Annotated Guide to Over 16,000 Business & Industrial Directories, Professional and Scientific Rosters, Directory Databases, & Other Lists & Guides of All Kinds. (Detroit: Gale Research, published annually.) The directories included cover the categories of business and commercial; manufacturing, mining, and transportation; cultural institutions; directories of individual industries, trades, and professions; engineering and computers; agriculture; the law and government; education, arts, and entertainment; health, medicine, and religion; hobbies and travel; and sports and recreation.

Guide to American Directories. (West Nyack, NY: Todd Publications, 1994.) Containing over 7,500 listings, this volume provides information on directories published in the U.S. and some foreign directories categorized under 300 industrial, technical, mercantile, scientific, and professional headings. It is designed to help businesspeople locate new markets for products. It also helps individuals, associations, researchers, direct mail users, advertisers, and others to find current information.

International Directories in Print. (Detroit: Gale Research.) This directory covers over 5,000 business and industrial directories, professional and scientific rosters, travel guides, biographical dictionaries, directory databases, directory issues of periodicals, and other lists and guides of all kinds published in more than 100 countries around the world. Entries include the title of the directory, publisher information, address, telephone, United States distributor (if applicable), and other details arranged by subject categories.

Business—General

The following directories provide valuable information in varied areas of business and industry:

AT&T Toll Free 800 Directory—Business Edition. (Parsippany, NJ: AT&T Communications, published annually.) Listed are over 100,000 business toll-free numbers.

Business Organizations, Agencies, and Publications Directory. (Detroit: Gale Research, published biennially.) This directory, containing over 24,000 organizations and publications, is a guide to trade, business, and commercial organizations; government agencies; stock exchanges; labor unions; chambers of commerce; diplomatic representation; trade and convention centers; trade fairs; publishers; data banks and computerized services; educational institutions; business libraries; information centers; and research centers.

Consultants and Consulting Organizations Directory. (Detroit: Gale Research, published annually.) Part I of this volume lists consultants in the U.S., its possessions, and other countries in the world. Part II contains a cross-index of subjects and a subject index of firms by location. Part III is an alphabetical index of individuals and an index of firms. Over 16,000 individuals and firms active in consulting are included in the directory.

The Corporate Directory of U.S. Public Companies. (San Mateo, CA: Walker's Western Research, published annually.) Contains over 10,000 publicly held companies with name, address, telephone number, officers, stock holdings, bonds, financial statements, subsidiaries, parents, products, SIC classification, employees, and geographic coverage.

Dial-A-Fax Directory. (Jenkinstown, PA: Dial-A-Fax Directories Corp, 1991.) Provides names, addresses, and fax numbers of over 250,000 businesses, government agencies, libraries, and other institutions and organizations in North America with fax numbers.

Directory of Corporate Affiliations. (New Providence, NJ: National Register Publishing Company, published annually.) This book lists over 5,000 U.S. parent companies with their domestic and foreign divisions, subsidiaries, and affiliates, as well as 60,000 "corporate children" and their parent companies. It includes five bi-monthly updating bulletins that report personnel changes, acquisitions, address changes, and other similar information.

Directory of Executive Recruiters. (Fitzwilliam, NH: Kennedy & Kennedy, Inc., published annually.) This cross-indexed directory lists 2,300 search locations in the U.S., Canada, and Mexico. It includes employment agencies operating on a fee-paid or contingency basis. The contents are arranged according to management functions, Standard Industrial Classification (SIC) codes, and geography. A companion, *International Directory of Executive Recruiters,* lists 650 search offices in 150 cities of 46 foreign countries.

Directory of Management Consultants. (Fitzwilliam, NH: Kennedy & Kennedy, Inc., published biennially.) This directory profiles 1,200 U.S. firms, including major companies and little-known specialists. It is cross-indexed by services offered, industries served, and geographical location. In addition to basic information such as name, address, telephone number, key contact, and branch offices, it also indicates firm size by number of professionals and revenue. It covers information on comparing leading consulting associations, on selecting a firm, and on the importance of professional affiliations.

Directory of Women Entrepreneurs. (Atlanta: Wind River Publications, Inc., published annually.) Includes name, address, telephone number, year founded, financial data, products, and SIC classification of over 3,200 women-owned businesses.

Dun's Directory of Service Companies. (Parsippany, NJ: Dun's Marketing Services, 1994.) Over 50,000 service businesses with 50 or more employees are profiled.

Government Contracts Directory. (Washington, D.C.: Government Data Publications, Inc., published annually.) All businesses receiving Federal government contracts over the past twelve months are profiled along with a description of the contracts received.

MacRae's Blue Book. (New York: Business Research Publications, Inc., published annually.) This series covers 40,000 manufacturing firms in the U.S. Volume 1 is a list of companies including address, products, and phone number; volume 2 contains product indexes.

Mail Order Business Directory. (West Nyack, NY: Todd Publications, 1995.) This directory provides the name, address, telephone number, services, and key personnel for 11,000 firms doing business by mail order.

National Directory of Addresses and Telephone Numbers. (Detroit: Omnigraphics, Inc, 1996.) Over 138,000 top U. S. firms in all areas of business are included with name, address, telephone, and fax numbers. Divided into two sections: white pages list all firms alphabetically by company name; yellow pages list companies alphabetically by business or product type.

Standard & Poor's 500 Directory. (New York: Standard & Poor's, 1994.) Profiles top 500 corporations in the United States, providing complete financial, management, operating, product, and plant information.

Thomas's Register of American Manufacturers and *Thomas's Register Catalog File* (16 volumes). (New York: Thomas Publishing Co., published annually.) Volumes 1 through 8 list products and services alphabetically. Volumes 9 and

10 alphabetically list company names, addresses, and telephone numbers, as well as branch offices, capital ratings, and names of company officials. Volume 10 is an index of brand names. Volumes 11 to 16 alphabetically list the companies cross-referenced in the first 10 volumes.

Training and Development Organizations Directory. (Detroit: Gale Research, 1994.) This directory gives detailed profiles of the activities and specialties of over 2,300 companies, institutes, and consulting groups that provide managerial and supervisory training courses for business firms and government agencies.

Ward's Business Directory. (Detroit: Gale Research, published annually.) Formerly, *50,000 Leading U.S. Corporations Directory.* This corporate marketing and financial directory covers over 140,000 manufacturers, public companies, and private firms. Companies are organized by SIC code and included are officers' names, numbers of employees, location of plants and offices, company earnings, assets, and financial ratios.

Computers

American Society of Computer Dealers - Membership Directory. (Honokus, NJ: American Society of Computer Dealers, published annually.) Information is provided for approximately 150 dealers, brokers, and lessors of midrange computer hardware.

Business Software Directory. (Medford, NJ: Learned Information, Inc., 1990.) Provides software titles and descriptions of products for over 10,000 suppliers of business software products.

Computer Graphics Directory. (Omaha, NE: American Business Information, Inc., published annually.) Provides name, address, telephone number, year of business incorporation, products, employees, and other details for nearly 3,500 suppliers of computer graphics materials.

The Computer Industry Directory. (San Jose, CA: Mentor Market Research, published annually.) Includes the company name, address, telephone number, line of business, products and services, key personnel, and other details on over 6,400 companies producing or distributing computer hardware or software products.

Computer Products Directory. (Collingdale, PA: Computer Products Directory, 1989.) Provides details on manufacturers, distributors, and mail order houses that manufacture or distribute computers, peripherals, computer supplies, and related products.

Computer Software Directory. (Omaha, NE: American Business Information, Inc., published annually.) Provides nearly 32,000 suppliers of computer software with company and product details.

Computer System Designers and Consultants Directory. (Omaha, NE: American Business Information, Inc., published annually.) Provides the names, addresses, telephone numbers, years in business, types of services, and size of company for nearly 22,000 computer system designers and consultants.

Computers and Computing Information Resources Directory. (Detroit: Gale Research, 1995.) Includes the name, address, telephone number, name of contact person, publications, year founded, target audience, products and prices, services, and area of research for all computer related information sources, including 1,500 consultants and training organizations, 650 trade and professional associations, 1,000 special libraries and information sources, 900 university computer and research sources, 600 for profit research services, 240 on-line services, 1,500 journals, 400 trade shows, 200 publishers, and 250 directories.

Computing Information Directory. (Pullman, WA: Hildebrandt, Inc., 1992.) Indexes and describes over 2,000 computer journals, 1,000 newsletters, 50 dictionaries, 300 directories and handbooks, 500 software sources, 400 hardware sources, and other computer information sources.

Computer Technology Industry Association Directory. (Lombard, IL: CTIA, 1994.) Presents company name, address, telephone number, key personnel, products, and other details for over 2,500 computer equipment dealers, producers, and resellers.

Data Entry Services Directory. (Philadelphia, PA: Market Access Co., 1989.) Provides names, addresses, telephone numbers, key personnel, descriptions of products and services, and other information for over 600 companies that specialize in data entry services on a service bureau basis, or selling equipment and systems useful for in-house data entry operations.

Data Processing Services Directory. (Omaha, NE: American Business Information, Inc., published annually.) Profiles nearly 10,000 companies in the data processing services business.

Directory of Top Computer Executives. (Phoenix, AZ: Applied Computer Research, published twice annualy.) This directory contains 2,000 organizations with names and addresses, subsidiary or division names, communications managers' names and titles, voice/data responsibilities, and telephone numbers. It is a reference tool for data communications designers and planners, conference organizers, vendors, and common carrier representatives. Non-industrial companies and commercial and governmental agencies are organized alphabetically by state and company name.

ICP Software Directory. (Indianapolis, IN: International Computer Programs, Inc., 1991.) Over 13,000 products supplied by over 4,000 companies are described. The nine volumes of this directory cover data center manager, system builder, business and financial management, accounting and human resources, insurance, banking, manufacturing and engineering, industrial specific applications, and developer index.

The Software Directory. (Pittsburg, PA: MENU Publishing, published annually.) Provides supplier name, address, telephone number, software products with descriptions, prices, and other details for over 100,000 suppliers of software products for microcomputers and minicomputers.

Who's Who in Electronic Commerce. (Potomac, MD: Phillips Business Information, published annually.) Includes details on computer service providers, value added networks, translation software, computer industry associations, consultants, and business and technical services.

Education

Students, teachers, and counselors in business will find the following publications valuable:

American Library Directory. (New York: R. R. Bowker, published annually.) This directory lists nearly 31,000 libraries in the United States and another 3,700 in Canada. Includes the library name, address, telephone number, name of the librarian, collection size, special collections, computer services, and other useful information.

College Media Directory. (New York: Oxbridge Communications, Inc., 1994.) This reference book provides a list of 3,500 two and four-year colleges and universities with campus addresses, telephone numbers, and names of the presidents and directors of student activities. It includes 4,800 student newspapers, magazines, and yearbooks, offering names of publication advisors, advertising rates, circulation information, print data, budget amounts, and sources of financing.

Directory of Organizations and Researchers in Educational Management. (Eugene, OR: Educational Resource Information Service, Clearinghouse on Education Management, 1984.) This directory covers 130 organizations in the field of educational management and research. Entries include the organization's name, address, telephone number, name of top executives, geographical area served, areas of specialization, publications, and other topics.

Directory of Overseas Educational Advising. (New York: College Board, 1992.) The directory provides the name, address, telex number, cable codes, and fax numbers of centers that can provide information on overseas educational opportunities for American students.

Directory of Postsecondary Institutions. (Washington, D.C.: National Center for Education Statistics, U.S. Department of Education, 1990.) Includes all postsecondary institutions in the United States, Puerto Rico, the Virgin Islands, the American territories in the Pacific, and the United States service schools. The entries include the name of the institution, address, telephone number, county, congressional district, year established, recent enrollment, tuition, room and board fees, religious or other affiliation, highest degree offered, and accreditation.

National Association of College Admission Counselors--Directory. (Alexandria, VA: National Association of College Admission Counselors, published annually.) Includes the names, addresses, telephone numbers, and corporate officers of over 4,000 organizational and individual members.

National Association of College Deans, Registrars and Admissions Officers— Directory. (Albany, GA: National Association of College Deans, Registrars and Admissions Officers, published annually.) Includes the names, addresses, telephone numbers, titles, and other pertinent information from about 325 member institutions.

National Faculty Directory. (Detroit: Gale Research, published annually.) This directory is a three-volume guide to nearly 700,000 college and university faculty members in the U.S. and Canada. Arranged alphabetically, it provides each individual's name, department, institution, address, and research interests. The directory includes a geographical listing of institutions covered.

Training and Development Organizations Directory. (Detroit: Gale Research, 1994.) Lists over 2,300 companies, institutes, graduate schools, consulting groups, and other organizations that provide training and development services for industry.

Environment

Sources of environmental publications that may be of interest to business people include the following:

Directory of Environmental Information Sources. (Rockville, MD: Government Institutes, Inc., 1992.) This directory covers several thousand governmental agencies, professional and scientific organizations, trade associations, and other groups involved with ecology and conservation. It also lists pertinent publications and audiovisual aids provided by each, along with names, addresses, and telephone numbers.

Directory of Environmental Investing. (Upland, PA: Diane Publishing, 1991.) Includes the names, addresses, telephone numbers, key executives, and pertinent information on over 150 companies involved in environmental services such as air pollution control, asbestos abatement, hazardous waste management, waste testing and analysis, nuclear waste handling, recycling, solid waste disposal, and waste-to-energy systems.

Directory of Resource Recovery Projects and Services. (Washington, D.C.: Institute of Resource Recovery, National Solid Wastes Management Association, published annually.) A directory of firms involved in recovering energy from solid waste materials.

Ecotechnics: International Pollution Control Directory. (Geneva, Switzerland: Ecopress Ltd., published biennially.) Lists 35,000 manufacturers and service organizations worldwide who are involved with pollution control, water and air pollution, solid wastes, noise, and vibration. Listings are by name, address, telephone and telex numbers, products, and services.

Energy Information Directory. (Washington, D.C.: National Energy Information Center, U.S. Department of Energy, published annually.) Includes a listing of all federal agencies, offices, and programs devoted to energy concerns. Also lists state energy offices, Department of Energy locations and programs, and DOE field facilities.

Financial

Many of the directories identified earlier under the heading of Business— General contain financial information in addition to the primary information of the directory:

America's Corporate Families: Billion Dollar Directory. (Parsippany, NJ: Dun & Bradstreet, Inc., published annually.) Lists more than 8,000 parent companies and nearly 50,000 domestic and foreign subsidiaries. Information provided includes DUNS number, name of company and principal officers, address, telephone number, banks, accounting firm, legal counsel, subsidiaries, sales, number of employees, stock information, and line of business.

Collection Agencies Directory. (Omaha, NE: American Business Directories, Inc., published annually.) Includes listings and information on over 7,000 collection agencies across the United States.

Directory of Security Analysts Societies, Analyst Splinter Groups, and Stockbroker Clubs. (Washington, D.C.: National Investor Relations Institute, published annually.) Lists 120 groups of security analysts, stockbrokers, and splinter groups (specialists in a single industry).

Dun & Bradstreet Million Dollar Directory. (Parsippany, NJ: Dun & Bradstreet, Inc., published annually.) This directory lists the top 50,000 companies, by asset size, in the United States. The companies are divided into the categories of utilities, transportation companies, bank and trust companies, brokerages, mutual and stock companies, insurance companies, wholesalers, retailers, manufacturers, and U.S. subsidiaries of foreign companies. Includes the names of company officers, addresses, telephone and FAX numbers, titles of key personnel, and detailed financial data.

Fairchild's Retail Stores Financial Directory. (New York: Fairchild Books, published annually.) This directory contains detailed financial information on all publicly held retail organizations in the United States.

Inc. 100. (Boston: The Goldhirsh Group, published annually.) Inc. Magazine lists the 100 fastest-growing, publicly held corporations in the United States. Includes the company name, headquarters address, telephone number, type of business, date incorporated, number of employees, return on equity, sales, and net income for the past five years.

Institutional Investor—M & A Directory Issue. (New York: Institutional Investor, Inc., published annually.) Lists by name, address, telephone number, and key personnel over 200 commercial banks and investment firms with mergers and acquisitions or LBO departments.

Institutional Investor—Public Finance Directory Issue. (New York: Institutional Investor, Inc., published annually.) Lists leading companies and personnel from investment and commercial banking companies with tax-exempt finance departments.

Food and Drugs

The following publications are available on the subject of food and drugs. They are published annually unless otherwise listed:

American Drug Index. (Philadelphia, PA: J. B. Lippincott Co., 1992.) This index lists 15,000 drugs, with information on manufacturers, composition, chemical formula, dosage forms, strength, and administration.

Bakers—Wholesale Directory. (Omaha, NE: American Business Directories, Inc., American Business Information, Inc.) Nearly 8,000 names, addresses, telephone numbers, and product listings for bakery products wholesalers are provided.

Bakery Production and Marketing—Red Book Issue. (Chicago: Gorman Publishing Co.) It lists over 2,000 wholesale, multi-unit retail, grocery chain, and co-op baking companies and plants in the U.S. and Canada that bake bread, cakes, cookies, crackers, pretzels, snack foods, and frozen bakery products. It also names some 1,200 middle people distributing these products. For major firms the listings include name, address, telephone number, type of operation, number of employees, sales, and brands. For smaller companies name, address, phone number, products, sales, and employees are listed.

Baking—Guide & Directory Issue. (Chicago: Putman Publishing Company.) Listed are over 2,500 manufacturers, suppliers, brokers, and distributors of ingredients, equipment, packaging, supplies, and services for the baked goods industry.

Beer and Ale Retailers Directory. (Omaha, NE: American Business Directories, Inc., American Business Information, Inc.) Nearly 13,000 retailers of beer and ale are identified by name, address, and geographical area of business operation.

Beer and Ale Wholesale Directory. (Omaha, NE: American Business Directories, Inc., American Business Information, Inc.) Over 5,000 wholesalers of beer and ale are identified by name, address, and geographical area of business operation.

Citrus & Vegetable—Farm Equipment Directory. (Tampa, FL: Citrus & Vegetable Magazine Company.) This directory provides a listing of all manufacturers of produce and citrus growing, handling, picking, and packaging equipment. Included are names, addresses, and telephone numbers.

Directory of the Canning, Freezing and Preserving Industries. (Westminster, MD: Edward E. Judge & Son, Inc., 1994.) Listed are over 1,700 food processors by name, address, and chief executives. The companies are also indexed by: geographical location, products under 375 product heads with the packers of each, and brands name.

Drug Topics Red Book. (Oradell, NJ: Medical Economics Books.) It lists wholesale druggists with names of buyers, officers, and executives, type of sales staff, and association affiliations. It also lists chain stores with basic information about stores, officials, and telephone numbers. Department stores are listed by name, address, and names of buyers in drugs and related areas. Manufacturers' sales agents are listed with pertinent information such as addresses, areas covered, and products sold. Discount houses are shown separately with useful information.

Food and Agricultural Export Directory. (Washington, D.C.: High Value Products Division, Foreign Agricultural Service, U.S. Department of Agriculture.) This directory lists federal and state agencies, trade associations, companies, and others who are able to assist U.S. businesses to develop their export potential.

Food Brokers Directory. (Omaha, NE: American Business Directories, Inc., American Business Information, Inc.) The names, addresses, and product and service categories of over 5,000 food brokers are listed.

Food Distributors—Specialty Foods Industry Directory. (Clearwater, FL: Gro Com Group.) Manufacturers, distributors, suppliers, exporters, and importers of specialty foods, equipment, and services are indexed.

National Frozen Food Association—Directory. (Hershey, PA: National Frozen Food Association.) Lists over 1,100 member companies worldwide, including distributors, packers, brokers, warehouses, suppliers, retailers, and food service operators.

Poultry Industry Directory. (Decatur, GA: Southeastern Poultry and Egg Association.) It covers 800 hundred egg, chicken, and turkey producers, processors, and other related suppliers. It also lists a number of state and national poultry trade organizations and university poultry departments.

Soya Bluebook. (Bar Harbor, ME: Soyatech, Inc.) Over 1,200 soybean processors, soy product manufacturers, and suppliers of equipment and services to the industry are covered. Company names, executives, addresses, telephone numbers, and products are included. Further information on this industry can be obtained from *Soyfoods Industry and Market: Directory and Databook*, (Lafayette, CA: Soyfoods Center.)

Sunflower Directory. (Fargo, ND: Sunflower Directory, published biennially.) This book covers 250 companies, trade associations, and government agencies concerned with sunflower agriculture in the U.S. and Canada. Included are company names, addresses, functions, and contact persons. Organizations are covered by function, location, and specialty.

Thomas Grocery Register. (New York: Thomas Publishing Co.) This is a three volume directory. Volume 1 covers about 1,800 supermarket chains, 4,300 brokers, and 4,200 wholesalers handling groceries, frozen foods, produce, meats, sundries, and hard goods. It also includes rack jobbers and warehouses. Volume 2 has a product index of more than 45,000 suppliers of food and nonfood products, equipment, machinery supplies, and services. Volume 3 lists over 50,000 companies, about 450 related trade associations, and food brand names.

U.S. Directory of Meat Processing Plants. (Fairfield, CT: Food Industries Directories.) This book covers 6,000 plants engaged in curing, smoking, canning, and freezing meats and manufacturing sausages and other meat specialties from purchased carcasses. It includes Canadian processors and gives names, addresses, telephone numbers, names of top executives, types of business, number of employees, and sales of each.

Industrial

The following publications are available on various topics of industrial activity. They are published annually unless otherwise listed:

Adhesives Redbook: Adhesives Age Directory. (Pasadena, CA: TC Publications.) About 2,000 manufacturers and suppliers to the adhesives industry, including manufacturers of adhesives and adhesive products; suppliers of machinery and equipment, compounding ingredients, adhesive chemicals and bases; consultants and related organizations are indexed. Included are names, addresses, telephone numbers, plant locations, products, number of employees, and names of chief executives.

Air Conditioning, Heating and Refrigeration News—Directory Issue. (Troy, MI: Business News Publishing Co.) This book lists about 1,600 manufacturers, wholesalers, factory outlets, exporters, and associations for the air conditioning, heating, and refrigeration industry. It gives names, addresses, key personnel, branches, and lists of products for each firm and pertinent information on individuals in the industry.

Air Freight Directory. (Annapolis, MD: Air Cargo, Inc., published six times annually.) This is a directory of 500 motor carriers who deliver and pick up air freight. Entries include airports served, firm name, address, telephone number, name of service manager, and services offered.

American Cement Directory. (Allentown, PA: Bradley Pulverizer Co.) This directory lists cement manufacturers in North, Central, and South America, including company name, address, telephone number, principal executives, product, and capacity for each firm.

American Coke and Coal Chemicals Institute—Directory. (Washington, D.C.: American Coke and Coal Chemicals Institute.) This directory provides the company name, address, telephone number, and executives for 55 producers of oven coke and coal chemicals, producers of metallurgical coal, tar distillers, and producers of chemicals.

American Concrete Institute—Membership Directory. (Detroit: American Concrete Institute, 1991.) Included are the names and addresses of over 18,000 engineers, architects, contractors, educators, and others interested in improving techniques of design, construction, and maintenance of concrete products and structures.

American Drop-Shippers Directory. (Medina, WA: World Wide Trade Service.) Included are the names, addresses, and products carried by over 350 firms that will drop ship orders direct to customers.

American Society for Industrial Security—Annual Membership Directory. (Arlington, VA: American Society for Industrial Security.) It lists 25,000 people involved in the security of offices, plants, institutions, proprietary data, databases, credit cards, and other articles of value. Each person is listed by name, address, and company or employer affiliation.

American Wood Preservers Institute—Member and Product Directory. (McLean, VA: American Wood Preservers Institute.) It covers firms producing pressure-treated wood products and their suppliers. The information given includes company name, address, telephone number, and products available.

Appliance—Appliance Industry Purchasing Directory. (Oak Brook, IL: Dana Chase Publications, Inc.) Listed are all appliance manufacturers and suppliers to appliance manufacturers. Entries include company name, address, and telephone number.

Best in Railroad Construction—Directory & Buyers' Guide. (Minneapolis: National Railroad Construction and Maintenance Association.) Approximately 50 member companies in the railroad industry, including contractors, suppliers, and engineers are indexed by name, address, telephone number, key executives, and products and services.

Brown's Directory of North American and International Gas Companies. (New York: Harcourt, 1978.) This source gives an alphabetical and geographical listing of over 1,800 U.S. gas distribution firms. It also includes Canadian and international firms, worldwide transmission lines, public service commissions, and gas associations.

Buyer's Guide to Manufactured Homes. (New York: Hawthorn Books Division, Elsevier-Dutton Publishing Co., Inc.) It lists approximately 125 manufacturers of mobile, modular, panelized, log, kit, and geodesic dome homes. The information includes manufacturers' names and addresses, type of homes manufactured, and areas served.

Directory of Building Codes & Regulations. (Herndon, VA: National Conference of States on Building Codes & Standards, published biennially.) Listed by name, address, and telephone are state offices responsible for enforcing building codes.

Directory of Central Atlantic States Manufacturers. (Boston: George D. Hall Company, published biennially.) Included are complete details on 22,000 companies operating in Maryland, Delaware, Virginia, West Virginia, North Carolina and South Carolina.

Dun's Industrial Guide: The Metalworking Directory. (Bethlehem, PA: Dun's Information Service, 1993.) The names, addresses, telephone numbers, SIC codes, and key personnel of over 65,000 metalworking plants and suppliers of metalworking equipment are provided.

Electronic Design's Gold Book. (Hasbrouck Heights, NJ: Hayden Publishing Co. Inc., 1992.) It includes nearly 10,000 electronic manufacturers and 1,400 distributors of electronic products. The directory gives names of companies, addresses, telephone numbers, names of executives, number of employees, financial information, trade and brand names, products or services, SIC numbers, and TWX and telex numbers.

Electronic Equipment/Supplies Directory. (Omaha, NE: American Business Directories, Inc., American Business Information, Inc.) Included are the names, addresses, and product offerings of over 15,000 suppliers of electrical equipment.

Fire Protection Reference Directory. (Quincy, MA: National Fire Protection Association.) Listed are the names, addresses, telephone numbers, and executives of all known producers of fire protection equipment in the United States.

Fleet Owner—Specs and Buyers' Directory Issue. (New York: McGraw-Hill.) It lists manufacturers and manufacturers' representatives of equipment and materials used by truck and bus fleets. The information includes company names, addresses, and telephone numbers. Some manufacturers are classified by products and others geographically.

Foundry Management & Technology—Where-To-Buy Directory. (Cleveland, OH: Penton Publishing Company.) Approximately 1,400 manufacturers of foundry products, manufacturers' representatives, dealers, and suppliers are indexed by name, address, and telephone number.

Lockwood-Post's Directory of the Pulp, Paper and Allied Trades. (New York: Miller Freeman Publications, Inc.) This is an annual directory for the pulp, paper and allied trades. Paper products are listed by state and city, as are products in allied industries. The classified section lists producers under product headings for the U.S. and Canada.

Machine Vision Industry Directory. (Dearborn, MI: Society of Manufacturing Engineers.) Suppliers of machine vision systems, equipment, products and services are listed.

Material Handling Engineering Handbook & Directory. (Cleveland, OH: Penton Publishing Company.) Covered are 2,000 manufacturers, material handling consultants, and several thousand distributors of material handling equipment. Included are company names, addresses, telephone numbers, and products distributed.

Material Handling Equipment Directory. (Omaha, NE: American Business Directories, Inc., American Business Information, Inc.) Included are the names, addresses, and product offerings of 5,200 materials handling distributors.

Metal Fabricators. (Omaha, NE: American Business Directories, Inc., American Business Information, Inc.) The names, addresses, and telephone numbers of over 2,000 metal fabricators are provided.

Metal Finishing—Guidebook & Directory. (Hackensack, NJ: Metals and Plastics Publications, Inc., 1979.) This directory identifies the names, addresses, telephone numbers, and other pertinent information on manufacturers and suppliers serving captive and contract metal and plastic finishing shops, and trade associations, and technical societies.

Metal Powder Producers and Suppliers Directory. (Princeton, NJ: Metal Powder Industries Federation, 1991.) Approximately 50 producers and suppliers of metal powders are identified.

Midwest Oil Register—Industry Segment Directories. (Tulsa, OK: Midwest Oil Register, Inc.) This firm publishes separate directories for segments of the petroleum and gas exploration, production, and distribution industries. Listings in these directories include company name, address, telephone number, executives, and specific information for each company. These directories are *Directory of Oil Marketing & Wholesale Distributors; Directory of Geophysical & Oil Companies Who Use Geophysical Service; Directory of Oil Well Drilling Contractors; Directory of Oil Well Supply Companies; Pipeline & Pipeline Contractors; Refining, Construction, Petrochemical, & Natural Gas Processing Plants of the World* (sometimes called *Directory of Oil Refineries); Directory of Electric Light & Power Companies;* and *Directory of Gas Utility Companies.* Also published by Midwest Oil Register are various regional directories covering different geographical regions of the U.S.

Molds—Manufacturers. (Omaha, NE: American Business Directories, Inc., American Business Information, Inc.) Nearly 3,000 mold manufacturers are identified by name, address, and key products and services.

Timber Harvesting—Wood/Woodlands Directory & Loggers' Guide. (Montgomery, AL: Hatton-Brown Publishers, Inc., published annually.) Includes the names, addresses, telephone numbers, and key executives of industrial timber corporations, manufacturers, and distributors of equipment used in harvesting and handling timber.

U.S. Industrial Directory. (Stamford, CT: Cahners Publishing Company, published annually.) Included in this three-volume set is "The Industrial Telephone/Address Directory," which provides over 54,000 company names, addresses, trade names, telephone numbers, and key products. Other volumes include product listings and supplier names.

Insurance

Readers interested in specific information on insurance may find these references helpful.

Best's Directory of Recommended Insurance Adjusters. (Oldwick, NJ: A.M. Best Co., Inc., published annually.) Over 1,200 American, Canadian, and foreign independent insurance adjusting offices recommended by insurance company groups, state and provincial governments, and trade associations are identified by name, address, telephone number and insurance specialty.

Best's Directory of Recommended Insurance Attorneys. (Oldwick, NJ: A.M. Best Co., Inc., published annually.) More than 5,000 American, Canadian, and foreign insurance defense law firms recommended by insurance companies and self-insurers are identified. Also includes shorthand reporters, law and medical consultants, testing laboratories, and special investigators. Includes names, addresses, telephone numbers, type of practice, and names of firm members.

Best's Safety Directory. (Oldwick, NJ: A.M. Best Co., Inc., published annually.) This directory is a reference source for manufacturers of safety devices, security systems, and pollution control products. It gives factual material relating to uses of safety devices and methods of combating hazards. Lists 2,000 manufacturers and distributors of safety equipment.

Marketing

Marketing, as a major area of business activity, offers many specialized directories of interest to all business students:

Adweek Agency Directory. (Lakewood, NJ: Adweek Directories, published annually.) Includes the agency name, address, telephone number, key personnel, major accounts, field served, billings, and other information for over 3,500 advertising agencies.

American Telemarketing Association—Membership Services Referral Directory. (Sherman Oaks, CA: American Telemarketing Association, published annually.) Member companies that supply telemarketing products and services are identified with names, addresses, telephone numers, markets served, and services offered.

American Wholesalers and Distributors Directory. (Detroit: Gale Research published biennially.) Includes the names, addresses, telephone numbers, products handled, and geographic area covered by over 18,000 wholesalers and distributors in the U.S.

Directory of Marketing Assistance for Minority Businesses. (Washington, D.C.: Information Center, Office of Minority Business Enterprise, U.S. Department of Commerce, 1974.) This directory lists 250 American Marketing Association members interested in working with minority business owners. It indicates each member's marketing specialty and interests and states whether the member provides services at no charge or requires reimbursement for out-of-pocket expenses.

Directory of Research Services Provided by Members of the Marketing Research Association. (Chicago: Marketing Research Association, 1976.) Over 800 marketing research companies and field service organizations are included with listings of names, addresses, telephone numbers, key executives, facilities, special capabilities, and services.

DSA Consumer Contact Directory. (Washington, D.C.: DSA Code of Ethics, Direct Selling Association, published annually.) This directory is part of the Direct Selling Association's (DSA) consumer education program designed to help consumers contact people responsible for customer satisfaction in 135 DSA member companies. Included are addresses and telephone numbers of companies that manufacture and distribute goods and services marketed by independent salespeople using the party plan or person-to-person methods.

Findex: The Worldwide Directory of Market Research Reports, Studies and Surveys. (Bethesda, MD: Cambridge Information Group, published annually with quarterly updates.) Indexes over 13,000 marketing studies. Most of the research reports mentioned in the book that are available for sale are very expensive. Contents typically pinpoint opportunities in very narrow market segments.

Franchise Annual Handbook and Directory. (Lewiston, NY: Info Press, Inc., published annually.) This book describes more than 5,300 franchise organizations, including U.S., Canadian, and overseas listings. Each listing includes a description of the franchise, the address of its headquarters, the number of franchised and company-owned units in operation, and the name and telephone number of the contact person. It features a sample franchise contract, an outline of the possible pitfalls of franchising, and details of the recently enacted franchising legislation.

International Directory of Marketing Research Companies and Services. (New York: American Marketing Association, published annually.) This annual edition provides listings for advertising companies worldwide. Coverage is especially good for the U.S. and Canada. Information is indexed by services offered, market/industry specialty, computer programs, trademarks/service marks, and by principal personnel.

Mail Order Business Directory: A Complete Guide to the Mail Order Market. (West Nyack, NY: Todd Publications, 1995.) The directory lists 11,000 mail order firms, including name, address, and products sold for each entry. It is classified by state and city.

MRA Research Service Directory. (See *Directory of Research Services Provided by Members of the Marketing Research Association* above.)

National Roster of Retailers Directory. (Cedar Rapids, IA: Stamats Communications, Inc., 2 vols., 1994.) This directory lists and describes the institutes, councils, and societies of the National Association of Retailers. The *National Roster of Realtors* includes names and addresses of all realtors (members of the National Association of Realtors) by boards in the U.S. and Canada.

Pharmaceutical Marketers Directory. (Boca Raton, FL: CPS Communications, Inc., 1990.) Lists over 7,000 marketing personnel with pharmaceutical companies, medical and biotechnology companies, advertising agencies with pharmaceutical clients, industry suppliers, and healthcare publications.

Research Centers Directory. (Detroit: Gale Research, published annually.) Lists over 11,000 university-related and other nonprofit research organizations in the U.S. and Canada.

Research Services Directory. (Detroit: Gale Research, 1992.) Over 4,000 commercial suppliers of research services are included. Covers names, addresses, telephone numbers, services provided, staff size, years in business, facilities, special equipment and services, and research specializations.

Source Directory of Lists Markets. (New York: Ed Burnett Consultants, Inc., 1992.) This is a reference tool for buying mailing lists and planning a direct mail promotion. It is divided into three major sections: business and consumer lists; businesses, professionals, and institutions; and mail order buyer lists. It is arranged and indexed alphabetically and by SIC code. The directory covers more than 7.6 million SIC records for businesses, professional offices, and institutions in the U.S. in its "master business file."

Standard Directory of Advertisers. (New Providence, NJ: National Register Publishing Co., published annually.) This two-volume set provides coverage of over 137,000 advertising personnel. Highlights detail who spends what, where they spend it, and who buys advertising.

Standard Directory of Advertising Agencies. (New Providence, NJ: National Register Publishing Co., published annually with quarterly updates.) This three volume set lists ad agencies including names, addresses, clients, and account billings.

Verified Directory of Manufacturers' Representatives (Agents). (New York: Manufacturers' Agent Publishing Co., Inc., published annually.) This volume lists over 16,000 manufacturers' representatives in the U.S., Puerto Rico, and Canada.

Minerals

References relating to minerals and related topics can be found in these sources:

Alaska Petroleum and Industrial Directory. (Anchorage, AK: Alaska Petroleum Information Corp., published annually.) This book gives an alphabetical listing of most industrial companies dealing in oil and gas pipelines, industrial services and suppliers, construction, transportation, mining, fishing, and timber, as well as of government and native organizations.

Coal Mine Directory. (Chicago: MacLean Hunter Publishing Corporation, published annually.) Lists all coal producing companies and their mines and plants for the United States and Canada. Includes company names, addresses, telephone numbers, types of mines, capacity and output, and number of employees. MacLean Hunter also publishes a series of regional and state mine directories.

Keystone Coal Industry Manual. (Chicago: MacLean Hunter Publishing Company, published annually.) This manual lists coal-producing companies; operating mines; sales agents and coal-exporting firms; utility, industrial, and cement plant customers; barge shipping lines; mining consultants; coke plants; and river dock facilities.

Society for Mining, Metallury and Exploration Directory. (Littleton, CO: SME, published annually.) Indexes 18,000 people engaged in the finding, exploitation, treatment, and marketing of all classes of minerals.

World Mines Register. (San Francisco, CA: Miller Freeman Publications, Inc., published annually.) Lists almost 1,700 firm headquarters, 1,700 active metal and minerals mining and processing operations in 103 countries, and over 11,000 mining executives. Specific information includes company names, addresses, executive, mines operated, holdings, financial data, and types of operation.

States

Information pertinent to specific states or groups of states can be found in the materials listed below. The directories listed are representative of other state directories. Industrial directories are also available for most states in book or microfiche form.

BNA's Directory of State Courts, Judges, and Clerks. (Washington, D.C.: BNA Books Division, Bureau of National Affairs, Inc., published biennially.) Included are approximately 13,000 state court clerks and judges in more than 2,100 state courts. Entries include court name, address, telephone number, court number, district or division, geographical area served, clerk name, and judge name and address.

California Manufacturers Register. (Anaheim: Database Publishing Company, 1994.) The material is presented in four sections. The alphabetical section includes company name, address, telephone number, SIC number, executives' titles and names, product or service description, divisions, home office, parent company, branch plants or offices, sales offices, affiliates, number of employees, date established, annual sales range, and export and/or import status. The geographical section lists plants, company name, address, and SIC number. The SIC section lists companies alphabetically. The products and services section lists SIC designations alphabetically with names and addresses of companies under each.

City & State Directories in Print. (Detroit: Gale Research, 1993.) Approximately 4,500 state business and industrial directories, buyer's guides, association membership lists, travel and restaurant guides, social service directories, city cross-reference directories, and other directories whose coverage is limited to single states are described.

Connecticut and Rhode Island Directory of Manufacturers. (Midland Park, NJ: Commerce Register, Inc., published annually.) The names, addresses, telephone numbers, plants, products, SIC classification, employees, financial data, and other details are provided for over 5,000 manufacturers in these two states.

Directory of New England Manufacturers. (Boston: George D. Hall Co., 1993.) The book is organized into four sections. In the alphabetical section, manufacturing concerns are listed with the names of the companies and their complete addresses. In the geographical section detailed information on New England manufacturing companies is listed by city and town. The banking section gives detailed information on New England banks listed by city or town. The product section lists manufacturers under product headings with complete addresses and SIC numbers. Included are 21,000 manfuacturers located in Connecticut, Maine, Massachusetts, New Hampshire, Rhode Island, and Vermont.

Directory of State Chamber of Commerce and Association of Commerce and Industry Executives. (Washington, D.C.: Chamber of Commerce of the United States, published annually.) Includes the names, addresses, and telephone numbers of state chambers of commerce and key personnel.

Directory of State and Federal Funds for Business Development. (Babylon, NY: Pilot Books, 1991.) Includes the addresses and telephone numbers of economic development offices in each state.

Directory of State & Local Mortgage Bankers Association. (Washington, D.C.: Mortgage Bankers Association of America, published twice annually.) Includes the names, addresses, telephone numbers, and operating information for all mortgage bankers associations.

Directory of Texas Manufacturers. (Austin, TX: Bureau of Business Research, University of Texas, Austin, 1993.) This two-volume directory lists firms alphabetically and geographically and includes a product section based on SIC codes and an index of products.

MacRae's Industrial Directory. (New York: MacRae's Blue Book Inc., Business Research Publications, Inc., published annually.) MacRae's publishes many state/regional industrial directories. Included among these are directories covering Maine, New Hampshire and Vermont; Maryland, DC and Delaware; Massachusetts and Rhode Island; North Carolina, South Carolina and Virginia; and several others.

Michigan Manufacturers Directory. (Detroit: Pick Publications, Inc., published annually.) The Master Geographical Section gives a complete listing of Michigan's 14,700 manufacturing operations, including firm names; addresses,

ZIP Codes; names, initials, and titles of all major executives from purchasing agent to president; products manufactured with SIC codes; number of employees, male and female; year established; export information; telephone numbers; plant square footage; and annual sales volume. The Alphabetical Section lists all manufacturers alphabetically with post offfice addresses and telephone numbers. The Products Section classifies Michigan's manufactured products by·SIC codes with post office addresses and telephone numbers. The Manufacturers' Representatives/Agents Section is a list of Michigan manufacturers' representatives and agents.

National Directory of State Agencies. (Gaithersburg, MD: Cambridge Information Group Directories, Inc., 1990.) Over 10,000 agencies, associations, and elected officials in the 50 states, District of Columbia, and U.S. possessions and territories, are listed by agency name, address, telephone number, and name of director.

State Franchising Regulations Directory. (New York: Frost & Sullivan, Inc., published annually.) This book compiles and summarizes state franchise statutes, rules, and regulations, as well as proposed legislation. It includes addresses of appropriate state administrative agencies, a review of the history of franchising, and an appendix comparing key features among the states that have enacted comprehensive franchise laws.

Travel

The following references can be useful to travel agents and businesspeople needing up-to-date information on travel:

AAA Bridge and Ferry Directory. (Falls Church, VA: American Automobile Association, published annually.) This volume covers toll facilities in the U.S., Canada and Mexico. It includes toll bridges; toll ferries; scheduled free ferry facilities; and steamship, rail, and bus services for the transportation of automobiles and passengers. For bridges, ferries, and steamship lines, the information includes terminal names and locations, size restrictions, tolls, schedules, crossing times and services. For rail and bus lines information includes fares, schedules, size restrictions, and terminal locations.

AIA Directory of Heliports and Helistops in the United States, Canada, and Puerto Rico. (Alexandria, VA: Helicopter Association International, published annually.) This book lists over 4,200 public, private, and hospital heliports. The information includes names, locations, addresses, telephone numbers, size of landing areas, services available, ownership and whether each heliport is for private or public use. Oil production sites and Forest Service landing areas are not included.

Airline Companies Directory. (Omaha, NE: American Business Directories Inc., American Business Information, Inc., published annually.) Includes information on scheduled and nonscheduled airlines, cargo carriers, equipment manufacturers, government agencies, associations, airports, and suppliers of goods and services to the industry worldwide. Each firm is listed by name, address, key personnel, and product or services offered.

Convention Hall Directory. (Washington, D.C.: American Society of Association Executives, published annually.) This directory, published in ASAE's *Association Management* magazine, gives the following information on three hundred convention halls, auditoriums, and arenas located in the U.S. and Canada: facility name, address, manager, telephone number, exhibit space, lodging facilities, storage space, parking, meeting rooms, capacity of rooms for meals and other functions, and distance to major hotels and business districts.

National Directory of Budget Motels. (Babylon, NY: Pilot Industries, Inc., published annually.) Included are the names, addresses, telephone numbers, services, and rates of all budget motels in the United States and Canada.

Official Airline Guide. (Oak Brook, IL: Official Airline Guides, published quarterly.) In addition to flight information, this indispensible directory provides facts on airports, ground transportation, and lodging.

World Aviation Directory. (Washington, D.C.: Aerospace and Defense Group, McGraw-Hill, published twice yearly.) This directory gives information on personnel of airlines, aircraft engine manufacturers, component manufacturers, and major aviation organizations, schools, and aviation groups, both domestic and foreign. There are over 35,000 listings.

Dictionaries

OBJECTIVES: This chapter will provide you with an understanding of the importance of business information dictionaries.

> **Introduction**
> **Dictionaries**
> - General Sources
> - Accounting
> - Advertising
> - Banking and Credit
> - Economics
> - Finance and Investments
> - Human Resources
> - Insurance
> - International Relations
> - Labor
> - Law
> - Management Information Systems (MIS) and Computers
> - Maps and Geography
> - Marketing
> - Production Management and Operations Research
> - Project Management
> - Real Estate
> - Retailing
> - Statistics

After reading this chapter you should be able to:

*Understand the broad range of dictionaries available to the business researcher.
*Realize the advantages of using a dictionary specifically written for your field of research.

INTRODUCTION

Dictionary: "A book containing words of a language arranged in alphabetical order, with explanations of their meanings, pronunciations, etymologies, and other information; a lexicon; a word book; any work which communicates information on an entire subject or branch of a subject, under entries or heads arranged alphabetically," *New Webster's Dictionary of the English Language*.

The items in this chapter are grouped under several broad topics. Since the selection of these topics is a very subjective process, you should examine additional similar topics as you read. Also, be sure to consult the introductory section of each dictionary. This material often explains very important features of the book and can help make your search more effective.

DICTIONARIES

General Sources

Abbreviations Dictionary, Augmented International Eighth Edition. (New York: Elsevier, 1992.) In its more than 1,000 pages, this book defines abbreviations from business topics to everything else under the sun: acronyms; anonyms; computer terminology; contractions; criminalistic terms; eponyms; geographical equivalents; governments agencies; historical, musical, and mythological characters; initialisms; medical and military terms; nations of the world; nicknames; ports of the world; shortcuts; short forms; signs and symbols; and slang. Also, 200 additional pages are devoted to airlines and airports of the world; astronomical constellations; bell code from bridge to pilothouse to engine room; birthstones; British counties; climatic regions; punctuation marks; earthquake data; the Greek alphabet; the Russian alphabet; railroads and steamship lines; wedding anniversary symbols; zodiacal signs, and another ten topics.

Biz Speak. (New York: Franklin Watts, 1986.) This light-hearted dictionary defines more than 2,000 words used in business with an emphasis on "the new and the humorous."

The Business Dictionary. (Englewood Cliffs, NJ: Prentice-Hall, 1984.) This is a very straightforward and easy to understand dictionary that is directed to a broad-based general audience. In addition there are ten useful appendices covering abbreviations, letter styles, the metric system, postal information, and other useful information.

A Concise Dictionary of Business. (New York: Oxford University Press, 1992.) This dictionary is intended for students of all kinds of business courses as well as businesspersons and their professional advisors including lawyers, bankers, accountants, advertising agents, and insurers. Topics covered include commerce; dealings in stocks, shares, commodities, and currencies; taxation and accountancy; marketing and advertising; shipping; insurance; business management and policy; personnel management and industrial relations; and banking and international finance. The English influence of Oxford University Press is evident in the definitions and an advantage for anyone dealing with countries within the United Kingdom.

The Concise Dictionary of Management. (New York: Routledge, 1986.) This contribution from Great Britain presents short, concise definitions which are more useful to reinforce one's knowledge than to expand it. It also allows insight into the point-of-view of the European businessperson.

Dictionary for Business & Finance. (Little Rock: The University of Arkansas Press, 1990.) This book, written by a practicing economist, addresses the need for an interdisciplinary dictionary covering legal, insurance, real estate, investment, marketing, accounting and banking terms as they relate to business and finance in their broadest interpretations. It is meant to be used by professionals, research librarians, and students from the high school level through graduate school.

Dictionary of Business and Economics. (New York: Free Press, 1986.) This provides a very broad coverage of terms related to business and economics, including price and income theory, real estate, business law, accounting, public finance, and private investing. Charts and graphs are used to clarify difficult concepts. Biographies of important economists, and their ideas, are also included. The book is meant to be understood by the lay person as well as the businessperson and professional economist.

Dictionary of Business and Management. (New York: John Wiley & Sons, 1992.) This book contains more than 8,000 entries in an attempt to present up-to-date word usage. The dictionary satisifies the needs of both the experienced person who demands precise information as well as the newcomer who seeks general information. Thirteen appendices include useful information such as: weights and measures, Celsius and Fahrenheit scales, metric conversion tables, Roman numerals, simple interest table, compound interest table, and a Summary of Major Business and Economic Events in the United States.

Dictionary of Business Terms. (Hauppauge, NY: Barron's Educational Series, 1994.) Areas covered include: accounting and taxation, advertising and direct mail, business law, communications and transportation, computers, economics, finance, insurance, law, management, marketing, real estate, and statistics. When a term has different meanings in these different areas, more than one definition is provided. There are three appendices: Abbreviations and Acronyms, Compound Interest Factors, and Economic Indicators.

The Dorsey Dictionary of American Government and Politics. (Chicago: The Dorsey Press, 1988.) This dictionary concentrates on the federal government and allows the reader a quick reference to subjects that often need updating. An example is the source of the elephant as a symbol of the Republican Party. The discussions of court cases, federal laws, government agencies and slang terms also contribute to the book's value. The appendices include The Constitution of the United States, a Guide to Federal Government Documents, a Guide to Statistical Information on American Government and a Guide to On-Line Data Bases on American Government. The individual definitions are enhanced by the inclusion of pertinent illustrations, additional references and addresses with telephone numbers where appropriate.

The MBA's Dictionary. (New York: Reston Publishing Company, 1983.) This book was written for undergraduate business majors, MBA students and managers in business and government. It contains definitions and discussions of many terms, processes, persons, organizations, laws, and court cases needed for business school courses and working in many fields of business. The book is a mini-encyclopedia for business managers and students. It contains many useful drawings and examples, slang terms definitions and informal processes. This book would be on a list of "must haves."

The MBI Dictionary of Modern Business and Management. (New York: Prentice-Hall, 1986.) The MBI stands for "Management Books Institute." The book provides insight and assistance on the broadest range of management issues and techniques within a single source. Topics include such terms as androgynous, behavior profile system, cellular telephony, strategic planning cognitive style positioning, ergonomics, corporation charters, dividends, stockholders, depreciation, and many other useful references. The entries are complete and well written.

The Modern American Business Dictionary: Including an Appendix of Business Slang. (New York: Quill, 1982.) This dictionary is intended to bridge the communications gap that often exists between entrepreneurs, bankers, lawyers, accountants, corporate executives, government officials, investors, and others in the business world. Terms used in over 50 fields are included. The book can also serve as a reference tool for consumers, educators, and business students.

Accounting

Dictionary of Accounting Terms. (Hauppauge, NY: Barron's Educational Series, Inc., 1987.) This book is directed to accountants, businesspersons, and students. Entries have been drawn from all areas within accounting, including financial accounting, managerial and cost accounting, auditing, financial statement analysis, and taxes. Over 2,500 terms are explained, many with substantial examples and data to further clarify the explanation. The book is complete enough to be used as a personal tutor.

Encyclopedic Dictionary of Accounting and Finance. (New York: Prentice-Hall, 1990.) This book is written for working professionals in the fields of accounting, finance, investment, and banking for day-to-day use in their practices and for technical research. Especially valuable are the clarity of the examples and the detail of the mathematics used in the sample problems. Topics covered include financial accounting, financial statement analysis, managerial/cost accounting, auditing, managerial finance, investments, financial planning, financial economics, and money and banking. Teachers may find many useful examples in this reference source. This book would be on a list of "must haves."

Kohler's Dictionary for Accountants, 6th ed. (New York: Prentice-Hall, 1983.) Approximately 4,500 terms are explained in this standard source.

Management Accounting Glossary. (New York: Institute of Management Accountants, Prentice-Hall, 1991.) This book is really a dictionary of terms used in the practice of management accounting. This glossary is designed to improve communication about financial matters both within the United States and internationally. Many definitions come from the Financial Accounting Standards Board and the Cost Accounting Standards Board as well as other similar organizations.

Advertising

Broadcast Communications Dictionary, 3rd ed. (Lincolnwood, IL: NTC Business Books, 1991.) This authoritative reference to the language used by broadcasters in English-speaking countries is for anyone seeking to communicate in this field. Covers programming, production, engineering, advertising, and other broadcast areas. Includes more than 6,000 technical, common and slang words unique to the business of broadcasting. Newly revised to include terms spawned by the development of today's satellite technology.

Dictionary of Mass Media & Communication. (New York: Longman, 1982.) This dictionary was written to solve communication problems caused by technical jargon and slang. It recognizes the widely varied backgrounds of persons working in the field of communications and their need to communicate with each other. The book is directed toward persons in advertising, TV and radio broadcasting, data processing, film, graphic arts, marketing, printing, public relations, publishing and the theater.

Dictionary of Trade Name Origins. (Lincolnwood, IL: NTC Business Books, 1990.) Coca-Cola, once advertised as an "Esteemed Brain Tonic and Intellectual Beverage," derives its name from two of its early ingredients, coca leaves and the cola nut. Maxwell House took its name from the Nashville hotel where the blend was first sold. This fascinating dictionary reveals the stories behind these and 700 other everyday trade names, whose origins and backgrounds were gathered first hand from the manufacturing companies themselves. In his introduction, internationally respected linguist Adrian Room explains how trade names are devised and examines the linguistic and legal pitfalls of the process. Appendices consider special aspects of trade name creation and give examples of computer-devised names.

Mass Media Dictionary. (Lincolnwood, IL: NTC Business Books, 1991.) The fast-changing world of media creates and discards terms every day. And for those working in the media, this is the single best source of accurate definitions for terms like abie, uplink, yupcom, and zero-frame dissolve. Printed in a clear, easy-to-read format, this encyclopedic resource features more than 20,000 terms commonly used in advertising, audience measurement, production, research, sound engineering, and other mass media fields. Entries are cross-referenced to related terms, and multiple definitions are provided for terms common to several media. Terms from leading-edge technologies are supplemented by older, less frequently used terms. An indispensable desktop reference for anyone involved in mass communications.

NTC's Dictionary of Mailing List Terminology and Techniques. (Lincolnwood, IL: NTC Business Books, 1990.) Covers the language, terminology, practices, and techniques of the mailing list industry. An ideal training tool for newcomers to direct mail, this comprehensive reference defines more than 1,500 terms. Where necessary, the easy-to-understand definitions and usages provided for each term are cross-referenced to synonyms or related terms. The usage preferred by mailing list authorities is noted. Includes insights into the rules, trade customs, and pitfalls associated with list rentals and usage.

Webster's New World Dictionary of Media and Communications. (New York: Simon & Schuster, 1990.) This dictionary provides accurate definitions to such commonly used terms as ADI, aliasing, cume, reach, poster, mat, matte, stacked ads, non-repro blue and residuals, plus many more. Written to satisfy the needs of professionals as well as general readers.

Banking and Credit

Dictionary of Banking. (New York: John Wiley & Sons, 1992.) This dictionary includes over 15,000 terms and incorporates the American Bankers Association's *Banking Terminology*. The entries include material from the entire financial services industry: insurance, banking, brokerage, capital structure, collections, commodities markets, credit, credit unions, government regulations and agencies, import-export, mortgages, personal finance, public finance, securities, transfers and trusts, and other areas.

Economics

The MIT Dictionary of Modern Economics. (Boston: MIT Press, 1992.) Fifteen contributors assisted in this effort. The results are worthwhile. For example, the entry for "iso-product curve" provides an excellent short discussion replete with a diagram showing three different curves for capital vs labor. A cross reference leads to "indifference curve" which also includes a diagram with the explanation. If we had a list of "must " books this dictionary would be on the list.

Finance and Investments

The A to Z of Investing. (New York: NAL Dutton, 1987.) From the "How To Use This Book" preface: "This book is an encyclopedic dictionary, defining

and explaining the thousand or so most used terms in the language of investment. . . . It includes the terminology of stocks and bonds, options and war-
rants, commodity and financial futures, mutual funds, pension accounts, gold
and silver, mineral and oil leases, interest-bearing bank accounts, life insurance,
real estate, collectibles and coins—in short, every kind of investment. . . .
Appendix B lists important sources of financial information. Appendix A
lists the stock and commodity exchanges where [investors] decisions may be
carried out and Appendix C the most important stock indexes and averages.''

Dictionary of Finance. (New York: Macmillan Publishing Company, 1988.)
This dictionary covers finance as well as economics, accounting, trading procedures in the securities and commodities markets, banking, private and public
financing, consumer and tax legislation related to finance. Of particular
interest are the portraits of famous economists which accompany their
biographies.

The Dow Jones-Irwin Guide to Personal Financial Planning. (Burr Ridge,
IL: Irwin Professional Publishing, 1986.) This publication contains over 3,000
entries related to personal financial planning. It is meant to be used by professionals and lay persons alike. The definitions are short and concise. It is
useful for accountants, lawyers, financial planners, insurance specialists, stock
brokers and bankers.

International Dictionary of the Securities Industry, 2nd ed. (Burr Ridge, IL:
Irwin Professional Publishing, 1989.) This dictionary stresses the stock market
of the United States but also covers international securities markets. Terms
in the French language, for example, are generally cross-referenced to their
English counterparts for definition. It is meant to be read by professionals
as well as new investors who may not have any background in this field.

Investment and Securities Dictionary. (Jefferson, NC: McFarland & Company, 1986.) This is a comprehensive summary of terms used in the markets
of stock exchanges, syndications, broker-dealers, investment managers, spon-
sors, and financial planners. The more than 2,000 entries include technical
words and phrases, industry agencies and associations, and regulatory bodies.
An appendix covering Prospectus and Offering Documents is included.
Another appendix is a complete alphabetical listing of every type of bond,
all of which may be cross-referenced to the glossary. The diagrams and
exhibits used extensively throughout enhance the readers' understanding and
make this information easier to comprehend.

The Investor's Dictionary. (New York: John Wiley & Sons, 1986.) This dictionary compiles traditional terms used by the 190-year-old securities exchange
system and the 140-year-old commodity and futures exchange system as well
as more recent developments in the financial markets. Investing areas include

antiques, art, bank depositories and securities, bonds, collectibles, commodity markets, currency trading, debentures, diamonds, exchanges, futures, government issues, insurance, investment trusts, legislation, metals, mortgage-backed bonds, mutual funds, oil investments, pass-through securities, pension plans, real estate/property ownership, stocks, tax-exempt bonds, tax shelters, and venture capital.

The Language of Commodities. (New York: New York Institute of Finance, 1985.) The commodity market refers to the market place of agricultural products. Key words and phrases are from the futures, options, forwards, and actuals markets. Words from the peripheral industries of shipping, import and export, insurance, banking and credit are also included. Examples are included to further explain certain concepts. The book is clearly written and can be easily understood by anyone interested in the commodities markets.

The New Palgrave Dictionary of Money & Finance. (New York: Groves Dictionaries of Music, 1992.) This three volume effort was assisted by an advisory board of twenty international scholars and practitioners. These three volumes can be described as a mini-encyclopedia rather than a dictionary in that most "definitions" are really essays which run several pages and even include a list of references.

Human Resources

Employee Benefits Dictionary. (Lanham, MD: Bureau of National Affairs, 1992.) From the preface, "Since the Employee Retirement Income Security Act (ERISA) was enacted in 1974, mountains of legislation and regulations have been issued in the employee benefits area. This, in turn, has given rise to a jargon that is peculiar to the field. It is almost impossible for someone new to this area of the law to deal with it effectively without having a working knowledge of its many 'terms of the art'." The book contains definitions and examples of confusing terms and jargon within the human resource field. Statutory and regulatory references appear where they are appropriate. An excellent dictionary from the user's perspective.

The Human Resources Glossary. (Saranac Lake, NY: AMACOM, 1991.) This comprehensive dictionary contains over 3,000 entries related to human resources. The book also contains the names, addresses, and other pertinent information about more than 130 associations and societies of interest to human resource practitioners.

Roberts' Dictionary of Industrial Relations, 4th ed. (Lanham, MD: Bureau of National Affairs, 1994.) New terms such as "dislocated worker," "concession bargaining," and "employee giveback" are covered this edition. The book includes information on new legislation and specific legal cases that have had a significant impact on the field of human resources. Definitions include examples and references to court cases where applicable. Cross-references are also used extensively.

Insurance

Dictionary of Insurance, 7th rev. ed. (Lanham, MD: Littlefield Adams, 1990.) Besides the basic terms in any field, each profession develops its own unique abbreviations and acronyms as a form of shorthand, but which if misunderstood can present additional problems, i.e., ACLU meaning both the American Civil Liberties Union as well as the American College of Life Underwriters. AAA may mean the American Automobile Association to some, the American Accounting Association to others, and the American Academy of Actuaries to those in the field of insurance. This book devotes approximately 500 pages of the text to definitions and explanations of specific insurance terms. Useful appendices include a Directory of Organizations Related to the Insurance Industry and a Directory of State Commissioners of Insurance.

Dictionary of Insurance Terms. (Hauppauge, NY: Barron's Educational Series, 1991.) This book offers essential information to those concerned with various forms of insurance such as life, health, pension plans, social security, individual retirement accounts, automobile, home, tenants, professional liability and umbrella policies, as well as employee benefit plans, workers' compensation, buy-sell insurance funded agreements, key person, business property and business liability, among others. It is also a reference source for practitioners who require succinct, technically accurate answers to insurance and risk management terminology questions. The insurance agent may even find this book helpful in marketing and servicing various insurance products. Over 2,500 entries are included.

The Insurance Dictionary; the A to Z of Life & Health, 3rd ed. (Chicago: Longman Financial Services, 1990.) Definitions cover not only life and health insurance terms but also a wide range of related subjects, including agent training and agency building concepts, retirement and estate planning, investments and securities, government benefit programs, and taxation as well as organizations and government agencies dealing with these topics. This reference tool is intended for all who work directly or indirectly with the insurance industry.

Insurance Dictionary. (Jefferson, NC: McFarland & Company, 1989.) This reference offers a comprehensive summary of industry words and phrases, including investment, actuarial, legal and marketing phrases. Also includes two appendices of State Insurance Commissioner names and addresses and Canadian Provincial Agency names and addresses.

International Relations

The International Relations Dictionary, 4th ed. (Santa Barbara, CA: ABC-CLIO, Inc., 1988.) From the Preface: "A format unique for dictionaries is used in this book. Entries are grouped into subject-matter chapters to parallel topics in more current international relations textbooks. In addition, terms are grouped together within each chapter under title rubrics that link relevant information. . . . Each entry in the book includes a definition of *Significance* so that the historical roots as well as the contemporary importance of the term can be studied." There are 12 chapters in this dictionary including: The Nature and Role of Foreign Policy, War and Military Policy, Diplomacy, American Foreign Policy, and International Law.

Labor

Biographical Dictionary of American Labor, 2nd ed. (Glenview, IL: Greenwood Press, 1984.) Devotes over 500 pages to thorough biographies of the people who contributed to America's labor movement. Background includes their date and place of birth, family relationships, education and the life key that helped each person achieve their place in the labor movement. Six appendices cover Union Affiliations, Religious Preferences, Place of Birth, Formal Education, Political Preferences and Major Appointive and Elective Public Offices.

Dictionary of Occupational Titles, 4th ed. (Washington, D.C.: U.S. Department of Labor, Bernan Press.) The Bernan Press takes the Labor Department's publication of the DOT, divides it into two volumes, separately binds each with a more substantial binder, and adds headings and text where necessary, making the publication more useful and more durable. The purpose of the book is to provide standardized occupational information to support job placement services. The DOT provides a structure for studying the millions of jobs in the U.S. economy by organizing groups jobs into "occupations" based on their similarities, and defines the structure and content of all listed occupations.

Law

Black's Law Dictionary, 6th ed. (Saint Paul, MN: West Publishing Co., 1990.) This dictionary has over 1,400 pages of definitions which are very clearly and thoroughly written. Many of the definitions are augmented by a case reference where the reader can obtain another definition as it was developed in case law.

Management Information Systems (MIS) and Computers

Dictionary of Computer Terms, 3rd ed. (Hauppauge, NY: Barron's Educational Series, 1992.) From the Preface: "This book is intended to help you understand what computers are, what they do, and how they do it. The entries cover a wide range of topics, including hardware, programming concepts and languages, operating systems, electronics, logic circuits, history of computers, and specific models of personal computers. . . . This book will also help you if you are interested in writing your own programs. We provide articles on nearly all of the programming languages in widespread use today, with sample programs in Ada, ALGOL, APL, BASIC, C, COBOL, FORTRAN, LISP, LOGO, Pascal, PL/1, and Prelog." Tables of flowchart symbols and logic symbols are also included.

Dictionary of Computing, 3rd ed. (New York: Oxford University Press, 1991.) From the Preface, "This edition contains, in a single alphabetical listing, nearly 4,500 terms used in computing and in the associated fields of electronics, mathematics, and logic. The branches of computing covered in this dictionary include: algorithms and their properties, programming languages and concepts, program development methods, data structures and files structures, operating systems and concepts, computer organization and architecture, hardware, including processors, memory devices, and I/O devices, computer communications, information technology, computer applications and techniques, major computer manufacturers, and legal aspects of computing." There is also a page of related symbols, including the Greek alphabet.

Dictionary of Information Science and Technology. (San Diego: Academic Press, 1992.) Over 1,000 entries and an extensive bibliography of over 300 references to both primary and secondary sources. Each term is followed by a key into the subject outlines at the back so that each term is given a context within a subject area. Each term is also annotated by one or more references to the literature.

Dictionary of Information Technology, 2nd ed. (New York: Oxford University Press.) The concept of information technology includes both management information systems and computers as well as many other subjects, including but not limited to cryptology, expert systems, on line information retrieval, cellular radio, fiber optics, global satellite communications systems, interactive video disks, local area networks, speech synthesis, videotext, and word processing. The authors lead into each definition with terms like, "In audiovisual aids," or "In computing," thereby creating a context for the reader as they read the definition. Helpful illustrations are also provided for some entries.

Historical Dictionary of Data Processing: Technology. (Glenview, IL: Greenwood Press, 1987.) This is one of a three-part series that also includes *Historical Dictionary of Data Processing: Organizations* and *Historical Dictionary of Data Processing: Biographies.* The breadth of series is indicated by the Chronology Appendix which begins at 3000 B.C. and cites the abacus.

207

The dictionary covers computers, electronic components, early calculating machines, software, special applications and projects, and general computer concepts. The tone and the approach of these books is suitable for the general reader as well as the specialist. A book for the "must" list.

Maps and Geography

Webster's New Geographical Dictionary. (Springfield, MA: Merriam-Webster, 1988.) This rather large volume has more than 47,000 entries, including 218 maps. The geographical terms section presents common terms in several languages. While coverage includes the world, emphasis is on the United States and Canada.

Marketing

Complete Multilingual Dictionary of Advertising, Marketing & Communications: English, French, and German. (Lincolnwood, IL: NTC Business Books, 1988.) This multilingual dictionary provides precise translations of more than 8,000 technical and general communications terms in three key languages. The most complete and authoritative reference of its kind, it is indispensable for all individuals and organizations involved of mass communications.

The Dictionary of Marketing. (New York: Fairchild Publications, 1987.) A note from the publisher recognizes the difficulty of creating a dictionary of marketing due to the dynamics of the topic. Yet, this dictionary is a comprehensive, non-technical review of marketing terms, including those used in direct marketing, marketing research, international marketing, advertising, salesmanship, wholesaling and retailing. Principal marketing trade associations have also been included. Several charts and graphs add to the definitions.

Dictionary of Marketing & Advertising, 2nd ed. (East Brunswick, NJ: Nichols Publishing, 1990.) Contributors to this book selected their own areas of expertise, so the result is a very understandable and well-written dictionary. The intended audience includes practitioners, managers, students and lay persons. The European origin makes this source very attractive to non-Europeans doing business in Great Britain or on the continent.

Dictionary of Marketing Terms. (Chicago: American Marketing Association, 1989.) Developed by professionals in several areas of marketing, this valuable resource includes over 2,000 concise definitions of terms and phrases. Through complete and detailed definitions, it offers information on all facets of present-day marketing and associated terminology ranging from finance issues to physical distribution, social marketing research, strategic marketing, pricing, global marketing and consumer behavior. This book is one of the most extensive references of marketing terms available.

The Marketing Glossary. (Saranac Lake, NY: AMACOM, 1992.) The subtitle, "Key Terms, Concepts, and Applications in Marketing Management, Advertising, Sales Promotion, Public Relations, Direct Marketing, Market Research and Sales," describes this book very accurately. There are over 1,400 entries covering both the theory and practice of marketing. These entries are encyclopedic in nature as contrasted with a few sentences or phrases. Three appendices add to the usefulness of the book: (A) Marketing and Media Trade, Commercial, and Business Organizations; (B) Marketing and Advertising Trade Publications; and, (C) Selected Bibliography: "How-To" Books in Marketing.

Dictionary of Marketing Research. (Detroit: St. James Press, 1987.) This resource is divided into Parts I and II plus appendices. Part I, the Alphabetical Index of Terms, is essentially the Index of the book. Part II, the actual dictionary of over 2,000 terms, is divided into seven chapters: Marketing and Media, Ancillary Sciences, Psychology, Statistics, Research Methodology and Theory, Research Practice, and Types of Research. The appendices include a checklist for marketing researchers as well as three different codes of ethics/conduct for practitioners. The actual entries also include descriptions of various publications complete with their addresses.

Production Management and Operations Research

APICS Dictionary, 7th ed. (Falls Church, VA: APICS, 1992.) Terms related to the production segment of business and the inventory systems which support the production cycle are explained. This field is often referred to as "industrial management" in university course work.

Project Management

A Project Management Dictionary of Terms. (New York: Van Nostrand Reinhold Company, 1985.) This dictionary was developed for managers and professionals who work in a project environment and was highly influenced by the Air Force Institute of Technology's "Compendium of Authenticated Systems and Logistics Terms," among other sources.

Real Estate

The Dictionary of Real Estate Appraisal. (Chicago: Appraisal Institute, 1993.) This book serves as a reference guide for the field of real estate appraisal. It reflects the interdependence of appraisal and other major professions involved in the interpretation of the marketplace, including accounting, agriculture, arbitration, architecture, banking, computer programming, construction, finance, insurance, law, and urban planning. Includes entries covering economics, environmental concerns, market analysis, and quantitative techniques. The list of sources consulted provides additional sources of information.

Real Estate Dictionary. (Jefferson, NC: McFarland & Company, 1988.) More than 1,100 terms from the areas of residential and commercial properties, investments in various forms, rules for mortgage loans, agencies, associations and regulatory bodies and the various rights and points of law affecting owners of real estate are covered. The book also includes a number of checklists for owners, buyers, sellers and investors. Various amortization tables and remaining balance tables are also included.

Webster's New World Illustrated Encyclopedic Dictionary of Real Estate, 3rd ed. (Englewood, Cliffs, NJ: Prentice-Hall, 1987.) Anyone working in any profession related to land can benefit from this book. The illustrations clarify many terms and give understanding to housing styles across the country. The over 150-page portfolio of forms is a very handy reference source by itself. The cross section of a house is useful.

Retailing

Fairchild's Dictionary of Retailing. (New York: Fairchild Books, 1984.) Words and phrases were assembled from word lists, glossaries, textbooks, periodicals, newspapers, and other sources. They are commonly used in retailing or areas closely allied to retailing such as wholesaling, advertising, or direct marketing. Specific retailing areas include, but are not limited to, stores, shopping centers, the supermarket industry, retail advertising, merchandising and display, and accounting in retailing as well as personnel and market research.

Statistics

A Dictionary of Statistical Terms, 5th ed. (White Plains, NY: Longman Scientific & Technical, 1990.) This publication is supported by the International Statistical Institute. The number of entries exceeds 3,000. Earlier editions were important because they contained many definitions of terms used in various countries. These have generally been discontinued as publications were developed to cover each language separately. See the several prefaces for additional information in this area. This book appears to be directed primarily at the professional statistician beyond the undergraduate college level, although terms and subjects covered at the undergraduate level are included.

Mathematical Dictionary for Economics and Business Administration. (Boston, MA: Allyn and Bacon, 1976.) Over 350 pages with over 2,000 entries covering such items as Minkowski's bounding hyperplane theorem and minimax strategy. Also includes an appendix of mathematical notation. The list of terms for the main text was obtained by searching the major journals in economics, operations research, finance, accounting and marketing.

Government Publications

OBJECTIVES: This chapter will provide you with an overview of important government publications along with sources of additional government publications.

> Introduction
> Federal Depository Libraries
> United States Government Bookstores
> Directories of Government Publications
> United States Department of Commerce
> United States Government Agencies and Departments
> Federal Information Centers
> State Government Information Sources

After reading this chapter you should be able to:

*Understand and use the major business resources published by federal and state government agencies.

INTRODUCTION

The United States Government is the single largest printer in the world. The Federal Government prints more pages of material every year than all book publishers in the United States combined. The job of printing all this material, and overseeing the printing of government material by outside printers, rests with the General Printing Office (GPO). The GPO was established by an act of Congress on March 4, 1861, the day that Abraham Lincoln was inaugurated as the sixteenth president of the United States.

The vast number of publications of the Federal Government are listed in the *Monthly Catalog of United States Government Publications* (referred to as MoCat) and in catalog and microfiche form in the *Publications Reference File (PRF)*. *MoCat* and *PRF* are publications of the GPO and are available from the Superintendent of Documents, U.S. Government Printing Office, Washington, D.C. 20402 or by calling (202) 512-1800. *MoCat* and *PRF* are also available online through services such as DIALOG, *Government Documents Catalog Service*, and *Online Catalog of the Library of Congress*.

FEDERAL DEPOSITORY LIBRARIES

The Federal Depository Library Program was enacted by Congress in 1813 to provide government publications to designated libraries throughout the

United States. The large, regional depository libraries (of which there are fifty-two) receive and retain at least one copy of nearly every Federal Government publication, either in print or microfilm form, for use by the general public. An additional 1,400 local depository libraries receive the most important federal government publications. Any local library can direct you to the Federal Depository Library nearest to you, or you can obtain a listing of these 1,400 libraries by writing to:

> Federal Depository Library Program
> U.S. Government Printing Office
> Superintendent of Documents
> Stop: SM
> Washington, DC 20402

Federal Depository Libraries receive free copies of government publications and, in return, agree to house these publications, provide reference assistance, make the publications available for general use, and provide for interlibrary loans. Regional depository libraries must keep all government documents permanently. All other depository libraries must keep government documents for a minimum of five years. Most depository libraries will keep the documents they receive much longer than this and, further, must request permission from the government before discarding documents.

A complete listing of the fifty-two regional depository libraries follows:

ALABAMA
AUBURN UNIVERSITY
LIBRARY
Documents Department
Montgomery, AL 36193
(334) 244-3650

UNIVERSITY OF ALABAMA
LIBRARY
Documents Department--Box S
University, AL 35486
(205) 348-6046

ARIZONA
DEPARTMENT OF LIBRARY,
ARCHIVES AND PUBLIC
RECORDS
1700 West Washington
Phoenix, AZ 85007
(602) 542-3701

ARKANSAS
ARKANSAS STATE LIBRARY
One Capitol Mall
Little Rock, AR 72201
(501) 682-2053

CALIFORNIA
CALIFORNIA STATE LIBRARY
Government Publications Section
P.O. Box 942837
Sacramento, CA 94237-0001
(916) 654-0069

COLORADO
UNIVERSITY OF COLORADO
LIBRARY
Government Publications Division
Campus Box 184
Boulder, CO 80309
(303) 492-8834

DENVER PUBLIC LIBRARY
Government Publications
Department
1357 Broadway
Denver, CO 80203
(303) 640-6249

CONNECTICUT
CONNECTICUT STATE
LIBRARY
Government Documents Unit
231 Capitol Avenue
Hartford, CT 06106
(203) 566-4971

FLORIDA
UNIVERSITY OF FLORIDA
LIBRARIES
Library West
Documents Department
Gainesville, FL 32611
(904) 392-0367

GEORGIA
UNIVERSITY OF GEORGIA
LIBRARIES
Government Reference Department
Athens, GA 30602
(706) 542-8949

HAWAII
UNIVERSITY OF HAWAII
LIBRARY
Government Documents
Collections
2550 The Mall
Honolulu, HI 96822
(808) 956-8230

IDAHO
UNIVERSITY OF IDAHO
LIBRARY
Documents Section
Moscow, ID 83843
(208) 885-6344

ILLINOIS
ILLINOIS STATE LIBRARY
Information Services Branch
Centennial Building
Springfield, IL 62756
(217) 782-7596

INDIANA
INDIANA STATE LIBRARY
Serials Document Section
140 North Senate Avenue
Indianapolis, IN 46204
(317) 232-3678

IOWA
UNIVERSITY OF IOWA
LIBRARIES
Government Documents
Department
Iowa City, IA 52242
(319) 335-5927

KANSAS
UNIVERSITY OF KANSAS
Documents Collection--Spencer
Library
Lawrence, KS 66045-2800
(913) 864-4660

KENTUCKY
UNIVERSITY OF KENTUCKY
LIBRARIES
Government Publications
Department
Lexington, KY 40506-0039
(606) 257-1631

LOUISIANA
LOUISIANA STATE
UNIVERSITY
Middleton Library
Government Documents
Department
Baton Rouge, LA 70803
(504) 388-2570

LOUISIANA TECHNICAL
UNIVERSITY LIBRARY
Documents Department
Ruston, LA 71272-0046
(318) 257-4962

MAINE
UNIVERSITY OF MAINE
Raymond H. Fogler Library
Tri-State Regional Documents
Deposits
Orono, ME 04469
(207) 581-1673

MARYLAND
UNIVERSITY OF MARYLAND
McKeldin Library--Documents
Division
College Park, MD 20742
(301) 405-9165

MASSACHUSETTS
BOSTON PUBLIC LIBRARY
Government Documents Department
Boston, MA 02117
(617) 536-5400 ext. 226

MICHIGAN
DETROIT PUBLIC LIBRARY
Sociology Department
5201 Woodward Avenue
Detroit, MI 48202-4093
(313) 833-1409

MICHIGAN STATE LIBRARY
P.O. Box 30007
Lansing, MI 48909
(517) 373-1300

MINNESOTA
UNIVERSITY OF MINNESOTA
Government Publications Division
409 Wilson Library
309 19th Avenue South
Minneapolis, MN 55455
(612) 624-5073

MISSISSIPPI
UNIVERSITY OF MISSISSIPPI
LIBRARY
Documents Department
University, MS 38677
(601) 232-5857

MISSOURI
UNIVERSITY OF MISSOURI AT
COLUMBIA
Ellis Library--Government
Documents
Columbia, MO 65201
(314) 882-6733

MONTANA
UNIVERSITY OF MONTANA
Mansfield Library
Documents Division
Missoula, MT 59812
(406) 243-6700

NEBRASKA
UNIVERSITY OF
NEBRASKA-LINCOLN
Love Library
Documents Department
Lincoln, NE 68588-0410
(402) 472-2562

NEVADA
UNIVERSITY OF NEVADA
LIBRARY
Government Publications
Department
Reno, NV 89557-0044
(702) 784-6579

NEW JERSEY
NEWARK PUBLIC
LIBRARY
5 Washington Street
Newark, NJ 07101-0630
(201) 733-7782

NEW MEXICO
UNIVERSITY OF NEW MEXICO
Zimmerman Library
Government Publications
Department
Albuquerque, NM 87131
(505) 277-5441

NEW MEXICO STATE LIBRARY
Reference Department
325 Don Caspar Avenue
Santa Fe, NM 87503
(505) 827-3824

NEW YORK
NEW YORK STATE LIBRARY
Empire State Plaza
Albany, NY 12230
(518) 474-5355

NORTH CAROLINA
UNIVERSITY OF NORTH
CAROLINA AT CHAPEL HILL
Davis Library
BA/SS Division
Chapel Hill, NC 27514
(919) 962-1151

NORTH DAKOTA
UNIVERSITY OF NORTH
DAKOTA
Chester Fritz Library
Documents Department
Grand Forks, ND 58202
(701) 777-4629

OHIO
STATE LIBRARY OF OHIO
Documents Department
65 South Front Street
Columbus, Ohio 43266-0334
(614) 644-7051

OKLAHOMA
OKLAHOMA DEPARTMENT OF
LIBRARIES

Government Documents
200 NE 18th Street
Oklahoma City, OK 73105
(405) 521-2502, ext. 252

OKLAHOMA STATE
UNIVERSITY LIBRARY
Documents Department
Stillwater, OK 74078
(405) 744-6546

OREGON
PORTLAND STATE
UNIVERSITY LIBRARY
Documents Department
P.O. Box 1151
Portland, OR 97207
(503) 725-4123

PENNSYLVANIA
STATE LIBRARY OF
PENNSYLVANIA
Government Publications
Section
P.O. Box 1601
Harrisburg, PA 17105
(717) 787-3752

SOUTH CAROLINA
CLEMSON UNIVERSITY
Cooper Library
Documents Department
Clemson, SC 29634
(803) 656-5174

UNIVERSITY OF SOUTH
CAROLINA
Thomas Cooper Library
Documents/Microform
Department
Green & Sumter Streets
Columbia, SC 29208
(803) 777-4841

TEXAS
TEXAS STATE LIBRARY
Public Services Department
P.O. Box 12927--Capitol Station
Austin, TX 78711
(512) 463-5455

TEXAS TECH UNIVERSITY
LIBRARY
Government Documents Department
Lubbock, TX 79409
(806) 742-2282

UTAH
UTAH STATE UNIVERSITY
Merrill Library, U.M.C. 30
Logan, UT 84322
(801) 797-2633

VIRGINIA
UNIVERSITY OF VIRGINIA
Alderman Library--Public
Documents
Charlottesville, VA 22093-2498
(804) 924-3133

WASHINGTON
WASHINGTON STATE LIBRARY
Documents Section
Olympia, WA 98504
(206) 753-4027

WEST VIRGINIA
WEST VIRGINIA UNIVERSITY
LIBRARY
Documents Department
Morgantown, WV 26506-6069
(304) 293-3051

WISCONSIN
STATE HISTORICAL LIBRARY
OF WISCONSIN
Government Publications Section
816 State Street
Madison, WI 53706
(608) 264-6525

MILWAUKEE PUBLIC LIBRARY
814 West Wisconsin Avenue
Milwaukee, WI 53233
(414) 286-3073

WYOMING
UNIVERSITY OF WYOMING
University Station
13th and Divison--Box 3334
Laramie, Wyoming 87201
(307) 766-2174

UNITED STATES GOVERNMENT BOOKSTORES

In addition to offering government publications through the mail from the Superintendent of Documents, the U.S. Government Printing Office operates twenty-three bookstores across the country. Each government bookstore carries the most popular government publications along with a selection of publications that are tailored to local interests. Any government publications not available at each bookstore can be specially ordered by that bookstore. The government bookstores accept all major credit cards. To find the government bookstore located closest to you, check the following listing:

ALABAMA
O'Neill Building
2023 Third Avenue North
Birmingham, AL 35203
(205) 731-1056

CALIFORNIA
Arco Plaza, C Level
505 South Flower Street
Los Angeles, CA 90071
(213) 239-9844

CALIFORNIA
Room 1023, Federal Building
450 Golden Gate Avenue
San Francisco, CA 94102
(415) 512-2770

COLORADO
World Savings Building
720 North Main Street
Pueblo, CO 81003
(719) 544-3142

Room 117, Federal Building
1961 Stout Street
Denver, CO 80294
(303) 844-3964

DISTRICT OF COLUMBIA
U.S. Government Printing Office
710 North Capitol Street NW
Washington, DC 20401
(202) 512-0000

Farragut West
1510 H Street NW
Washington, DC 20005
(202) 653-5075

FLORIDA
Room 158, Federal Building
400 West Bay Street
Jacksonville, FL 32202
(904) 353-0569

GEORGIA
Room 100, Federal Building
275 Peachtree Street NE
P.O. Box 56445
Atlanta, GA 30303
(404) 347-1900

ILLINOIS
Room 1365, Federal Building
219 South Dearborn Street
Chicago, IL 60604
(312) 353-5133

MARYLAND
Retail Sales Outlet
8660 Cherry Lane
Laurel, MD 20707
(301) 953-7974

MASSACHUSETTS
Room G-25, Federal Building
Sudbury Street
Boston, MA 02203
(617) 720-4180

MICHIGAN
Suite 160, Federal Building
477 Michigan Avenue
Detroit, MI 48226
(313) 226-7817

MISSOURI
120 Bannister Mall
5600 East Bannister Road
Kansas City, MO 64137
(816) 765-2256

NEW YORK
Room 110, 26 Federal Plaza
New York, NY 10278
(212) 264-3825

OHIO
1st Floor, Federal Building
1240 East 9th Street
Cleveland, OH 44199
(216) 522-4922

Room 207, Federal Building
200 North High Street
Columbus, OH 43215
(614) 469-6955

PENNSYLVANIA
Robert Morris Building
100 North 17th Street
Philadelphia, PA 19103
(215) 636-1900

PENNSYLVANIA
Room 118, Federal Building
1000 Liberty Avenue
Pittsburgh, PA 15222
(412) 644-2721

TEXAS
Room 1C50, Federal Building
1100 Commerce Street
Dallas, TX 75242
(214) 767-0076

9319 Gulf Freeway
Houston, TX 77017
(713) 228-1187

WASHINGTON
Room 194, Federal Building
915 Second Avenue
Seattle, WA 98174
(206) 553-4270

WISCONSIN
Room 190, Federal Building
517 East Wisconsin Avenue
Milwaukee, WI 53202
(414) 297-1304

DIRECTORIES OF GOVERNMENT PUBLICATIONS

The millions of Federal Government publications are far too numerous to list in one chapter of a book. Therefore, the listings that appear in the following sections are limited to the government publications that would be of most value to businesspeople. There are, however, entire directories of government publications available. These sources provide more detailed listings than can be found in this chapter. The most useful of these directories are identified in the following list:

Directory of Government Document Collections & Librarians. (Bethesda, MD: Congressional Information Service, Inc., 1993.) This directory lists all libraries that contain government documents, the collections that can be found at each library, libraries that contain specialized collections of government documents, sources of state government information, and addresses of important government agencies.

Free Publications from U.S. Government Agencies. (Englewood, CO: Libraries Unlimited, Inc., 1989.) This source provides a listing of all publications that are available free from the Federal Government and explains how to obtain them. The publications are listed by subject area, including public affairs, crime, education, energy, economics, environment, consumer affairs, health, and alcohol and drug abuse.

Government Reference Serials. (Englewood, CO: Libraries Unlimited, Inc., 1988.) This directory of over 600 pages contains more than 50,000 government publications listed by nearly 100 topic areas. The four major sections of the directory are titled: General Government Publications, Social Sciences, Science and Technology, and Humanities.

Guide to Information from Government Sources. (Radnor, PA: Chilton Book Company, 1992.) Contained in this guide are a listing of all United States Government agencies and departments, with a listing of the publications of each; a listing of all database sources of government information; and a subject area listing of government publications.

Guide to Popular U.S. Government Publications. (Englewood, CO: Libraries Unlimited, Inc., 1993.) This guide lists the more popular Federal Government publications over fifty subject areas, with a short description of each publication and information on how to obtain the publication.

Subject Guide to U.S. Government Reference Sources. (Englewood, CO: Libraries Unlimited, Inc., 1985.) This source contains a detailed listing of government publications by subject area, with details on how to obtain the publications. The topic areas indexed are: general works, library science, anthropology and ethnology, economics and business, education, geography, history, law, political science, recreation and hobbies, sociology, statistics and demography, urbanology, agriculture, astronomy, biology, chemistry, data processing, earth science, energy, engineering, environment, mathematics, medical science, physics, transportation, architecture, fine arts, literature, music, performing arts, philosophy, and religion.

Subject Bibliographies of Government Publications. (Detroit, MI: Omnigraphics, Inc., 1992.) This very detailed directory of nearly 1,000 pages lists government publications, classified by 234 subject areas, and the specific agency or department source of each publication.

The Government Directory of Addresses and Telephone Numbers. (Detroit, MI: Omnigraphics, Inc., 1996.) This is a comprehensive guide to federal, state, county, and local government offices in the United States. Addresses and telephone numbers provided for every government office.

United States Government Publications Catalog. (Washington, DC: Special Libraries Association, 1988.) This detailed guide contains an alphabetized listing of all serials published by the Federal Government, the publishing agency, information on how to get on the mailing list for the serials, and cost, if any, of each publication.

U.S. Government Publications for School Library Media Centers. (Englewood, CO: Libraries Unlimited, Inc., 1991.) This directory provides a history of government publications; a guide to indexes of government publications; information on ordering government publications; and a listing of government publications, divided into fifty-four subject areas.

Using Government Information Sources. (Phoenix, AZ: Oryx Press, 1994.) This is a basic reference guide to finding United States Government documents and information sources. Government information sources are identified by subject area, government agency of origin, type of statistical data, and special information sources. There is also an introduction on how to undertake a government information search.

UNITED STATES DEPARTMENT OF COMMERCE

While there are many important sources of government information, the Department of Commerce is the single most important source for business and economic data. One division of the Department of Commerce, the Bureau of the Census, is the largest gatherer of statistical information in the country. The original census, first undertaken in 1790, was the Census of Population. Today, the job of the Bureau of the Census has been expanded to include ten different censuses (described below), all of which are of interest to the business researcher. Data from the Bureau of the Census is generally of very high quality, is often very detailed, and is usually available on computer tapes or diskettes in addition to print format. Census data is available in most libraries and can be obtained from the United States Department of Commerce, Bureau of the Census, Room 2428, Federal Building #3, Washington, DC 20233 or by fax at (301) 763-4191.

The *Census of Agriculture* is undertaken every five years in years ending in "2" and "7" (that is, in years such as 1992 and 1997). This census provides detailed data arranged by state and county on the number of farms, farm types, farm acreage, land-use practices, agricultural employment, livestock, crops raised, and the value of farm land and farm output. This census is supplemented by the annual publications *Agricultural Statistics* and the *Commodity Yearbook*.

The *Census of Government* presents information on the general characteristics of state and local governments, including government employment, size of payroll, indebtedness, operating revenue, costs of government operation, and types of programs. This census is undertaken in years ending in "2" and "7."

The *Census of Housing*, which is undertaken in conjunction with the *Census of Population*, is published every ten years (in years ending in "0".) This census includes information on number of dwelling units, type of structure, size, building condition, occupancy, water and sewerage facilities, monthly rent, average value, and household appliances. For large metropolitan areas, statistics are provided by zip code and block areas. In the ten-year interim between censuses, housing data is updated in the yearly *American Housing Survey*.

The *Census of Manufacturers* is undertaken in years ending in "2" and "7." This census categorizes manufacturers by type, using 450 classifications. For each classification, statistics include number of establishments, quantity of output, value added, capital expenditures, employment, wages, value of inventories, sales by type of customer, and water and energy consumption. The *Annual Survey of Manufacturers* provides information for the years between the census publications, while the *Current Industrial Reports* contains monthly information for selected industries.

The *Census of Mineral Industries*, undertaken in years ending in "2" and "7," includes information similar to that found in the *Census of Manufacturers*, broken out by 50 mineral industries. Important information provided includes establishments by type, employment, production, value of shipments, capital expenditures, cost of supplies, payroll, power usage, and water consumption. The *Minerals Yearbook*, published by the Bureau of Mines of the Department of the Interior, provides yearly updates to the census information in a slightly different format.

The *Census of Population* is undertaken every ten years in years ending in "0." This census reports detailed information about the population by geographic areas. Detailed breakdowns are provided by sex, marital status, age, education, race, national origin, family size, employment and unemployment, income, housing, and other socio-economic characteristics. This census is updated by the yearly *Current Population Reports*.

The *Census of Retail Trade* is undertaken every five years in years ending in "2" and "7." This census contains detailed statistics on retail establishments classified by type of business. Statistics presented include number of stores, sales volume, employment, payroll, and value of inventory. The data is presented by region, state, county, SMSA, and city. Updates can be found in a report titled *Monthly Retail Trade*.

The *Census of Service Industries*, undertaken in years ending in "2" and "7," contains information on dollar sales, employment, and number of units, classified by type of business. The information is available by small geographic areas. Current information can be found in the *Monthly Selected Services Receipts* reports.

The *Census of Transportation* is also undertaken in years ending in "2" and "7." Detailed information is reported in three major areas: passenger travel, truck and bus data, and transportation of commodities by class of carrier.

The *Census of Wholesale Trade*, undertaken in years ending in "2" and "7", provides statistics on over 150 types of wholesale business types. Information includes sales, services performed, warehouse space, employment, expenses, and customers. Information is presented by region, state, county, SMSA, and city. Current updates can be found in the report of *Monthly Wholesale Trade*.

In addition to the Bureau of the Census, there are many other divisions of the Department of Commerce that publish information of interest to the business researcher. Selected other reports are presented in the following list. These reports can be found at most libraries or can be obtained by writing to the United States Department of Commerce, Bureau of Economic Analysis, Washington, DC 20230.

The *County and City Data Book* is published every five years and serves as a convenient source of statistics gathered from the various censuses. The data included, divided by city and county, are: population, education, employment, income, housing, banking, manufacturing output, capital expenditures, retail and wholesale trade, mineral output, agricultural activity, and government employment and expenditures.

County Business Patterns is an annual publication, arranged by county, containing statistics on the number of businesses, their type, employment, payroll, inventories, and sales.

The *Federal Statistical Directory* lists the names, addresses, and telephone numbers of key people involved in gathering statistical data for the Department of Commerce. It is a useful means of identifying who in the Federal Government might be of some help in locating specific types of data.

The *Handbook of Statistical Indicators* contains nearly 100 leading indicators designed to serve as barometers of current business activity and forecasters of future business conditions.

Historical Statistics of the United States from Colonial Times to 1970 contains information on the social, economic and political history of the country. Annual historical data on some 12,500 different statistics are presented, providing a rich historical view of change in the United States.

The *State and Metropolitan Area Data Book* contains information on population, housing, government, manufacturing, retail and wholesale trade, services, employment, wages, and selected other topics for each state and the SMSAs within each state.

The *Statistical Abstract of the United States* is published annually. It contains over 1,500 tables summarizing a wide range of economic, demographic, social, and political information taken from various other Federal Government publications. This publication is intended to serve as a convenient reference guide. Sources of more detailed information are provided under each of the tables in the *Statistical Abstract*.

The *Survey of Current Business* is published monthly. This publication includes nearly 3,000 different statistical data series covering such topics as general business indicators, commodity prices, construction and real estate activity, personal consumption expenditures by major product types, foreign transactions, income and employment by industry, transportation and communications activity, and many other topics.

The *U.S. Industrial Outlook* covers recent trends and provides five-year forecasts for over 350 manufacturing, wholesale, retail, and service industries.

The above list provides only a brief overview of the more important publications of the Department of Commerce. For a complete listing of all of the publications of this very important government department, you can write to United States Department of Commerce, Bureau of Economic Analysis, 1401 K Street, NW, Room 705, Washington, DC 20230 or send a fax to (202) 523-7538.

UNITED STATES GOVERNMENT AGENCIES AND DEPARTMENTS

There are far too many government departments and publications to make note of them all. The directories listed earlier in this chapter provide details on additional government sources of information. In this section, important government agencies and departments are identified, the types of information they gather are summarized, and the more important publications of each department are listed. Any government document can be secured by writing to the Superintendent of Documents, U.S. Government Printing Office, Washington, DC 20402. Keep in mind, as well, that all government documents can be found in the Regional Federal Depository Libraries.

Please note that many departments within the Federal Government were undergoing reorganization at the time of publication.

Central Intelligence Agency
Washington, DC 20505

The CIA gathers and reports information on foreign developments, primarily in the business-related areas of economics, science and technology, and politics, as well as such United States Government concerns as congressional affairs, military operations, and relations with foreign governments. Types of public information provided by the CIA can be obtained by calling (703) 351-2053.

Consumer Product Safety Commission
Washington, DC 20207-001

This commission is responsible for identifying and reporting on product defects. Important publications include *A Compilation of Laws Administered by the U.S. Consumer Product Safety Commission, Handbook and Standards for Manufacturing Safer Consumer Products,* and *Meetings of the Consumer Product Safety Commission.*

PLEASE PRINT OR TYPE ALL INFORMATION

ORDER FORM

MAIL TO:

U. S. Government Printing Office
Superintendent of Documents
Mail Stop: SSOP
Washington, DC 20402–9328

Customer's Telephone No.'s

Area Code	Home
Area Code	Office

MASTERCARD/VISA ACCEPTED

Date Customer Order Number

Credit Card No.

Customer's Name and Address

Expiration Date
Month/Year

ZIP

Deposit Account Number

TO PLACE YOUR ORDER BY PHONE CALL OUR ORDER DESK AT 202-783-3238, MONDAY THROUGH FRIDAY, 7:30-4 EASTERN TIME

Stock No.	Quantity	Unit of Issue	List ID	☐ Publication	Title of	☐ Subscription	Unit Price	Total

TOTAL ENCLOSED $

SHIP TO: (If different from above)

ZIP

Unit of Issue	Explanation
EA	Each - single copy
KT	Kit of multiple items in a special container
PD	Pad containing multiple sheets
PK	Package containing multiple copies
SE	Set of multiple items
SU	Subscription

[THIS FORM MAY BE REPRODUCED]

GPO Form 3430
(R 11-91)

PRELIM. 13

224

Department of Agriculture
Chief of Records
Administrative Services Division
14th and Independence Avenues SW
Washington, DC 20250

The Department of Agriculture provides detailed farming data on many topics, including economic analyses and forecasts, rural population information, farm loans, farm improvements, farm safety, value of farming operations, quality of farm output, animal statistics, forestry operations, wilderness preserves, Indian affairs, ecological activities, and agricultural research. Important publications include *Agricultural Economics, Agricultural Outlook, Agricultural Research, Agricultural Statistics, Extension Review, FARMLINE, Foreign Agriculture, Agricultural Insurance, Agricultural Productivity,* and *Research Outlook.*

Department of Defense
Director, Freedom of Information and Security Review
The Pentagon
Room 2C757
Washington, DC 20301

The DOD reports on contracts and contractors for defense work as well as providing information on the Armed Forces, civil defense, military research, and national security. Important publications include *ADP Security Manual, Civil Defense, Defense Indicators, Engineer, How to Do Business with the Defense Supply Agency, Labor Productivity, Planning U.S. Security, Selling to the Military,* and *Subcontracting Possibilities.*

Department of Education
400 Maryland Avenue SW
Washington, DC 20202-0100

The DOE compiles statistics on all facets of public education in the United States. The various offices of the DOE include Accounting and Financial Management Services, Office of Bilingual Education and Minority Language Affairs, Civil Rights Office, Education Research and Improvement, National Center for Education Statistics, Elementary and Secondary Education Office, Grants and Contract Service, Postsecondary Education Office, Higher Education Programs, Special Education and Rehabilitative Services, Special Education Programs, National Institute on Disability and Rehabilitative Research, Rehabilitation Services Administration, and the Office of Vocational and Adult Education.

Department of Energy
1000 Independence Avenue SW
Washington, DC 20585

This department maintains statistics on energy research, technology, resource applications, solar energy, conservation, fuel supplies, fuel imports, energy reserves, domestic energy production, energy usage, data on producing companies, and related statistics. Important publications include *Analysis of Petroleum Company Investments, Energy Information Administration Annual, Energy Information Directory, Energy Insider, Energy Research Abstracts, Materials Management, Monthly Energy Review, Monthly Petroleum Price Report, Monthly Petroleum Statistics Report, Quarterly Energy Report,* and *Statistics of Privately Owned Electric Utilities.*

Department of Health and Human Services
Office of Public Affairs
Hubert H. Humphrey Building
200 Independence Avenue, SW
Room 1187
Washington, DC 20201

HHS contains the Alcohol, Drug and Mental Health Administration, Civil Rights Commission, Family Assistance Office, Food and Drug Administration, Office of the Surgeon General, Health Services Administration, National Center for Health Statistics, Centers for Disease Control and Prevention, Office of Public Affairs, the Social Security Administration, the Office of Policy and External Affairs, Food and Drug Administration, Health Resources and Services Administration, the National Cancer Institutes, National Institutes of Health, and many other important consumer service agencies. Detailed statistics covering all aspects of health, education, foods and drugs, national welfare, and senior citizen information can be obtained from this department. Among many important publications are *American Education, Educational Directory, The Federal Experience, Resources in Education,* and *National Health Statistics.*

Department of Housing and Urban Development
Program Information Center
451 7th Street SW
Washington, DC 20410-1047

HUD provides information on mortgage insurance programs, neighborhood rehabilitation programs, rents, urban preservation programs, urban land development, housing registrations, and land values. Selected publications include *Business Packaging, Customer Relations Training Manual, HUD Newsletter, Guide for Environmental Assessment,* and *Statistical Yearbook of the United States.*

Department of the Interior
Room 5316
Main Interior Building
1849 C Street NW
Washington, DC 20240

This department maintains and provides information on national parks and historic land areas, and it contains the National Parks Service, Fish and Wildlife Service, Bureau of Indian Affairs, and the Bureau of Land Management.

Department of Justice
10th & Constitution Avenues, NW
Washington, DC 20530

This department contains the Office of the Attorney General of the United States, Office of Civil Rights, Bureau of Prisons, Office of the Inspector General, United States Criminal Division, the Federal Bureau of Investigation, Immigration and Naturalization Service, Interpol (US), and the National Institute of Justice.

Department of Labor
200 Constitution Avenue NW
Room S2002
Washington, DC 20210

The DOL publishes data on labor practices, health conditions, employment, pensions, collective bargaining, worker's compensation, job training, unemployment, employment by job categories, wages, unions, economic growth, and other labor-related statistics. Important publications include the *Consumer Price Index, Retail Price Index, Wholesale Price Index, Fuel Price Index, Electric Price Index, Capital Stock Estimates, Consumer Expenditure Studies, Employment and Earnings, Current Wage Developments, Directory of Labor, Directory of National Unions, Federal Contract Compliance Manual, Monthly Labor Review, Federal Labor Laws, Job Openings,* and *Worklife Magazine.*

Department of State
Freedom of Information Staff
2201 C Street NW
Room 1512
Washington, DC 20520

Data gathered and published by the State Department includes foreign aid payments, aid to developing countries, population planning statistics, foreign population statistics, and information on foreign agreements. Popular publications include *Countries of the World, Department of State Bulletin, Official Record of United States Foreign Policy,* and *Update from State.*

Department of Transportation
Office of the Secretary
Freedom of Information Officer
400 7th Street NW
Room 9421
Washington, DC 20590

The DOT compiles statistics on Coast Guard operations, maritime operations, Great Lakes pilotage, ports, commercial vessels, aircraft and airline information, motor vehicle statistics, highway data, mass transit information, and almost anything related to transportation. Important publications include *Aeronautical Information, Basic Flight Information, Air Traffic Control Handbook,* and *Transportation Department Directory.* Publications from DOT are available in many specialized areas of transportation interest.

Department of the Treasury
Public Disclosure Office
15th & Pennsylvania Avenue NW
Washington, DC 20220

This department compiles statistics on banks, trust companies, financial institutions of all types, corporate financing and shareholder data, import and export information, tax data by different categories of business, and information on not-for-profit corporations. This department publishes all tax booklets used by individuals and corportations as well as the *Treasury Bulletin, Statistics of Income, Economic Indicators,* and the *Treasury Department Directory.*

Department of Veterans Affairs
810 Vermont Ave. NW
Washington, DC 20420

The VA compiles statistics on all aspects of veterans affairs and is divided into the offices of Veterans Health Administration, National Cemetary Systems, Academic Affairs, Clinical Programs, and Veterans Benefits, among others.

Environmental Protection Agency Library
401 M Street, SW
Room 1132, West Tower
Washington, DC 20460

The EPA compiles statistics on all environmental interests including information on noise, air, and water, pollution; waste management; and pollutants. It offers many publications on laws, regulations, and areas of concern relating to all areas of the environment.

Equal Employment Opportunity Commission
Office of Communications and Legislative Affairs
1801 L Street NW
Washington, DC 20507

This commission maintains a library that provides industry-by-industry hiring data and related statistics. Information is also available on all issues concerning employment laws and regulations.

Federal Communications Commission
Economic Studies Branch
1919 M Street NW
Room 530
Washington, DC 20554

The agency maintains information on cable television companies, communications licensing, licensing applications, radio and television broadcasting, foreign communications, telephone communications, satellite communications, and financial data on broadcasting companies. Popular publications of this agency are *Actions Alert, FCC Report, Feedback, Political Broadcasting Primer,* and *The Public and Broadcasting.*

Federal Maritime Commission
Office of the Secretary
800 N Captal Street NW
Washington, DC 20573

This agency controls and documents how carriers handle inquiries and complaints, maintains statistics on maritime tariffs and maritime traffic, maintains an inventory of maritime vessels, and compiles selected maritime shipping information.

Federal Trade Commission
Public Reference Branch
6th and Pennsylvania Avenues NW
Room 130
Washington, DC 20580

The FTC regulates trade practices, trade advertising, debt collection, and credit reporting. It compiles various statistics in these areas. Among the many important publications of this commission are *Advertising, Buyers Guide,*

Consumers Guide, Corporate Planning, Drug Product Selection, FTC Decisions, Report on Mergers and Acquisitions, Mass Media, Statutes and Decisions, Quarterly Report for Manufacturing, Mining and Trade Operations, and *What's Going on at the FTC?*

General Services Administration
Director, Office of Information
18th and F Streets NW
Room 6111
Washington, DC 20405

The GSA controls the process of government buying and supplies disbursements. Information is compiled on all government purchasing including strategic materials, government buildings, construction, utilization and disposal of property, and government data processing operations. All government contracting information is available through the GSA. Important publications include *Competitive Bidding for Construction Contracts with the GSA, Government Business Opportunities, Guide to Specifications and Standards of the Federal Government, List of Procurement Commodities, Public Laws, Quality Control System Requirements,* and *Weekly Compilation of Presidential Documents.*

Interstate Commerce Commission
Freedom of Information Officer
12th and Constitution Avenue NW
Room 2215
Washington, DC 20423

The ICC is responsible for the regulation of interstate commerce by railroads, freight forwarders, motor carriers, and water carriers. The commission compiles and provides detailed data on the interstate movement of commodities. Often-requested ICC reports include *Amtrak, The ICC Annual Report, Motor Carrier Regulation,* and *Weekly Review.*

National Aeronautics and Space Administration
Public Information Service Chief
300 E Street SW
Washington, DC 20546

NASA is responsible for administering the space program and compiles and provides information on all space-related activities. This includes space research, construction, testing of space vehicles, and satellite information. Important publications include *Cosmic, NASA Directory, NASA Patents Bibliography, NASA Tech Briefs, Outlook for Space,* and *Scientific and Technical Aerospace Reports.*

National Labor Relations Board
Division of Information
1099 14th Street NW
Room 710
Washington, DC 20570

The NLRB is responsible for monitoring labor activities and handling unfair labor practices, and it compiles statistics and case histories of such activities. Much of the information compiled by the NLRB is published in the *NLRB Annual Report*, which is available to all interested parties by writing to this agency.

National Science Foundation
Freedom of Information Officer
4201 Wilson Boulevard
Arlington, VA 22230

This foundation is responsible for regulating scientific research grants. Grant proposals, grant applications, and grant evaluations are available on request.

Nuclear Regulatory Commission
Washington, DC 20555

The NRC is responsible for licensing all nuclear facilities and materials and for the building and monitoring of nuclear waste sites. Copies of all licenses and applications made to this commission are available upon request. Also available are statistics on nuclear power plants, nuclear exports and imports, and nuclear transportation. Publications available include *Nuclear Regulatory Commission Rules and Regulations, Nuclear Safety,* and *Power Reactor Events*.

Securities and Exchange Commission
Public Reference Section
450 5th Street NW
Washington, DC 20549

The SEC collects and maintains statistics on over 12,000 public corporations in the United States. Elaborate financial information on United States businesses is available from *10K—Annual Report Filings, 10Q—Quarterly Report Filings, 8K—Current Company Developments Filings, 13D—Major Stockholder Status Filings, 14D—Subjects of Tender Offers Filings, List of*

Registered Investment Companies, SEC Decisions and Reports, SEC News Digest, and *SEC Monthly Statistical Review.*

Small Business Administration
Freedom of Information and Privacy Officer
409 3rd Street SW
Washington, DC 20416

The SBA collects and provides information on all aspects of starting, owning, and operating small businesses. Among the many publications are *Analyzing Your Cost of Marketing, Buying and Selling a Business, Choosing a Form of Business Organization, Finding a New Product for Your Company, Human Factors in Small Business, Learning About Your Market, Managing for Profits, Practical Business Use of Government Statistics, Profitable Plant Layout, Small Business Guide to Government, Starting and Managing a Small Business, United States Government Purchasing and Sales Directory,* and *Small Business in the American Economy.* In addition, the SBA conducts many seminars for small business operators.

The United States Information Agency
301 4th Street SW
Washington, DC 20547

The United States Information Agency publishes information on all aspects of broadcasting in the United States and from the United States to foreign countries. Details on broadcast services and broadcast laws can be obtained from this agency.

United States International Trade Commission
500 E Street SW
Washington, DC 20436

This commission is responsible for regulating international trade, ensuring conformance to international trade laws and regulations, monitoring international trade, and compiling detailed statistics on international trade.

The above listing does not include all Federal Government agencies, bureaus, commissions, and departments but only those that might be of most use to the business researcher. A more complete listing can be found in some of the directories identified earlier in this chapter, especially *The Government Directory of Addresses and Telephone Numbers.*

FEDERAL INFORMATION CENTERS

Business researchers interested in government information that is beyond what has been presented here, or interested in finding out if information of personal interest is available from the government, can visit, telephone, or write one of the Federal Information Centers maintained by the General Services Administration. There are over 90 Federal Information Centers located across the United States. A complete listing of the locations and 800 numbers for these centers follows.

ALABAMA
Birmingham, Mobile
(800) 366-2998

ALASKA
Anchorage
(800) 729-8003

ARIZONA
Phoenix
(800) 359-3997

ARKANSAS
Little Rock
(800) 366-2998

CALIFORNIA
Los Angeles, San Diego, San Francisco, Santa Ana
(800) 726-4995
Sacramento only
(916) 973-1695

COLORADO
Colorado Springs, Denver, Pueblo
(800) 359-3997

CONNECTICUT
Hartford, New Haven
(800) 347-1997

FLORIDA
Ft. Lauderdale, Jacksonville, Miami, Orlando, St. Petersburg, Tampa, West Palm Beach
(800) 347-1997

GEORGIA
Atlanta
(800) 347-1997

HAWAII
Honolulu
(800) 733-5996

ILLINOIS
Chicago
(800) 366-2998

INDIANA
Gary
(800) 366-2998
Indianapolis
(800) 347-1997

IOWA
From all points
(800) 735-8004

KANSAS
From all points
(800) 735-8004

KENTUCKY
Louisville
(800) 347-1997

LOUISIANA
New Orleans
(800) 366-2998

MARYLAND
Baltimore
(800) 347-1997

MASSACHUSETTS
Boston
(800) 347-1997

MICHIGAN
Detroit, Grand Rapids
(800) 347-1997

MINNESOTA
Minneapolis
(800) 366-2998

MISSOURI
St. Louis
(800) 366-2998
From elsewhere in Missouri
(800) 735-8004

NEBRASKA
Omaha
(800) 366-2998
From elsewhere in Nebraska
(800) 735-8004

NEW JERSEY
Newark, Trenton
(800) 347-1997

NEW MEXICO
Albuquerque
(800) 359-3997

NEW YORK
Albany, Buffalo, New York,
Rochester, Syracuse
(800) 347-1997

NORTH CAROLINA
Charlotte
(800) 347-1997

OHIO
Akron, Cincinnati, Cleveland,
Columbus, Dayton, Toledo
(800) 347-1997

OKLAHOMA
Oklahoma City, Tulsa
(800) 366-2998

OREGON
Portland
(800) 746-4995

PENNSYLVANIA
Philadelphia, Pittsburgh
(800) 347-1997

RHODE ISLAND
Providence
(800) 347-1997

TENNESSEE
Chattanooga
(800) 347-1997
Memphis, Nashville
(800) 366-1998

TEXAS
Austin, Dallas, Ft. Worth,
Houston, San Antonio
(800) 366-2998

UTAH
Salt Lake City
(800) 359-3997

VIRGINIA
Norfolk, Richmond, Roanoke
(800) 347-1997

WASHINGTON
Seattle, Tacoma
(800) 726-4995

WISCONSIN
Milwaukee
(800) 366-2998

STATE GOVERNMENT INFORMATION SOURCES

In many cases, the business researcher might be interested in publications of various state governments. While a complete listing of state government publications is not possible, as they vary from state to state, there are agencies that can be contacted in each state to determine what type of state government information is available. An alphabetical listing, by state, of agencies and individuals responsible for administering state documents is provided. These sources can be contacted for further information.

ALABAMA
Alabama Department of Archives and History
Archival Services Division, State Publication Section
624 Washington Avenue, Montgomery 36130-0100
(205) 242-4152
FAX: (205) 240-3109
Keeta Kendall (State Publications Librarian)

ALASKA
Alaska State Library
Division of Libraries, Archives and Museums
State Publications Distribution and Data Access Center
P.O. Box 110571,
Juneau 99811-0571
(907) 465-2927
Fax: (907) 465-2665
Patience Frederiksen (Head, Documents Section)

ARIZONA
Arizona State Library
Department of Library, Archives and Public Records
1700 West Washington, Room 200
Phoenix 85007
(602) 542-4035
Louise Muir (State Documents Librarian)

ARKANSAS
Arkansas State Library
Documents Services Section
One Capitol Mall,
Little Rock 72201
(501) 682-2326
Mary Brewer (Documents Coordinator)

CALIFORNIA
California State Library
Government Publications Section
P.O. Box 942837
Sacramento 94237-0001
(916) 654-0261
Thomas Andersen

COLORADO
Colorado State Library
State Publications Library
201 East Colfax Avenue, Room 314
Denver 80203-1740
(303) 866-6728
Fax: (303) 866-6938
Catherine McLaughlin (State Publications Consultant);
James Shubert (Director, Library Services)

CONNECTICUT
Connecticut State Library
Government Information Services
231 Capitol Avenue,
Hartford 06106
(203) 566-4971
Fax: (203) 566-3322
Albert Palko (Library Specialist);
Linda Katzoff-Grodofsky (Librarian)

DELAWARE
Delaware State Library
Bureau of Archives and Records Management
Hall of Records, P.O. Box 1401
Dover 19901
(302) 739-5318
Howard Lowell (State Archivist)

FLORIDA
Florida State Library
Documents Section
R. A. Gray Building
Tallahassee 32399-0250
(904) 487-2651 ext. 136
Lisa Close (Documents Librarian)

GEORGIA
Georgia Department of Education
Division of Library Services
Twin Towers E
205 Butler St., Room 2066
Atlanta 30334
(404) 656-2461
Joellen Ostendorf

HAWAII
Hawaii State Library
Hawaii Documents Center
478 South King Street
Honolulu 96813
(808) 586-3543
Fax: (808) 586-3584
Clarissa Pon Sin (Hawaii
Documents Librarian)

IDAHO
Idaho State Library
325 West State Street
Boise 83702
(208) 334-2150
Stephanie Nichols (Documents
Librarian)

ILLINOIS
Illinois State Library
Illinois Documents Section
300 South 2nd Street
Springfield 62701-1796
(217) 782-4887
Liz Alexander (Illinois Documents
Coordinator)

INDIANA
Indiana State Library

Serials/Documents
140 North Senate Avenue
Indianapolis 46204-2296
(317) 232-3678
Fax: (317) 232-3728
David Lewis (Indiana State
Documents Coordinator)

IOWA
State Library of Iowa
East 12th and Grand Avenues
Des Moines 50319
(515) 281-4102, 6718
Fax: (515) 281-3384
Nancy Lee (State Documents
Depository Librarian)

KANSAS
Kansas State Library
Reference Division
Capitol Building, 343 North
Topeka 66612
(913) 296-3296
Fax: (913) 296-6650
Bill Sowers (State/Local
Documents Librarian)

KENTUCKY
Kentucky Department for Libraries
and Archives
Public Records Division
P.O. Box 537
Frankfort 48602
(502) 875-7000 ext. 207
Fax: (502) 564-5773
Bill Richardson (State Publications
Coordinator)

LOUISIANA
Louisiana State Library
P.O. Box 131
760 Riverside North
Baton Rouge 70821-0131
(504) 342-4929
Fax: (504) 342-3547
Grace Moore (Recorder, State
Documents)

MAINE
Maine State Library
Documents Section
State House, Station 64
Augusta 04333-0064
(207) 289-5600
Elaine Stanley (State Documents
Librarian)

MARYLAND
Enoch Pratt Free Library
State Publications Depository
and Distribution Program
400 Cathedral Street
Baltimore 21201
(410) 396-1234
Kathleen Fay (Program
Administrator)

MASSACHUSETTS
State Library of Massachusetts
Room 341, State House
Boston 02133-1099
(617) 727-6279
Fax: (617) 727-5819
Bette L. Siegel (Documents
Librarian)

MICHIGAN
Michigan State Library
P.O. Box 30007
717 West Allegan
Lansing 48909
(517) 373-1300, 0640
Fax: (517) 373-3381, 8933
F. Anne Diamond (Government
Information Specialist)

MINNESOTA
Minnesota Legislative Reference
Library
645 State Office Building
St. Paul 55155
(612) 296-3398
Fax: (612) 296-9731
Helen Whipple (Head, Technical
Services)

MISSISSIPPI
Mississippi Library Commission
P.O. Box 10700
1221 Ellis Avenue
Jackson 39209
(601) 359-1036
Barbara Smith

MISSOURI
Missouri State Library
P.O. Box 387
620 West Main
Jefferson City 65102-0387
(314) 751-3075
John D. Finley (Head, State
Government Documents)

MONTANA
Montana State Library
Reference and Information Resources
1515 East 6th Avenue
Helena 59620
(406) 444-3004
Fax: (406) 444-5612
Harold L. Chambers (Collection
Management Librarian)

NEBRASKA
Nebraska Library Commission
Nebraska Publications Clearinghouse
The Atrium
1200 N. St., Suite 120
Lincoln 68508-2023
(402) 471-4016
Fax: (402) 471-2083
Karen Lusk (State Documents
Librarian)

NEVADA
Nevada State Library
Captiol Complex
100 Stewart St.
Carson City 89710
(702) 687-5160
Fax: (702) 687-8330
Ann Brinkmeyer (Head, Tech
Services)

NEW HAMPSHIRE
New Hampshire State Library
20 Park Street
Concord 03301
(603) 271-2239
John McCormick (Supervisor
Reference and Information
Services)

NEW JERSEY
New Jersey State Library
CN-520
Trenton 08625
(609) 292-6294
Robert E. Lupp (Supervising
Librarian, New Jersey State
Government Publications)

NEW MEXICO
New Mexico State Library
325 Don Gaspar Avenue,
Santa Fe 87501-2777
(505) 827-3805
Norma McCallan (State
Documents Librarian)

New Mexico State Records Center
and Archives
Rules and Publications Division
404 Montezuma Avenue
Santa Fe 87503
(505) 827-7332
Fax: (505) 827-7331
Vickie J. Ortiz (Management
Analyst)

NEW YORK
New York State Library
Cultural Education Center
Empire State Plaza
Albany 12230
(518) 474-5355
Mary Redmond (Principal
Librarian)

NORTH CAROLINA
North Carolina Department of
Cultural Resources
State Library of North
Carolina, Government and
Business Services Branch
109 East Jones Street
Raleigh 27601-2807
(919) 733-3270
Fax: (919) 733-5679
Cheryl W. McLean (State
Documents Librarian)

NORTH DAKOTA
North Dakota State Library
Liberty Memorial Building
604 East Boulevard
Bismarck 58505-0800
(701) 224-4622
Fax: (701) 224-2040
Susan Pahlmeyer (Head Reference
Librarian); Mark Bowman (Head
Tech Services)

OHIO
State Library of Ohio
Documents Section
65 South Front Street
Columbus 43215
(614) 644-7061
Fax: (614) 466-3584
Clyde W. Hordusky (Documents
Administrator)

OKLAHOMA
Oklahoma Department of
Libraries
Public Services, Wright Building
200 Northeast 18th Street
Oklahoma City 73105
(405) 521-2502
Fax: (405) 525-7804
Vicki Sullivan (Oklahoma Publica-
tions Clearinghouse Librarian)

OREGON
Oregon State Library
State Library Bldg
Salem 97310-0640
(503) 378-4277, ext. 240
Richard Myers (Documents
Librarian)

PENNSYLVANIA
State Library of Pennsylvania
Law/Government Documents
Section
P.O. Box 1601
Harrisburg 17105
(717) 787-3273
Fax: (717) 783-2070
Judith Weinrauch (Reference
Librarian); John Geschwindt
(Government Depository Librarian
Advisor); Eugene Smith (Section
Head); Randall Tenor (Reference
Librarian)

RHODE ISLAND
Rhode Island State Library
300 Richmond St.
Providence 02903-4222
(401) 277-2473

SOUTH CAROLINA
South Carolina State Library
P.O. Box 11469
1500 Senate Street
Columbia 29211
(803) 734-8666
Fax: (803) 734-8676
Mary Bostick (Documents
Librarian)

SOUTH DAKOTA
South Dakota State Library
700 Governors Drive
Pierre 57501-2291
(605) 773-3131

Margaret England (Documents
Librarian)

TENNESSEE
Tennessee State Library and Archives
403 Seventh Avenue North
Nashville 37243-0312
(615) 741-2764
Beverley Banasiewicz (Librarian);
Sandy Mannshen (Librarian)

TEXAS
Texas State Library
Information Services Division
P.O. Box 12927
1201 Brazos
Austin 78711
(512) 463-5455
Fax: (512) 463-5436
Chris Fowler (Coordinator, State
Publications Clearinghouse)

UTAH
Utah State Library
2150 South 300 West, Suite 16
Salt Lake City 84115
(801) 466-5888
Lenn S. Anderson (State Publications Librarian)

VERMONT
Vermont Department of Libraries
Reference and Law Services
109 State Street
Montpelier 05609-0601
(802) 828-3268
Fax: (802) 828-2199
Patricia Klinck (State Librarian)

VIRGINIA
Library of Virginia
Documents Section
11th Street at Capitol Square
Richmond 23219
(804) 786-2175
Gwen Goff (Collections Develop-
ment Manager)

WASHINGTON
Washington State Library
Documents Center
P.O. Box 42464
16th and Water Streets
Olympia 98504-2464
(206) 753-4027
Ann Bregent (Documents
Librarian)

WEST VIRGINIA
West Virginia Library
Commission
1900 Kanawha East
Charleston 25305-0620
(304) 588-2045
Fax: (304) 588-2044
Carol Vandevender (Librarian)

WISCONSIN
Wisconsin Reference and Loan
Library
2109 South Stoughton Road
Madison 53716
(608) 221-6165
Fax: (608) 221-6178
Loretta Harmatuck (Government
Services Librarian); Leonard Tessen
(Reference and Documents
Assistant)

WYOMING
Wyoming State Library
Government Publications
Depository
2301 Capitol Avenue
Cheyenne 82002-0060
(307) 777-6333
Fax: (307) 777-5920
Venice N. Brown Beske
(Documents Librarian)

13

Audiovisual Aids

OBJECTIVES: This chapter outlines the sources and uses of audiovisual material for the business information researcher.

> **The Audiovisual Media**
> **Personal Computers and CD-ROMs**
> **Computer Projection Panels**
> **Video Projectors**
> **Information to Help You Develop and Use Audiovisual Material**
> **Sources of Audio Visual Media**
> **Additional Sources of Material**
> - Economics and Demographics
> - Labor
> - MIS and Computers
> - Management and Human Resources
> - Maps
> - Marketing
> - Advertising
> - Sales
> - Production Management and Operations Research
> - Non-Profit Associations

After reading this chapter you should be able to:

*Gain an appreciation for the many sources of business information to be found in non-print formats.

*Understand the opportunity of supplementing your learning process, training program, sales representation, or other business activity by adding visual aids to your useful sources of information.

*Realize that fewer cataloging aids may be available to assist you in locating audiovisual media but that sources of the information can be logically located through other available cataloging and reference aids.

*Understand that the term "audiovisual" has been expanded recently and that the media now available will be expanded even further in the next few years.

THE AUDIOVISUAL MEDIA

We use the term "audiovisual" in its broadest sense. Earlier editions of this book discussed radio, reel-to-reel audio tape, and records. Now, as the year 2000 is on the horizon, number of audiovisual media has been greatly expanded. Technology continues to provide more opportunity for individuals to diversify every aspect of their lives, and audiovisual has also benefited.

241

In the 1970's the technology-oriented vacationer was proudly using color "slide film." In the 1980's the tech buffs had switched to large video cameras. In the 1990's, high-tech tourists are using smaller palm-sized mini-cams. Satellite dishes that were a curiosity in the early 1980's are now common; and cable, which has only slowly become available to most of us, may soon be augmented by systems with ten times the capacity of today's networks.

This chapter emphasizes sources of information available in different media rather than the media themselves--although the most recent media developments are briefly discussed.

Since some of the items might not be easily found in a library, the listings of sources in this chapter include a phone number, and sometimes an address, for your convenience. These listings are not an endorsement of any of these items, nor are they meant to be exhaustive. Given the rapid rate of technological change, it is a good idea to ask the business librarian if a newer version of the source is available. You can often find additional information by reading the periodicals in your subject field. You can find these periodicals in the library by referring to other chapters of this book.

PERSONAL COMPUTERS AND CD-ROMS

One of the newest audiovisual media is the personal computer equipped with software for word processing and a CD-ROM for creating a multimedia presentation. Only a few years ago 64K personal computers were the standard. Now the WINDOWS(TM) environment suggests a minimum of 4MB RAM. The attachment of CD-ROM sub-systems, complete with stereo sound, to these computer systems is becoming commonplace. (K equals 1000 bytes, MB equals one megabyte or approximately 1,000,000 bytes. Each byte is capable of storing a single letter or digit. RAM refers to random access memory, typically the memory inside the computer where the programs are run. CD-ROM means Compact Disc - Read Only Memory, which means it can be written upon only once but then later read, or retrieved, as often as needed.)

When used for music only, which is the most common use at present, the CD-ROM can be recorded to provide music for over one hour. We refer to these CD-ROM's more simply as a "CD." When the CD-ROM is used with a personal computer we tend to refer to it more formally as a CD-ROM and a large amount of information, such as a complete encyclopedia, may be stored on the disc. Technically speaking, 630 MB of text can be stored on a CD-ROM. When this is compared to the 4MB referred to above with respect to WINDOWS(TM) you can begin to understand the tremendous capacity of the CD-ROM, and, therefore, the interest in this medium. (We can also begin to comprehend the complexity of recording music with this technology, since only about one hour of music utilizes all the storage space on a disk.)

What information is available on CD-ROMs for use with a properly configured personal computer, often referred to as a "Multimedia Computer"? While we can provide an answer to this question today, we know that by the time this book is printed the answer will be different. For most of the other types of information in this book, the passage of time is less crucial with respect to the value of the information presented. Some of the dictionaries described in Chapter 11 will retain their value for 5 to 10 years. In the case of CD-ROM's, a single day may make a difference in the amount and nature of the information available.

The most current source for titles of material available on CD-ROM is, and will likely continue to be, magazines directed to the users of personal computers. The on-line database searching process can also be used to determine currently available CD-ROMs. Here is a short description of some CD-ROMs available today.

DeLorme, P.O. Box 298, Main Street, Freeport, Maine 04032. (207) 865-1234; Fax (207) 865-9291. *Street Atlas USA* and *MapExpert* are produced by DeLorme. These two CD-ROMs contain street maps for all streets in the U.S. Such a description almost sounds impossible to comprehend—but it is true. Each atlas also shows highway numbers, points of interest, and bodies of water. The maps can be imported into another software program, Paintbrush(TM) for printing. *MapExpert* has more functions than *Street Atlas USA*, such as allowing the user to add notes to the map before printing them. Each program works within the WINDOWS(TM) environment.

Gale Research, 835 Penobscot Bldg., Detroit, MI 48226. (800) 877-GALE.

CD-ROMs in Print: An International Guide to CD-ROM, CD-I, CDTV & Electronic Book Products. (Print Volumes). This guide to CD-ROM products claims comprehensive international coverage of some 8,000 titles. Each entry has up to 25 items of information, including many of the following: producer of the database, coverage dates of information/data on CD, frequency of updating, computer hardware requirements (e.g. amount of memory, compatibility of the CD with different types of computers and computer peripherals), description of search software and operating system, print and/or online equivalents, availability from U.S. and non-U.S. distributors, and networking or site license fees and stipulations. Eight indexes include the following options for looking up individual CD products: alphabetical arrangement by the title of the CD product, subject index including such topics as Bibliographies & Indexes, computer tools such as Clip-art, industries from Agriculture & Animal Husbandry to Travel & Tourism, and branches of knowledge such as Biology and Women's Studies, U.S. distributor index, non-U.S. distributor index, database provider index (meaning the entity producing the database), software provider index, publisher index, and a separate Macintosh index. Special features include essays on topics such as the growth of the CD publishing industry and trends in the Japanese segment of the industry.

CD-ROMs in Print (CD-ROM Version). Same information as in above print version, but this database is also searchable by 27 information variables.

New Media Source, 3830 Valley Centre Drive, Suite 2153, San Diego, CA 92130. (800) 344-2621. This company sells CD-ROMs by mail and discounts their prices. A list of titles in various disciplines is available.

Omnigraphics Inc., Penboscot Building, Detroit, MI 48226. (800) 234-1340, Fax (800) 875-1340, distributes *CD-ROM Directory*. Task Force Pro Libra, published annually. Full details on 6,000 CD-ROM and multimedia CD titles and 3,800 companies worldwide. Product listings include: publisher and distributor, subject matter, type, language, geographical and date coverage, online/print sources, content description, price, update frequency, retrieval software, system and network requirements, and ISBN/ISSN numbers. Also available in CD-ROM format.

The Oxford English Dictionary, 2nd ed. This dictionary, available on CD-ROM, contains 615,000 entries, featuring 249,000 etymological listings, 137,000 pronunciation guides, and 2.4 million illustrative quotations. (By comparison, the 2,600 page *Webster's Third International Dictionary* has 450,000 entries.)

Software Toolworks World Atlas MPC. This CD-ROM package includes 240 color maps, 4,400 statistical maps, and a 300-article database of geographical information on topics such as ethnic groups, climate, natural resources, and economics.

Software Toolworks U.S. Atlas. A companion program to the above package, this program contains over 1,000 statistical maps for data on states and counties in the United States.

COMPUTER PROJECTION PANELS

The personal computer screen has evolved from a black-and-white image to full color on even relatively low-cost systems. However, using a 15-inch color monitor for meetings and group presentations in classrooms or offices has some inherent difficulties. Fortunately, technology has offered a solution to this problem.

Computer projection panels allow you to use your computer in a meeting and project the image on your monitor to a large screen. These projection panels are placed on top of an overhead projector and essentially duplicate your monitor output and allow it to be projected, via the light source of the overhead projector, to the screen. You can then operate your computer to bring up additional images and project them in whatever order you choose.

When a presentation/projection system is added to the personal computer and the CD-ROMs are joined with appropriate software, the user can create audiovisuals that can serve a multitude of purposes from teaching, training, or sales to uses limited only by the imagination.

Now, the output of all your software programs can be presented in a group environment without having to first make slides or overhead projection images. You can work in "real time" and respond to "what if" questions from the audience. Imagine the possibilities of redesigning a vehicle as a result of suggestions from focus group members during the actual group session, or responding to a question of increasing the advertising budget and projecting the increase in sales or profit.

Prices for black-and-white computer projection panels are around $1,000, while the color models were in the $4,000 - $5,000 range. As with most devices, there are certain optional extras which can add a few additional hundred dollars to the price.

VIDEO PROJECTORS

Most users of video tapes in business and education still rely on the television screen to show their videos. Large cabinets have been designed to hold the screen and video player and elevate the screen to be seen by the audience. Projectors are now available that can project your video tape to a larger screen for group presentations. These projectors weigh about 20 pounds and can be placed on a table or desk to project the video to a screen. The easiest parallel is to think of a slide projector and how it is used. Now we can project our video tape with (sound of course). Prices are in the $2,800 to $3,500 range.

INFORMATION TO HELP YOU DEVELOP AND USE AUDIOVISUAL MATERIALS

Audiovisual aids often must be prepared for meetings, conferences, and seminars. The following companies and publications can provide valuable help as you develop and use various audiovisual materials. These sources also discuss the educational process, and how learning can be enhanced with audiovisual materials. They should be helpful to trainers in business as well as persons with responsibilities for any other person or group of persons, such as sales managers, department managers, and human resource persons.

Audiovisual Fundamentals: Basic Equipment Operation & Simple Materials Production, by John R. Bullard, Bill Martin and Calvin E. Mether, 4th edition. (Madison, WI: William C. Brown Co., 1989. (319) 588-1451.)

The Best Book of Harvard Graphics, by John Mueller. (Sams, 1991. (800) 428-5331.) This book provides the business professional with a comprehensive tutorial covering the fundamentals of one of the most popular graphics software packages.

Complete Audiovisual Guide for Teachers & Media Specialists, by Jacquelyn Peake and Carol Ann Tarter Petersen. (Englewood Cliffs, NJ: Prentice Hall, 1989.) This is a very basic book and includes a discussion of opaque projectors, overhead projectors, projection screens, overhead transparencies, mounting transparencies, using slides and coordinating them with tapes, cameras and lenses, creating bar graphs and pie charts, film, filmstrips, chalkboards, whiteboards, flip charts, bulletin boards, flannel, Velcro and magnetic boards, posters, pictures, maps, specimens, models, audio tapes, computer graphics, desktop publishing, and all-inclusive graphic systems. Relevant pictures and examples are included.

Desktop Video, by Michael Wells. (White Plains, NY: Knowledge Industry Publications, Inc., 1990. (914) 328-9157.) Learn to use your computer to produce video information programs.

Dynamic Graphics, Inc., 6000 N. Forest Park Drive, Peoria, IL 61614. (800) 255-8800. This company produces art packages for different themes. The prepared art packages are principally black and white line art, special effect photos, and duotones. A catalog is available.

Electronic Learning: From Audiotape to Videodisc, by Jerome Johnston. (Hillsdale, NJ: Lawrence Erlbaum Associates Publishers, 1987.) It includes a discussion of instructional methodology as well as information on the media inferred in the title. The information on the videodisc should be useful to many readers.

Executive Handbook of Business Film and Videotape, by Michael Cook. (Michael Cook, Inc., 200 W. 79th St., New York, NY 10024.) This handbook covers 38 aspects of corporate film production.

How to Produce Your Own Videoconference, by Georgia Mathis. (White Plains: Knowledge Industry Publications, Inc., 1987. (914) 328-9157.) This book includes information on uplinks, downlinks, satellites, production equipment, technicians and other experts, remote locations, and more.

The Instructional Media Library, James L. Lipsitz, ed. (Englewood Cliffs, NJ: Educational Technology Publications Inc, 1981. (201) 871-4007.) This is a sixteen-volume set of books covering everything from books to videodiscs.

Instructional Video, by Stuart DeLuca. (Stonehill, MA: Butterworth-Heinemann, 1991.) This production describes video and audiovisual media, plus it explains how to create instructional video, with an emphasis on equipment and production processes.

Integrating Telecommunications into Education, by Nancy Roberts, et al. (Englewood Cliffs, NJ: Prentice Hall, 1990.) This source describes the nature of telecommunications activities and provides specific examples in banking, shopping, travel, research, and other aspects of business. The book includes a discussion of simulations, electronic mail, bulletin boards, uploading and downloading, commercial database services, databases and national networks, and the inclusion of these in an educational environment. Schools and businesses can benefit from this information.

Libraries Unlimited, Inc., P.O. Box 6633, Englewood, CO 80155. (800) 237-6124. This company publishes five books that discuss audiovisual technology:

> *Audiovisual Technology Primer*, by Albert J. Casciero and Raymond G. Roney (1988). An excellent handbook for the practicing media specialist.
> *Multi-Image Slide/Tape Programs*, by Ron Slawson (1988). A presentation of state-of-the-art production techniques in five short chapters.
> *501 Ways to Use the Overhead Projector*, by Lee Green (1982). A complete guide to producing transparencies and more.
> *Nonprint Production for Students, Teachers, and Media Specialists: A Step-by-Step Guide*, 2nd ed., by James L. Thomas (1988). Many different techniques are covered.
> *Creative Slide/Tape Programs*, by Lee Green (1986). A book for the novice.

The Multimedia Directory, by C. J. O'Brien, ed. (Phillips Publishing Inc, 1993. (301) 340-2100.) This is a directory of interactive video, CD-ROM, CD-I, DVI, video compression software, desktop video, and hardware.

Stock Photo Deskbook, 4th ed., by R. Persky, ed. (New York: The Photographic Arts Center Ltd., 1992. (212) 838-8640.) This is a 320-page book of worldwide sources of stock photographs for publishers, graphic artists, and picture editors.

SOURCES OF AUDIOVISUAL MEDIA

Several indexes of audiovisual materials are described in this section. In addition, details on specific audiovisual items are presented to show the breadth and diversity of such aids. Once you are on the job, you will likely subscribe to magazines in your field and join professional societies related to your career. Check the publications of these societies and pertinent trade journals for advertisements of materials you can use.

You can check special collections or government and corporate libraries for audiovisual material. For example, Detroit Public Library has a special collection, as you might expect, related to the automobile industry. They have a collection of photographs and repair manuals that likely is not duplicated elsewhere. The library of Lawrence Technological University has a special collection of architectural materials and reference books donated by Albert Kahn. These libraries, and others with special collections are a valuable yet little known source of audiovisual materials. Ask your librarian about special collections as part of every library project.

Ambrose Video Publishing, Inc., 381 Park Avenue South, Suite 1601, New York, NY 10016. (800) 526-4663; Fax (212) 685-5486. This company, the exclusive distributor of Time-Life Video, markets a complete collection of training videos, courses, and business documentaries. Topics include stress management; workplace literacy; management skills, including performance appraisal, time management, and communication skills; sales training, including selling skills, negotiation skills, small group presentations, effective writing for sales, and stress management for sales persons; secretarial skills; health videos, including ones on AIDS, smoking, battered wives, drugs, alcoholism, and other topics; entrepreneurial videos; banking subjects; personal finance topics; and additional videodisc training programs targeting reading and writing skills. Write for a catalog with full descriptions and prices.

AV Market Place, (New York: R.R. Bowker, published annually.) This is the most comprehensive directory of audio and video products, manufacturers, services, and suppliers in the United States and Canada. It lists over 1,300 products or services and over 6,900 companies that supply them. The Products, Services & Company Index is organized by audio, audio visual, computer systems, film, video, programming, and miscellaneous. The companies are then further indexed by state to ease your search. A separate Periodicals section lists and describes periodicals in the AV market. There is also a multi-page section of reference books covering all areas of audiovisual activity. It contains information on related associations, state and local film and TV commissions, awards and festivals, and AV-oriented conferences and exhibits. Several references from this source are listed above.

Books on Cassette, Audio Editions®, P.O. Box 6930, Auburn, CA 95604. (800) 231-4261; Fax (916) 888-7805. This company creates and sells audio cassettes in many different subject areas, including business and management. Five pages of their catalog feature business and management titles, including: *Making the Most of your Money*, written and read by Jane Bryant Quinn; *Sam Walton: Made in America*; and similar works.

Bureau of the Census (U.S.) Public Information Office (301) 457-3100; or Data User Services at (301) 457-4100. The Bureau offers many of its reports on computer readable media. Much of the information described in Chapter 12 is available.

Business Currents Index. (Insight Datasystems, Inc., 723 Washington St., Newton, MA 02160. (800) 876-1245.) This is a PC-based database, of 13 leading business magazines (at the time we reviewed their literature). Searching the database is similar to the searching techniques described in our database chapter. Full text is then available via a telephone call. Updated monthly.

The Canadian Film & Video Information & Research Service. (Ottowa, Ontario: Canadian Film Institute, 1985. (613) 232-6727.) This was formerly titled, *Guide to Film, Television & Communication Studies in Canada.*

Dartnell, 4660 Ravenswood Ave., Chicago, IL 60640. (800) 621-5463; Canada (800) 441-7878; Fax (312) 561-3801. Dartnell offers top-quality, highly effective training films and videos on such vital business topics as sales training, motivation, customer service, supervisory and management development, employee relations, human resources, and professional development. A sampling of titles includes: *Do You Have Any Objections?*, *The Human Nature of Quality,* and *Supercharged Selling—The Power to be Your Best.* Some audio cassette programs are also offered. A 46-page catalog is available.

D.E. Visuals, 3595 N.W. 83rd Ave., Sunrise, FL 33351. (800) 736-6438. This company offers 8 slide-tape packages in the areas of marketing, retailing, fashion merchandising, and general business. They also offer nearly 100 video programs on all areas of marketing, retailing, wholesaling, merchandising mathematics, personal selling, advertising, branding, and personal developments. These visual units are packaged with a script, discussion questions, and a quiz. A catalog is available.

Educational Film - Video Locator, by 4th edition, Leigh Carol Yuster, ed. (New Providence, NJ: R. R. Bowker, 1990. (908) 464-6800.) This catalog lists 52,000 videos and films available for rental from the consortium of College & University Media Centers.

Educators Progress Service, Inc., 214 Center St., Randolph, WI 53956. (414) 326-3126. This company publishes several guides yearly covering various audiovisual media, all of which are available for use on a free basis. While the information is designed for educators, it includes many items which could be used by businesspeople and university students in business. Many of the films are made available by firms in particular industries. A special section of each guide covers those titles that are available in Canada. The guides include title, subject, and source indexes. The current guides include:

> *Educators Guide to Free Films*, 54th ed., John C. Diffor and Elaine N. Diffor, eds. (1994). Over 1,800 titles are described and referenced as to source, time and intended audience.
>
> *Educators Guide to Free Filmstrips and Slides*, by 46th ed., John C. Diffor and Elaine N. Diffor, eds. (1994). This guide includes 186 filmstrips, 313 sets of slides, 128 audiotapes and 3 sets of transparencies. Several of the slide sets are of foreign countries (such as Turkey, Finland, or Taiwan).
>
> *Educators Guide to Free Videotapes*, 39th ed., by James L. Berger, ed. This guide lists 2,581 items with 874 being new to this edition. Over 100 of these are classified as "business and economics." The description includes the content of each item, running time, and type of videotape. Items which can be retained permanently are flagged.
>
> *Guide to Free Computer Materials*, 10th ed. Features include comprehensive annotations of each title; indexed by title, subject and source; and includes a glossary of computer technology. Over 2,500 titles of Shareware for various computers are included.

Eva-Tone, 4801 Ulmerton Rd., Clearwater, FL 33520. (813) 577-7000. Eva-Tone produces records on a flexible material that can be mailed or included in a publication as an insert. They are one of the largest independent audiocassette duplicators, sheetfed printers, and automated direct mail facilities in the United States.

Executive Seminars in Sound. (Nation's Business, Executive Seminars Division. (800) 321-4949.) Eight 45-minute audio cassettes deliver practical, proven techniques that you can implement right away, including *How To Get Your Ideas Across, Your Role As a Decision Maker, Better Management of People, How To Live With Your Own Success*, and four others.

Film and Video Catalog. (Michigan State University Instructional Media Center, East Lansing, MI 48826. (517) 353-3960.) The university distributes this catalog on an IBM-compatible floppy disk. The program accompanying the disk allows the end user to search for specific subject areas or keywords. The data may then be printed if desired.

Films for the Humanities & Sciences. (P.O. Box 2053, Princeton, NJ 08543-2053. (800) 257-5126; or (609) 452-1128.) Although it might first appear to offer little to the person interested in business, this source offers a 4-part series, *Made in America*, which looks at American industry, as well as individual titles of *Who's the Enemy, The Automobile Story, Winners and Losers*, and *American Industrial Policy*. Additional titles are related to management skills, office skills, and other work-related themes. A catalog is available.

Going Online for Business Information. (Learned Information, Inc., 143 Old Marlton Pike, Medford, NJ 08055-8707. (609) 654-6266. 1988.) This 20-minute video shows how online searching can provide quick, concise, and up-to-the-minute information in all areas of business and finance. The presentation explains the computer equipment required and gives a sampling of the various types of business information available online. Additional print material is supplied.

InfoPower. (Information USA. (301) 942-6303.) This is a collection of sources of government information, which includes the Federal Government as well as lower levels of government. Many individual items are available free. Both disk and CD-ROM versions are available. They can be searched as a database with software provided with the disks.

Insight Media, 2162 Broadway, New York, NY 10024. (212) 721-6316. This organization sells a wide variety of VHS video tapes on the following topics (among others): women at work, safety, ethics, office procedures, attitude, consumer economics, legal issues and office procedures, job searching, resumes, appearance, computers in the office, desktop publishing, communicating, getting along, listening and body language. Catalog available.

Modern Talking Picture Service, Inc., 5000 Park St. North, St. Petersburg, FL 33709. (813) 541-7571. Modern distributes corporate-sponsored videos, films, and teaching materials on a free-loan basis to educators and community groups. Modern's latest Resource Guide can be obtained by writing to the company.

National Information Center for Educational Media [NICEM], a Division of Access Innovations, Inc., P.O. Box 40130, Albuquerque, NM 87196. (800) 468-3453, (505) 265-3591; Fax (505) 256-1080.

In 1958, the University of Southern California, with a partial grant from the U.S. Office of Education, began to electronically catalog non-print instructional materials included in their master file. The project was named NICEM. The project was expanded, and in 1967 NICEM contracted with McGraw-Hill to publish the first bound NICEM indexes to provide wider, faster, and easier access to the data.

In 1977, NICEM took its place in the technological revolution by going online on DIALOG Information Retrieval Service. In 1984, the NICEM database was purchased from USC by Access Innovations, Inc. Within a year, NICEM became available on CD-ROM, and its computer retrievable versions became known as *A-V Online*.

NICEM restructured its print indexes, refined and enhanced the master file, and now adds 20,000 records per year to the database.

Today, the full NICEM file of 380,000 records is available as *A-V Online* on DIALOG File 46, updated quarterly. A 60,000-unit subset, titled *Training Media Database*, is carried on Executive Telecom's Human Resource Information Network. *A-V Online* is available on CD-ROM from SilverPlatter and in MARC format for cataloging as *NICEM A-V MARC* on BiblioFile CD-ROM from The Library Corporation.

Along with the expansion of its product line, NICEM has continued to grow with the media revolution of the past three decades. Not limited strictly to curriculum materials, NICEM covers a broad spectrum of non-print media useful at every level of education, instruction, training, and research. Librarians, media specialists, curriculum planners, teachers, human resource professionals, and researchers can select from NICEM's listings, which are available from more than 20,000 production and distribution sources.

All subject areas that apply to learning, from preschool through professional, are covered in the database, including vocational and technical education, management and supervisory training, health and safety, history, psychology, fine arts, engineering, literature, and drama. Furthermore, NICEM is rich in non-English language materials, documentaries, avant-garde works, genre titles, self-help, and guidance programs.

Formats cataloged include film, video, videodisc, audio, filmstrip, CD-ROM, and software, as well as slide, transparency, motion cartridge, and record. Print indexes from NICEM (available from Plexus Publishing, Inc. 143 Old Marlton Pike, Medford, NJ 08055-8750; (609) 654-6500, Fax (609) 654-4309):

> *Film & Video Finder*, 4th edition, June 1994. Three volumes, 3700 pages, covering 110,000 films and videos. The most comprehensive reference of educational Audiovisual (AV) materials. Includes information on content, audience level, format, running time, date of release, and the purchase/rental source.
> *Index to AV Producers & Distributors*, 9th edition, June 1994.
> *Audiocassette & CD Finder*, 3rd edition, 1993. 925 pages covering 29,000 audiocassettes. Hardbound guide to educational and literary materials on audiocassettes and CD-ROMs. Includes index and a description of the content, audience level, format, running time, date of release and purchase or rental information.
> *Filmstrip & Slide Set Finder*, 1st edition, June 1990. A three

volume, 3,000 page guide to 35mm educational filmstrips and slide sets.

Online files from NICEM:

A-V Online, DIALOG File 46 Contact: Knight-Ridder Information, 2440 El Camino Real, Mountain View, CA 94040. (800) 334-2564, (415) 254-7000; Fax (415) 254-7070.

Training Media Database, Human Resource Information Network. Contact: Executive Telecom System International, College Park North, 9585 Valparaiso Court, Indianapolis, IN 46268-1130. (800) 421-8884; (317) 872-2045; Fax (317) 872-2059.

CD-ROMs from NICEM:

A-V Online. Contact: SilverPlatter Information, 100 River Ridge Drive, Norwood, MA 02062-5026. (800) 343-0064; (617) 769-2599; Fax (617) 769-8763.

NICEM A-V MARC. Contact: BiblioFile/The Library Corp. Research Park, Inwood, WV 25428-9733. (800) 624-0559; Fax (304) 229-0295.

Additional search services are also available from NICEM. Contact: NICEM (800) 468-3453; (505) 265-3591; Fax (505) 256-1080.

Nation's Business®. (800) 253-6000. This publication is from the U.S. Chamber of Commerce. The Circulation Department of this periodical has many additional business and management audio/visual items for sale. Some titles include: *The Power of Customer Service* (audio or video with a workbook), *How to Get Things Done* (audio or video with a workbook), *Start and Manage Your Business For Success* (VHS only), and *Business Writing* (audio with workbook). They also offer several business aids ready to use on your personal computer. These packages include the software on a disk and a book describing the software. Titles include *Personnel Readyworks, Letterworks, Sales Letterworks,* and *Legal Letterworks.*

1995 International GIS Sourcebook, (GIS World, Inc., Fort Collins, CO. (800) GIS-WRLD.) In recent years a whole new computer industry called GIS (Geographic Information Systems) has developed. GIS uses census and other sources of information to allow the user to identify areas of opportunity for new businesses and many other purposes. This source is a 702-page directory of marketers of GIS hardware and software, with descriptions of their products.

Pyramid Film & Video, Box 1048, Santa Monica, CA 90406. (800) 421-2304. This company distributes sponsored films, sound filmstrips, and videocassettes in many subject areas, including business. A catalog is available.

Tutor/Tape, 107 France St., Toms River, NJ 08753. (800) 256-2396; in NJ (908) 270-4880. Tutor/Tape is a division of Tutor College Services, a nonprofit educational research organization. This organization specializes in audio tapes only. They provide more than fifty programs in a dozen topical areas including marketing, advertising, small business, selling, accounting, business law, economics, and management. The company also produces tapes that are meant to help students, such as *Student's Survival Kit*; *8 Steps to the Dean's List*; and *Spelling*. Some titles are available with slides, filmstrips, transparencies, or workbooks. There are also tapes on topics in science and religion. If you are looking for an audio tape on any topic, we suggest you call for their catalog. In addition, they maintain "a file of ALL tapes ever published."

Videos for Business Training, David J. Weiner, ed. (Detroit: Gale Research Inc., 1990. (800) 877-GALE.) This is a 500-page guide to 16,000 video titles for training purposes. It includes a brief description of the programs, targeted users, available formats, length, producers, and distributors. It also includes addresses and phone numbers for obtaining the videos.

Washington Researchers, Ltd., 2612 P Street, NW., Washington, DC 20007-3062. (202) 333-3533. This firm will do business research for clients. They also sell several video tapes which teach you how to do research, including *How to Find Information About Private Companies, How to Find Information About Foreign Firms, How Competitors Learn your Company's Secrets,* and *How to Get Top Results From Your Business Research Professionals*. Call for a catalog and more titles.

ADDITIONAL SOURCES OF AUDIOVISUAL AIDS LISTED BY BUSINESS AREA

The above references are general and cover many subject areas. The following items are more limited in their use, so they are classified by more specific business topics.

Economics/Demographics

U.S. Data Diskettes. (Chase Econometrics, 150 Monument Rd., Bala Cynwyd, PA 19004. (215) 667-6000.) There are 3 different series of data diskettes: U.S. Consumer Market Diskettes, U.S. Industry Diskettes, and U.S. Economic Diskettes. Classified as a service, the information on these diskettes are updated frequently to maintain the data's currency. This data includes information on retail sales, consumer price indexes, housing activity, monthly producer prices, population statistics, industrial production, leading economic indicators, and many other series of data.

Labor

Films and Videotapes for Labor. (AFL-CIO, Department of Education, [American Federation of Labor and Congress of Industrial Organizations], 815 16th St. N.W., Washington, DC 20006. (202) 637-5153.) This catalog, published by the Film Division, lists a number of films relating to unionism, civil liberties, and political education. It currently contains more than 80 pages and is updated periodically. Anyone teaching or working in a labor environment should consider sending for this catalog.

MIS/Computers

Libraries Unlimited, Inc. P.O. Box 6633, Englewood, CO 80155. (800) 237-6124. Twelve computer instruction videos are available, and more will be announced soon, including ones for WINDOWS(TM). The videos are designed to be used by persons while they are working at their computer. A catalog describing these videos is available.

Career Encounters #4: Information Science. (NICEM, 1989. 28 minutes.) A visit to a state-of-the-art library with an emphasis on information science. It includes explanations of how information is created, stored, and retrieved by information professionals.

PBS Shareware Catalog and Reference Guide. (Public Brand Software, P.O. Box 51315, Indianapolis, IN 46251. (800) 426-3475; (317) 856-4144.) Shareware is a marketing method, not a type of software. With shareware, you try it before you buy it. This catalog contains over 2,000 shareware programs, many of them useful for businesses. There is often little or no cost. PBS also publishes the *Beginner's Resource Guide.*

Management/Human Resources

The Blanchard Trilogy: Values and Vision, by Dr. Ken Blanchard. (Video Publishing House, Inc., 30 minutes. (800) 824-8889.) Dr. Blanchard presents a three-part method for managing for success: exceeding customers' expectations, empowerment of employees, and an emphasis on financial stability.

CRM Films. (800) 421-0833; This company offers many videos related to management and human resources. They have a catalog and also a preview policy for their videos. Some topics and titles include: employee involvement—*Dealing with Conflict, Working with Difficult People*; customer satisfaction—*Now, That's Service, Who Are You, by the Way*; personal effectiveness—*Speaking Effectively, After All, You're the Supervisor*, and *Performance Appraisal.*

Preventing Burnout. (Great Performance. (800) 433-3803.) This video helps people regain a sense of control by showing them how to cope with, and insulate themselves from, on-the-job stress. Features information on how to set limits, develop detached concern, and turn energy sappers into energy refreshers.

The Story Behind the Space Shuttle Challenger Disaster, by J. Marcus (Mark) Maier. (SUNY-Binghamton, NY. (607) 777-6723.) The commission investigating the Challenger tragedy found that the decision-making process which contributed to the fatal launch was "seriously flawed." Maier utilizes this Commission and its findings in this compelling three-part, affordable video program and instructional module appropriate for courses on organizational behavior, management, ethics, organizational culture, power and politics, science engineering or society and technology.

Stress Management Video. (Great Performance. (800) 433-3803.) This video uses a three-step process to help people recognize and cope with stress as well as change life's stressors, instead of being consumed by them.

Time Management Video. (Great Performance. (800) 433-3803.) This video tailors time management to personality type. People learn to identify their time type, how to set personal goals, and what they can do to improve their time habits.

Trial By Fire: The Ross Perot Story and *America Under Fire.* (Video Publishing House, 34 minutes; 31 minutes. (800) 824-8889.) These two videos tell the story of Ross Perot and his candid personal assessment of the crisis in leadership in America today. These videos were made before the election of November, 1992.

World Class Quality: The Customer Will Decide, by Tom Peters. (Video Publishing House, 72 minutes. (800) 824-8889.) Peters travels to Germany and interviews several persons at small- to mid-size companies, who tell him to focus on the product, because when benefits for the customer are maximized, profits will inevitably follow.

Maps

See the discussion of CD-ROMs above.

Commercial Atlas & Marketing Guide. (Skokie, IL: Rand McNally; published annually.) Includes U.S. maps of retail sales, manufacturing and population, population and sales data for all zip codes, population and income data by county, by Metropolitan Statistical Area, and Basic Trading Area. It also includes full-color maps of every state in the country, plus much more information, and suggestions for the use of the data.

Intelligent Charting, Inc., 600 International Drive, Mount Olive, NJ 07828. (800) 321-7002; (201) 691-7000. This company makes custom maps. Data for the maps can be supplied by this company or the client, and typical map characteristics can be specified by the buyer. Map sizes vary from 8½ x 11 to 36 x 48. Maps can be printed on different paper stock or transparency film.

MarketMap, Rand McNally Business Reference Products (BRP), P.O. Box 7600, Chicago, IL 60680. (800) 332-RAND; in Illinois (312) 673-9100. Maps in color or black-and-white of U.S. cities, counties, and states, as well as also certain Canadian maps. Map sizes vary from 24x28 to 30x38 and can be mounted or framed.

PC Globe and *PC USA*. These two software programs allow you to print maps providing specific related information, including economics, politics, chief languages, population demographics, travel and tourist information, and even mean temperatures for both international locations and U.S. cities and states. These programs are generally available at your local computer software retailer.

ZIP Code Atlas and Market Planner. (Skokie, IL: Rand McNally.) This is a looseleaf collection of 11" x 15½" full-color maps of all 50 states. Five-digit zip code area boundaries are printed in black on transparent overlays. Many other features and data are included to help in the analysis of business problems and opportunities.

Marketing

Doing Business in Asia. (P.O. Box 68618, Indianapolis, IN 46268-2555. (800) 526-8926; (317) 297-6142.) This is an integrated series of four video programs (each 60 minutes) covering Taiwan, Japan, Korea, and Hong Kong. Each is supplemented with discussion guides (24 pages). The tapes present the views and opinions of several business persons and others with knowledge of the particular area. The videos are available to rent or purchase.

Professional Displays, Inc. (800) 222-6838; (416) 291-2932. This is a source of displays for trade shows or other presentations. A brochure is available.

RMI Media Productions, Inc. 2807 West 47th St., Shawnee Mission, KS 66205. (800) 745-5480. This company offers a wide variety of VHS and U-Matic tapes covering all aspects of marketing, sales, retailing, wholesaling, channels of distribution, logistics, public relations, pricing, telemarketing, and more. A catalog is available.

257

Advertising

The Ad and the Id: Sex, Death, and Subliminal Advertising, by Bernard McGrane, Ph.D. (University of California Extension Center for Media & Independent Learning, 1992. (510) 642-0460.)

This eye-opening video shows how advertisements, which are often artistically and psychologically brilliant, employ powerful subliminal images to influence and motivate consumers to buy.

The Best TV and Radio Commercials, (Advertising Age Marketing Dept., 220 East 42nd St., New York, NY 10017. (212) 210-0283. Published annually.) Two separate tapes, one video and one audio, of those commercials felt to be the best of a given year.

Mastering the Media, (Advertising Age, 220 East 42nd St., New York, NY 10017.) This series includes individual tapes on the different media available including magazines, yellow pages, outdoor, television, direct mail, newspaper, radio, and other alternative media. A workbook is also available.

Sales

See also Ambrose Videos above.

38 Proven Ways To Close That Sale. (Nation's Business, 87 minutes. (800) 253-6000.) A VHS tape to help you read prospects, overcome objections, and close the sale. It is applicable to retail sales, industrial sales, business-to-business selling, and other types of sales situations.

Breakthrough Selling. (Great Performance. (800) 433-3803.) These eight audio tapes teach important selling skills, including: prospecting, referral selling in the world of capital goods and services, solving complaints, sales presentations and closing, self-motivation, and time management. Additional reminder cards are included.

Contact Plus Professional®. (Contact Plus Corporation, 1992. (800) 366-9876.) DOS-based contact management software. It fully supports WordPerfect®.

Getting Through to Buyers...While Others Are Screened Out, by Art Sobczak. (Business By Phone, Inc. (402) 895-9399.) A video to train persons in telephone selling techniques. It includes information on planning the call as well as making the call. Additional information is included in a 17-page workbook.

Prosell: Contact Management Software. (Sales Management Systems. (800) 444-9945; (206) 391-0710.) DOS-based computer software to assist in managing the information flow related to the selling function, including sales

call reports, contact notes history, expense tracking and reports, lead tracking, sales management reports, appointment calendar/scheduler, plus additional features, including telemarketing support.

Sell Well—Because Healthy Salespeople Sell More. (Great Performance. (800)
433-3803.) These 4 audio tapes and three personal action guidebooks help
you to achieve success by showing you how to increase your stamina, how
to turn stress into success, which foods to eat for high-performance, and why
better health results in better sales.

Success Strategies For Unlimited Selling Power, by Donald J. Moine, Ph.D.
and Kenneth Lloyd. (Nightingale-Conant. (800) 323-3938.) These 12
audiocassettes teach the process of selling by teaching you to tune in on your
prospects' and customers' nonverbal cues and then lead the sales call to its
successful conclusion. Some topics include: *The Proven Tools of Mesmeriz-
ing Selling, The Psychology of Trust and Rapport, Success with Story Tell-
ing,* and *Scripting Your Word Magic.* A workbook is included.

Successful Closing Techniques. (Dartnell. (800) 621-5463.) This is a 4-page
bulletin program that is sold on a subscription basis. Every two weeks a new
bulletin is sent to you for each of your salespeople. Each bulletin contains
a "how to" sales message describing a particular closing technique.

Tom Hopkins International, Inc., P.O. Box 1969, Scottsdale, AZ 85252.
(800) 528-0446; in Arizona, (602) 949-0786; Fax (602) 949-1590. 15 audio
albums and eight video programs are available to assist sales people in
developing their sales ability. A free 24-page catalog of sales training aids
is available.

Production Management/Operations Research

Manufacturing Insights®, Case Study Videos. (Society of Manufacturing
Engineers. One SME Drive, P.O. Box 930, Dearborn, MI 48121-0930. (800)
733-4763.) This is a series of 46 videos covering the latest technological advances. Each program shows state-of-the-art manufacturing systems and processes in action. The case studies bring you inside the plant, where you will
see what other companies are doing to improve their operations. Some titles
include: *Total Quality Management, Total Productive Maintenance,
CAD/CAM, Personal Computers in Manufacturing, Flexible Small Lot Production for Just-In-Time, Lasers in Manufacturing, Composites in Manufacturing,* and many more. A catalog is available.

Just-in-Time Production Video Course, by Richard J. Schonberger. (APICS,
1986. (800) 444-2742; (703) 237-8344.) One of the most comprehensive overviews available on Just-in-Time (JIT) production, Schonberger's video
training program demonstrates to professionals how to use the JIT system

for reducing inventory levels, streamlining production, reducing costs, and improving quality. The eight-part program demonstrates how lower inventory levels lead to better forecasting and scheduling abilities as well as faster feedback on defects and their causes. Additional materials include a text, workbook, and transparencies.

Videoplus JIT Course, by David W. Baker, Inc. & Associates. (APICS, 1989. (800) 444-2742; (703) 237-8344.) This course addresses the complete spectrum of JIT issues in twelve units: an overview, technology management, people management, systems management, a simulation exercise, setup reduction, total quality focus, supplier partnerships, total employee involvement, performance measurements, transition from MRP to JIT, and steps to implementation. Additional materials include a workbook, leader guide, and support services.

Videoplus MRP II Course, by David W. Baker, Inc. & Associates. (APICS, 1989. (800) 444-2742; (703) 237-8344.) A learning tool for companies involved in MRP II. The course covers the key MRP II issues in twelve units; an overview, top management planning, master scheduling, material planning, capacity planning, bills of material, inventory status, routings, purchasing, shop floor control, performance measurement, and steps to success. Additional materials include a workbook, leader guide, and support services.

Videoplus Solution Series, by David W. Baker, Inc. & Associates. (APICS, 1989. (800) 444-2742; (703) 237-8344.) This series provides 20 hours of learning time in each of several distinct subject areas: manufacturing cycle time reduction, employee work teams, lot size reduction, total quality management, setup reduction, data base integrity, performance measurements, getting started in JIT or MRP, improving manufacturing flow, the planning and scheduling process, laying the foundation for world-class performance, total quality basics, and problem solving techniques. The videos are available individually.

Non-Profit Associations

American Society of Association Executives (ASAE), 1575 Eye Street, NW, Washington, DC 20005. (202) 626-2748. This Society has several audio tapes, video tapes, and books designed to increase the effectiveness of managers of non-profit associations.

14

International Sources

OBJECTIVES: This chapter will expose you to international business information sources. This includes material published in other countries, but focuses primarily on sources published in the U.S. that cover most other countries.

> **Introduction**
> **International Information Sources**
> - Handbooks and Almanacs
> - Yearbooks and Encyclopedias
> - Directories
> - Dictionaries
> - Indexes

After reading this chapter you should be able to:

*Understand the basic facts regarding the international business network.
*Locate facts, figures, and other information resources worldwide.

INTRODUCTION

In recent years we have witnessed the creation of more and more business information with an international flavor. Reflecting actual changes in the business community worldwide, business information publishers are discovering new markets and interests in business information around the globe. This book is no exception in recognizing the importance of this information to your research. This chapter will lead you through many of the leading handbooks, directories, guides and indexes that are available to you for conducting research in the international business community. Most of the publications covered are printed in the English language. Countries or areas of the world that are emphasized are: Canada, Mexico, Europe, and the Pacific Rim.

INTERNATIONAL INFORMATION SOURCES

Handbooks and Almanacs

Asia-Pacific Securities Handbook, 2nd ed. (Hong Kong: Phillip Jay Publishing, Ltd., 1994.) A comprehensive guide to Asia-Pacific securities markets. Presented are analyses of the newer markets and a feature on tax implications of trading in this region. Market overviews are provided for the following countries: Australia, Bangladesh, China, Hong Kong, India, Indonesia, Japan, Malaysia, Nepal, New Zealand, Pakistan, Philippines, Singapore, South Korea, Sri Lanka, Taiwan, and Thailand.

Caribbean Economic Handbook, 2nd ed. (Detroit: Gale Research, 1995.) Economic details are given for each major island. Smaller islands are also covered. Statistics, trends, and future outlooks are provided.

Chisholm's Handbook of Commercial Geography, 20th ed. (Essex, England: Longman Group, Ltd., 1980.) This volume deals with factors relating to the production, distribution, and exchange of commodities throughout the world. In addition, it deals with commodity transportation, agricultural products, timber, and furs of many countries ranging from temperate to tropical climates. The first edition was published in 1889.

Cracking Latin America: A Country by Country Guide to Doing Business in the World's Newest Emerging Markets. (Chicago: Probus Publishing Co. Inc., 1993.) A comprehensive guide that provides valuable information to the novice foreign trader. Useful for listings of distribution channels, import/ export contacts, etiquette, and profiles of finance and politics. Includes coverage of Central and South America.

East European Economic Handbook, 2nd ed. (Detroit: Gale Research, 1995.) Separate chapters on each of the seven countries covered give such economic details as industrial output, economic planning, etc. The countries covered include Bulgaria, Czechoslovakia, Germany, Hungary, Poland, Romania, and the former Yugoslavia.

European Marketing Data and Statistics. (Detroit: Gale Research, 1994.) An invaluable collection of statistics pertaining to the marketing of major commodity products such as washing machines, automobiles, etc. Coverage includes most European countries.

German Trade Fairs: A Handbook for American Exhibitors and Exporters. (Washington, D.C.: International Trade Administration, U.S. Department of Commerce, 1986.) Includes a listing of over 90 major business fairs in Germany.

Handbook of International Business. (New York: John Wiley & Sons, Inc., 1988.) This book explains the impact on international business of international financial flows, balance of payments, currency exchange rates, government subsidies, trade barriers, and other factors.

Handbook of International Business and Management. (Cambridge, MA: Basil Blackwell, 1990.) This handbook provides an overview of managing businesses engaged in international trade.

Handbook of International Management, Ingo Walter and Tracy Murray, eds. (John Wiley & Sons, Inc.: New York, 1988.) Covered in this handbook are the economic, legal, and political aspects of managing international businesses.

Handbook of Joint Venturing, by John D. Carter. (Burr Ridge, IL: Irwin Professional Publishing, 1988.) After exploring joint venturing in general, the handbook examines joint ventures in health care, construction, real estate, telecommunications, information technology, banking and financial services, retailing, and natural resources.

Handbook on Financing U.S. Exports, 4th ed. (Washington, D.C.: Machinery and Allied Products Institute, 1984.) Covers the Export-Import bank (EXIMBANK), financing foreign trade, trade laws, foreign loans, private funding, export credit, the use of commercial banks for export loans, export insurance, and EXIMBANK programs and services.

International Handbook of Production and Operations Management, by Ray Wild. (Falls Church, VA: APICS, 1990.) This source covers recent developments in production and operations management, current practices, and proposals for future improvements, including examples from businesses around the world.

International Management Handbook, by John V. Terry. (Fayetteville, AK: University of Arkansas Press, 1992.) An eclectic volume that features chapters covering management perspectives on Western Europe, the Middle East, the Commonwealth of Independent States, China, and Pacific Rim countries. Good source for brief biographical sketches of international management theorists as well as extensive listings for central banks, stock exchanges and travel information.

International Marketing Data and Statistics. (Detroit: Gale Research, 1994.) This data handbook provides information similar to its European counterpart, but coverage is restricted to Asia, Africa, the Americas, and Oceania.

Pacific Rim Almanac, by Alexander Besher. (New York: HarperPerennial, 1991.) An invaluable almanac which provides detailed chapters on marketing, trade, finance, society, customs, ecology, infrastructure, and a prognosis for the future. Also important are the 10 appendices which cover statistics, investments, companies, trade groups and information networks.

U.S.-Eastern European Trade Sourcebook, William S. Loiry, ed. (Chicago: St. James Press, 1991.) Listings of both U.S. and East European trade contacts are provided. Included are attorneys, consultants, financing sources, and government agencies. Names, addresses, telephone or telex numbers, and descriptions of services are provided.

World's Emerging Stock Markets: Structure, Development, Regulations and Opportunities, Keith K. Park and Antoine W. Van Agtmael, eds. (Chicago: Probus Publishing Co. Inc., 1993.) This title is a good place to obtain overviews of stock exchanges in Asia, Latin America, Europe, and the Middle

East; over 18 countries are featured in detail. Also highlighted are the top companies within each market.

Yearbooks and Encyclopedias

Containerization International Yearbook. (London: National Magazine House, published annually.) This source provides data on world container ports and terminals, large container ships, container equipment, container leasing companies, container repair companies, ship brokers, and container shipping insurance companies.

Countries of the World and Their Leaders Yearbook. (Detroit: Gale Research, published annually). This reference provides information on all countries in the world. Included are lists of government leaders and diplomats, U.S. embassies and consulates with personnel, and detailed descriptions of each country's economy, history, language, and culture. Also included are world health conditions, visa requirements, custom regulations, maps, and detailed statistics.

Encyclopedia of Associations—International Organizations. (Detroit: Gale Research, published annually.) Lists approximately 2,000 non-profit associations worldwide. Information on each organization includes contact person, activities, purposes, publications, meetings, and geographic coverage.

Information Industry Directory. (Detroit: Gale Research, published annually.) This two-volume set is a comprehensive international guide to over 5,000 information services in 65 countries. Entries include software and hard copy data services.

The Europa World Yearbook. (Detroit: Gale Research, published annually.) This publication is a clear favorite for obtaining descriptive and statistical information on any country in the world. Each entry includes the sections: Location, Language, Climate, Religion, Flag, Capital, Recent History, Defense, Economic Affairs, Social Welfare, Public Holidays, and Weights and Measures. The statistical section covers: Area and Population, including Employment, Births, Marriages, and Deaths. Statistical tables also detail the performance of the country's economy including: Agriculture, Forestry, Fishing, Mining, and Industry. Valuable economic data can also be found for Finance, State Budget, Balance of Payments, External Trade and Principal Trading Partners. Data for Transport, Tourism, Communications Media, and Education complete the statistical analysis. In addition to this comprehensive array of statistics, each entry also provides a synopsis of the country's Constitution and current information on the government including Head of State, Council of Ministers, Ministries, Legislature, Political Organizations, Judicial System, and Diplomatic Representation. The presentation goes on to further outline the country's Religion, Press (including information on key newspapers and periodicals). Banks, Insurance Companies, Chamber of Commerce Offices, Foreign Trade Companies, and Trade Unions are typically listed by name, and include addresses, phone numbers, and descriptions of business activities.

It is also worth noting that detailed coverage is provided for international organizations, including the United Nations, Regional Commissions, Other Bodies, Specialized Agencies, and Other International Organizations. Names, addresses, and telephone numbers, along with an in-depth analysis of mission and performance are provided where applicable.

Exporter's Encyclopedia, Joseph Douress, ed. (Parsippany, NJ: Dun & Bradstreet Information Services, published annually.) This encyclopedia is a comprehensive world marketing reference guide divided into sections covering market information for specific countries, firms specializing in international business, laws and legislation, international trade associations, government agencies, shipping practices, and reference data on weights and measures of overseas ports. The guide covers over 180 countries.

International Encyclopedia of Population, John A. Ross, ed. (New York: Columbia University Press, 1982.) Over 135 articles are presented, covering populations in different countries of the world. Each report includes population demographics, composition, growth rates, fertility, marriage and divorce statistics, mortality rates, internal migration, urbanization, the labor force, ecology, and resources.

International Encyclopedia of the Social Sciences. (New York: Free Press, 1977.) This encyclopedia informs readers of the progress made in the various fields of the social sciences as well as providing factual information in the areas of politics, economics, history, jurisprudence, anthropology, penology, sociology, ethics, philosophy, and psychology.

International Financial Statistics Yearbook. (Washington, D.C.: International Monetary Fund, published annually.) This extremely important publication is the first source to consult for statistics on international monetary reserves, monetary aggregates, interest rates by leading world economies, exchange rates, commodity prices around the world, national accounts, international banking, balance of payments by leading economies, and country financial tables.

International Petroleum Encyclopedia. (Tulsa: PennWell Books.) This is a country-by-country review, with maps, of the oil industry. It lists active oil and gas fields and gives directory information on oil companies and government agencies, a census of tankers, and other industry statistics.

International Trade Statistics. (Geneva: General Agreement on Tariffs and Trade, published annually.) An important overview of statistics on merchandise trade by region and by product. All value figures are expressed in United States dollars.

International Yearbook of Trade Statistics. (New York: United Nations, published annually.) Provides basic economic data for individual countries, trade statistics, currency values, commodity prices, balance of trade data, and trade by country.

The Statesman's Yearbook, Brian Hunter, ed. (New York: MacMillan Publishing Co., published annually.) This publication provides statistical and historical references for the governments of the world. Each edition includes up-to-date political, economic, and social data.

Statistical Abstract of Latin America, James W. Wilkie, ed. (Los Angeles: UCLA Latin American Center Publications, University of California, published annually.) Excellent yearbook furnishing country-by-country analysis of foreign trade, financial flows, and national accounts. Also useful for demographic and infrastructure statistics.

Statistical Yearbook. (New York: United Nations, 1993.) This yearbook is a leading source for locating economic and demographic statistical data on over 270 countries.

World Currency Yearbook. (Brooklyn, NY: International Currency Analysis, Inc., published annually.) Formerly titled *Pick's Currency Yearbook*, this one-of-a-kind publication has been updated annually since 1955. Information provided includes monetary legislation, currency values, transfer regulations, and clearing and compensation agreements. It also includes important unofficial data on market and currency developments and values.

World Facts and Figures. (New York: John Wiley & Sons, published annually.) Provides current data on 222 countries. This annual is divided into 6 sections, including physical characteristics of countries, land areas, city data, cultural features, population, and publications.

World Insurance Yearbook. (London: Financial Times, published annually.) This yearbook provides an overview of the world insurance industry. Covered are 30 national markets, including outlines of general socioeconomic and risk background in 40 additional countries. Also included are legal and regulatory conditions.

Yearbook of International Organizations. (New York: K.G. Saur, Inc., published annually.) Lists over 20,000 international organizations, ranging from international committees to universal and regional intergovernmental organizations to national groups concerned with international issues.

Yearbook of the United Nations. (Norwell, MA: Kluwer Academic Publishers, published annually.) This yearbook is the main reference source of the United Nations. It provides topical accounts of U. N. decisions, data on subjects such as drug control, disaster relief, human rights, trade and industrial development, and aid to refugees and children. Also included are data on terrorism, hostage taking, and international legal actions.

Directories

There are many directories available for identifying and researching foreign and international companies and individuals. Following are representative directories that are considered the most useful for everyday needs and the most likely to be found in your library:

America's Corporate Families and International Affiliates. (Bethlehem, PA: Dun & Bradstreet Information Services, published annually.) This is a key directory for tracking U.S. companies and their foreign operations. Arrangement is alphabetical by country and by company within each country. Entries include name, address, sales information, contacts, and business description. Indexing includes SIC, geographic, and company name.

American Export Register. (New York: Thomas International Publishing Co., published annually.) This is a directory of American manufacturers who offer products for sale overseas. It provides a reference for international buyers seeking American goods. Lists over 38,000 manufacturers, with addresses, telephone, fax and telex numbers, and overseas markets. The directory covers three thousand product categories. It is indexed alphabetically in English, French, German, Japanese, and Spanish. Some features are: lists of U.S. Chamber of Commerce offices, U.S. Foreign Service posts, and banks engaged in world trade.

Anglo-American Trade Directory, 1993. (London: American Chamber of Commerce.) This directory covers approximately 13,000 British and American businesses interested in exporting and foreign investment. The listings are by name, address, phone number, cable address, chief executive or contact, trading interests, name of distributor, subsidiary, and agent or other connection.

Blue Book of Canadian Business. (Toronto: Canadian Newspaper Services International, published annually.) A key source for Canadian business information. This directory provides profiles of leading Canadian companies, rankings of major Canadian companies, and indexing of companies. Inclusion is based on a company having revenues of $10 million or more or assets of $5 million or more. The profile section is unsurpassed for its descriptions of leading companies and is more detailed than most standard directories.

In addition to names and addresses, the book also contains histories, management philosophy, and other company involvements.

Brazil Company Handbook. (Rio de Janeiro: IMF Editoria, 1993.) Arranged by major industries, this handbook provides public company information including background, officers, major stockholders, sales, markets, balance sheet ratios, and other stock information. Also includes information on the economy, investments and stock exchanges.

Canadian Company Handbook. (Toronto: Globe and Mail Publishing, published annually.) Use this directory for current information on all Toronto Stock Exchange 300 companies, former 300 companies and other public companies. Arrangement is alphabetical within major industry groupings and entries include stock symbol, ratios, synopsis, charting, and rankings.

Canadian Key Business Directory. (Mississauga, Ontario: Dun & Bradstreet Canada, Ltd., published annually.) Published yearly since 1975, this directory is very useful for broad numbers of company listings. Over 20,000 Canadian companies are featured, with each entry providing name, address, key officers, telephone numbers, and brief information on products or services.

Canadian Trade Index. (Bristol, PA: International Publications Service, published annually.) A standard directory of over 14,500 Canadian companies listing brief directory information. Includes names, addresses, telephone or telex numbers, and contacts.

Directory of American Firms Operating in Foreign Countries. (New York: World Trade Academy Press, 1991.) This directory provides detailed information on over 2,600 companies with over 19,000 plants operating outside the U.S.

Directory of Foreign Firms Operating in the United States. (New York: World Trade Academy Press, 1992.) This directory verifies links between foreign companies and their American counterparts. Covers approximately 1,600 foreign firms that have substantial investments in the U.S. Listings are by country or by name of the company.

Directory of Foreign Manufacturers in the United States, Jeffrey S. Arpan and David A. Ricks, eds. (Atlanta: Georgia State University, 1993.) Provides useful information on foreign companies operating in the U.S. This directory focuses on manufacturing and allows you to search by state, industry, and name of company.

Directory of Multinationals, John Stopford, ed. (New York: Stockton Press, 1992.) Covers 450 multinational companies with assets in excess of $1 billion. Complete financial details are presented in this two-volume set.

East-West Business Directory. (West Nyack, NY: Todd Publications, 1992.) Complete operating details are provided for 825 companies that have capital participation from countries in East Europe, in the former Soviet Union, and former Yugoslavia.

Eastern European Business Directory. Frank X. Didik, ed. (Detroit: Gale Research, 1992.) Profiles over 7,000 companies and organizations in Bulgaria, Czechoslovakia, Hungary, Poland, Romania, the former East Germany, and the Commonwealth of Independent States.

Economic World Directory of Japanese Companies in the U.S.A. (New York: Economic Salan, Ltd., 1986.) The names, addresses, telephone numbers, products, top managers, revenue, and other financial data are provided for over 850 U.S. companies with Japanese ownership.

European Directory of Business Information Libraries. (London: Euromonitor, 1990.) A unique listing of over 500 key European business library collections located in 17 Western European countries that belong to the European Economic Community. Entries include name, address, telephone or telex numbers, availability, description of collections, services, and publications.

European Wholesalers and Distributors Directory. Linda Irvin, ed. (Detroit: Gale Research, 1992.) Provides company names, addresses, telephone numbers, revenues, management personnel, year founded, products carried, and geographic area covered for over 5,000 wholesalers and distributors operating in Europe.

Global Company Handbook. (Princeton, NJ: Center for International Financial Analysis & Research, 1993.) This CIFAR directory set is one of a very limited number of directories to provide abbreviated financial statements and key business ratios for companies covered. In all, over 7,500 companies in over 48 countries are profiled. The directory also features rankings of companies, industry ratios for comparing specific company performance and analysis of accounting standards in all countries covered.

Hong Kong Trade Directory. (Clearwater, FL: Selective Books, Inc., 1987.) Names, addresses, telephone and fax numbers, products, and other details are provided for approximately 300 manufacturers in Hong Kong.

Hoover's Handbook of World Business 1995-1996, Gary Hoover, ed. (Austin, TX: Reference Press Inc.) This publication provides complete financial and operating details on over 165 companies around the world that dominate the industries in which they operate.

International Directory of Company Histories. (Chicago: St. James Press, 1993.) This nine-volume set briefly describes most of the major companies in the world. Entries include company logo, legal name, date of incorporation, number of employees, sales, stock exchanges, ownership, and concise history of development.

International Directory of Corporate Affiliations. (Wilmette, IL: National Register Publishing, published annually.) One of the leading directories for determining who owns what worldwide. By looking up the name of the company in the master index you can find what the relationship is to its parent company, subsidiaries, divisions, or plants. Information includes sales or revenues when available, names, addresses, telephone numbers, and products or services.

International Directory of Market Research Organizations. (Atlanta, GA: MacFarlane & Co., published biennially.) Information is provided on over 1,700 market research companies operating in 75 countries.

International Directory of Marketing Research Companies and Services. (New York: American Marketing Association, published annually.) Also known as the *Green Book*, this directory is the best source to use to identify marketing companies in over 60 countries. It includes extensive coverage of the United States. A detailed services index complements the package.

International Multi-level Marketing Reference Book and Resource Directory, by Jannette Tappan. (Norwood, MA: Communications by Design MLM, 1988.) Covers over 800 companies in the multi-level marketing industry, and suppliers or services and generic products to the industry.

International Shipping and Shipbuilding Directory. (London: Benn Publications, 1990.) This directory lists several thousand ship owners, managers, and shipping lines. Also lists container companies and services, building and repair firms, and suppliers of ships' machinery and equipment. Includes company names, addresses, telephone and telex numbers, and cable addresses. The directory lists major executives and agents of associated companies and data on the capacity of ships.

Kelly's Business Directory. (New York: International Publications Service, published annually.) Long considered the best directory for British companies, this publication also is international in scope. Alphabetically lists over 80,000 companies, followed by product or service listings, and geographical listings by country.

Kompass. (West Sussex, England: Reed Information Services Ltd., published annually.) This directory set provides listings of European, Asian/Pacific, and American companies. Countries covered include Australia, Hong Kong, Indonesia, India, Japan, Korea, Malaysia, Philippines, Singapore, Taiwan, Thailand, Australia, Israel, Poland, Portugal, Slovenia, Tunisia, Brazil, and Mexico, to name a few. The directories have a considerable reputation because of their long publishing record and the fact that they contain listings for companies impossible to find elsewhere. Over 20 different county directories are available, and most of the directories are published in the language of the featured country.

Major Business Organizations of Eastern Europe and the Commonwealth of Independent States. (London: Graham & Trotman, 1993.) Over 2,000 organizations in Eastern Europe and countries of the former Eastern Bloc are profiled. Included are government agencies as well as trade groups involved with manufacturing, foreign trade, and finance. Names, addresses, and telephone or telex numbers, contacts, services, and commodities traded are described.

Major Companies of Europe, 1993-94. (London: Graham & Trotman.) Over 4,000 of the largest companies in Europe are profiled, with standard directory information provided. A companion set is the *Medium Companies of Europe*, which covers 4,500 companies. The break-off point for medium industrial companies is anything with annual sales below $90 million.

Major Companies of the Arab World, 1993-94. (London: Graham & Trotman.) Another directory in the Major Companies series, this volume is particularly useful for its comprehensive inclusion of all Arab countries including, Lebanon, Iraq, etc. Most major companies are profiled and sales data is provided even for some of the private companies. Standard directory information is furnished for all companies, including key contacts and product or service descriptions.

Major Companies of the Far East and Australasia, 1993-94. (London: Graham & Trotman.) Published in 3 volumes, this set covers Southeast Asia, East Asia, Australia, and New Zealand. Basic directory information is provided for over 4,500 companies.

Marconi's International Register. (Larchmont, NY: Tele Cable, published annually.) This directory of foreign and international companies has been published for over 90 years. It contains basic information, including name, address, telex and telephone numbers, as well as product lines. Coverage of non-American and non-British companies is excellent.

Mexico Company Handbook. (Rio de Janeiro: IMF Editoria, 1993.) Arranged by major industries, this handbook provides public company information including background, officers, major stockholders, sales, markets, balance sheet, ratios, and other stock information. Also includes information on the economy, investments, and stock exchanges.

Moody's International Manual. (New York: Moody's Investors Service, Inc., published annually.) Since 1981 this directory service has been the first choice for researching major international public company information. Contained in four volumes, including an update volume, arrangement is geographical by country and includes company history, property, subsidiaries, directors, income/balance sheet, debt, and other stock information. Special features cover stock exchange indices, international stock splits, foreign consumer price indices, and import/export statistics.

Principal International Businesses. (London: Dun & Bradstreet International, Ltd., published annually.) Published yearly since 1974, this directory provides coverage of approximately 60,000 businesses in over 130 countries. Entries are similar to other Dun & Bradstreet directories, with name, address, telephone number, officers, industry groupings, sales, number of employees, and also indicators as to whether the company is involved with import/export. Additional access points let you research the company using an industry index (SIC) or by geographical area.

Trade Directories of the World. (Queens Village, NY: Croner Publications, published monthly.) Formerly *Croner's Reference Book for World Traders*, this directory contains the latest information on business and trade directories in the U.S. and foreign countries.

United States Importers and Exporters Directory. (Phillipsburg, NJ: Journal of Commerce, 1990.) Included are over 30,000 manufacturers with import and export interests. Provided are company names, addresses, telephone numbers, names of chief executives, markets served, products and services, brokers used, bank references, ports, and other information.

United States-Italy Trade Directory. (New York: Italy-American Chamber of Commerce, 1986.) Over 4,000 American importers of Italian commodities and a listing of Italian exporters' agents are given. Trade names, Italian manufacturers represented in the U.S., and over 700 American firms with business interests in Italy are listed. The guide describes income tax, exchange, taxation, and tariff regulations.

U.S.-Belgium Trade Directory. (New York: Belgium American Chamber of Commerce in the U.S., 1985.) This directory contains detailed facts about companies engaged in trade between the two countries. Also provides, guidelines for engaging in trade with Belgium.

U.S.-Mexico Trade Pages: Your Single Source for Transborder Business, by Kara Kent. (Washington, D.C.: The Global Source, 1994.) This is a book designed to answer most transborder questions. Lists trade fairs, research centers, consultants, marketing, legal and accounting firms as well as transportation specialists.

Venezuela Company Handbook. (Rio de Janeiro: IMF Editoria, 1993.) Arranged by major industries, this handbook provides public company information including background, officers, major stockholders, sales, markets, balance sheet ratios, and other stock information. Also includes information on the economy, investments and stock exchanges.

Worldscope Company Profiles. (New York: Worldscope/Disclosure Partners, published annually.) This extensive directory set (8 volumes) is similar in content to the CIFAR directories and is also an exclusive source of financial performance information on international companies and industries. Five of the volumes profile industrial companies and the other 3 volumes cover financial and service companies. Total company coverage is approximately 7,000 companies within 24 countries. The financial information is quite detailed with, on the average, 23 different ratio indicators per company.

Dictionaries

English-Spanish Banking Dictionary. (Madrid: Editorial Paraninfo SA, 1978.) A useful guide for Spanish business idioms. Arranged in two separate sections, one in English and one in Spanish. Terms are provided with concise definitions.

Harrap's French and English Business Dictionary. (Edinburgh: Chambers Harrap Publishers, Ltd., 1991.) This dictionary includes terms and expressions used in a wide variety of commercial contexts: banking, stock exchange, accountancy, insurance, commerce, and law. Inclusion is based on terms found in the standard business media sources; everyday non-commercial meanings are not included.

The International Business Dictionary and Reference, by Lewis A. Presner. (New York: John Wiley & Sons, 1991.) This dictionary is "one of a kind" in providing a truly comprehensive and accurate cross-disciplinary interpretation of the vocabulary of international business. Its unified alphabetical arrangement allows the user to locate business terms used in North America, Latin America, the Caribbean, Western Europe, Eastern Europe, the Middle East, Africa, and Asia. Terms are thoroughly defined within a business context, with descriptions sometimes involving several pages. Appendices include: Foreign Exchange Contracts Vocabulary, Foreign Exchange Risk Vocabulary, Uniform and Non-Uniform Terms of Trade: Incoterms and Non-Incoterms, International Organizations, International Law Vocabulary, and Selected Information Sources.

The International Development Dictionary, by Gerald Fry and Galen Martin. (Santa Barbara: ABC-CLIO, 1990.) A useful work that provides a basic grounding in the thought of international development. Not intended to be comprehensive, this guide provides coverage of key development thinkers, leaders, and practitioners. Basic development concepts are also discussed with arrangement in broad categories: economic, agricultural and rural, political, sociocultural, human resource, environmental, and technology transfer.

International Dictionary of Management, by H. Johannesen and G.T. Page. (East Brunswick, NJ: Nichols/GP Publishing, 1990.) With over 6,500 entries, this dictionary is comprehensive in its coverage of management terms used in primarily the U.S. and the U.K. The arrangement is dictionary style with numerous cross-references where warranted.

Japanese Business Dictionary, by Boye De Mente. (Rutland, VT: Charles E. Tuttle Company, Inc., 1991.) This dictionary is important for anyone involved in doing business with Japanese speaking people. In a very easy to use alphabetical arrangement, English business terms are translated and rendered in both standard Hepburn romanization as well as the author's own easily interpretable phonetic system.

Key Words in International Trade. (Paris: ICC Publishing, 1989.) This is a quick and easy to use glossary of key business terms in five languages: German, Spanish, French, Italian, and English. Words are arranged in spreadsheet format for instant referral.

Standard Dictionary of Advertising, Mass Media, and Marketing: English-German, by Wolfgang J. Koschnick. (New York: Walter de Gruyter, 1987.) A dictionary-style arrangement is employed, concentrating on industry terms. Translations are provided in German for the English terms.

Talking Business in French. (New York: Barron's, 1993.) This dictionary is one of Barron's Bilingual Business Guides. It provides both English to French and French to English access. Translated definitions are usually no more than one or two words. Other features of the guide include basic phrases; key words for specific industries; abbreviations, weights and measures; postal service; time zones; etc. A truly business-type travel guide. Other editions include: German, Italian, Japanese and Spanish.

Indexes

Predicasts F & S Index: International. (Cleveland, OH: Predicasts, Inc., published monthly with quarterly and annual cumulations.) This index is unmatched for locating information on companies or products and services worldwide. As with other Predicasts' indexes, this publication makes use of an enhanced SIC classification in arranging the article entries. Access is also provided by company name and by geographical area. The focus is primarily on trade literature and government economic reports.

274

Worldcasts. (Cleveland, OH: Predicasts Inc., published quarterly.) This service is similar to its companion *F & S Index: International* in that each is solely dedicated to international coverage and each makes use of an exclusive indexing arrangement. This latter service, however, provides coverage of primarily economic forecasting data, sometimes projecting beyond five years into the future. The economic events include standard indicators such as GNP, CPI, employment, factory demand, etc. Other events more specific to narrow industry segments are also included, with data drawn from key trade publications worldwide.

15

Research Foundations and Associations

OBJECTIVES: This chapter will provide you with an overview of the importance of foundations and associations for your business information research.

> **Introduction**
> **Foundations and Associations**
> **Other Sources**

After reading this chapter you should:
*Have an understanding of the nature of foundations and associations.
*Appreciate the unique areas of research that many of these groups support.
*Know how to conduct research by contacting these groups directly.

INTRODUCTION

Research foundations are generally nonprofit organizations established to collect, analyze, and disseminate information in a given field. Many foundations were created by philanthropists who left funds in trust for research, office facilities, and the personnel necessary for their operations. Additional funds are derived from subscriptions to journals and fees for books, pamphlets, and special studies. According to recent figures found in the *National Data Book of Foundations*, (New York: The Foundation Center) there are over 30,000 research foundations in the United States with total assets of $122 billion dollars.

Associations differ from foundations in that they are commonly founded by professional or trade groups who share a mutual interest in a given field. Typically they have as their goals self-education, professionalism, and an increased understanding of their field among their membership and the general public. To accomplish these goals they usually publish a journal, hold conferences, create educational programs for members and non-members, and publish related materials written by staff employees, members or other interested individuals. Current data reveals that there are over 22,000 associations in the United States, with the largest number concentrated in the areas of business, commerce, and trade.

Within this broad category of "associations" it is helpful to distinguish between those that have as their main goal the advancement of knowledge and those that are geared towards furthering their members' business needs. The former group includes such organizations as the American Management Association, the American Marketing Association, and the American Statistical Association. These are known as professional associations. The second group includes such organizations as the American Gas Association,

Direct Mail Marketing Association, and the Distilled Spirits Council Association of the U.S., Inc. The associations in this group are better known as trade associations.

Professional associations are aligned along the lines of the professions. It is likely that a profession may have several associations representing narrow specialties of its members or focusing on important subjects and special interests. Many of the larger professional associations also support a myriad of committees and task forces, which have the charge of developing professional standards, codes of ethics, public relations, and producing governmental and legislative issue papers.

A trade association is a voluntary, non-profit organization of business members, usually in one branch of industry. The primary objective of a trade association is to assist members with common problems in several of the following areas: accounting principles; business ethics; commercial research; industrial research; standardization; statistics; trade promotion; and relations with government, labor, and the general public.

Trade associations make significant contributions to our economy and the business world. They collect, organize and publish data in directories, fact books, newsletters, and journals, which are invaluable resources in their fields. In some cases, the existence of strong and powerful trade groups entices commercial publishers to produce periodicals aimed at membership, thereby adding to literature available for that field.

Both trade and professional associations are involved with lobbying government for their special interests that may or may not coincide with the interests of other such groups or the general public. This common governmental interaction also helps to stimulate the amount of information created to support a particular field or industry.

All such associations are sources of unique business information. Much of this information can be found in libraries, but you can obtain much more by contacting the proper foundation or association directly. Associations are generally cooperative and helpful in responding to requests for information. In fact, trade associations can often supply a great deal of information without charge.

Because of the large number of foundations and associations, they cannot all be listed in this text. Instead, several are described below, and publications are mentioned where available. The listing comprises both organizations that are in the mainstream of business as well as those that might be less well known but make a significant contribution to the world of business.

If you don't find what you are looking for in the following descriptions, examine the sources that follow at the end of the chapter under "Other

Sources'' for further listings. These sources should also provide current telephone numbers, addresses, membership totals, year founded and fax numbers to fill most of your research needs. The descriptions are arranged alphabetically by name.

FOUNDATIONS AND ASSOCIATIONS

Academy of International Business. This group has been in existence for over 30 years and specializes in international business education. In addition to providing a newsletter, a directory of members, and the *Journal of International Business Studies*, they sponsor an employment service and offer awards and grants for students in the field.

Administrative Management Society (AMS). One of the older, larger, and more respected management associations, this group includes a mixture of business owners, business faculty, and information system managers. They are heavily involved with publishing and produce monographs, salary surveys and other research reports. They also sponsor the Certified Administrative Manager (CAM) program.

Advertising Research Foundation. Since it was founded in 1936, the Advertising Research Foundation has been considered one of the leading associations for advertising and marketing facts and statistics. This association serves both advertising schools and the advertising trade. They maintain an extensive library and produce numerous publications, including the prestigious *Journal of Advertising Research*.

Aerospace Industries Association of America (AIA). In existence since 1919, this trade association is very powerful in its corporate membership and government involvement. Considered a leading source for aerospace information, AIA compiles most of the available statistics on the industry. Their annual publication, *Aerospace Facts and Figures* is regarded as the starting place for anyone researching this field.

AFL-CIO (American Federation of Labor and Congress of International Organizations). As the largest labor organization in U.S. history with over 14 million members, this organization maintains a sizable staff and is involved with all aspects of labor. Numerous committees and departments allow for subject specialization. Their library is an excellent starting place in pursuing labor research.

Agriculture Council of America. Comprised of larger farming cooperatives, agribusiness, and independent farmers, this trade association collects and disseminates facts and statistics about this industry. Publications, newsletters and research reports are available.

Air Conditioning Contractors of America. This is a typical trade association that has numerous committees, gears its activities towards its specific industry, maintains educational programs, provides research and information, and offers services to maintain and promote the livelihood of this industry.

Aluminum Association. This association consists of aluminum producers and manufacturers. It is the definitive source for information in this area. The association produces a commercially available electronic database, publishes several reports and journals, and produces the annual publication, *Aluminum Statistical Review*, a must for any research project on this subject.

American Accounting Association. The American Accounting Association is involved with accounting education and research. Members receive *The Accounting Review* and *Accounting Education News*. Several sections are available for membership activity including international accounting, auditing, and taxation. College accounting students are welcome as associate members.

American Apparel Manufacturers Association. This group coordinates industry activities of major apparel manufacturers in the nation through many committees, divisions, and councils. They publish directories of the industry as well as salary surveys, consumer information, and other technical aids.

American Assembly of Collegiate Schools of Business. This association provides accreditation for schools offering undergraduate and graduate educational programs. They publish newsletters, directories, and produce salary and other statistical surveys.

American Automobile Manufacturers Association of the United States. This group consists of automobile, bus, and truck manufacturers in the nation. They are primarily involved with researching and disseminating information about the performance of the industry, environmental issues, safety concerns, and governmental industry activities. They publish the important *Motor Vehicle Facts and Figures* and *World Motor Vehicle Data Book*. Both sources are a must for research within this industry.

American Bankers Association (ABA). The premier association for the banking industry, this organization encompasses both educators as well as practitioners. This is a major source for all types of banking and finance facts and statistics. Among other services, they provide course work and training through the "American Institute of Banking" and other programs, impact legislation, conduct conferences, and offer awards and fellowships. Their information services include maintaining a library for their 10,000 plus members, publishing several leading journals (including the *ABA Banking Journal*), and numerous newsletters and bulletins. The ABA *Banking Literature Index* is considered a key source for searching through banking periodical literature.

American Council of Life Insurance. This group consists of legal reserve life insurance companies authorized to do business in the U.S. There are also associate members whose business lies outside the U.S. Although this association produces numerous pamphlets, monographs, and other services, it is best known for its annual *Life Insurance Fact Book*. This work is an excellent source for current facts and statistics on the life insurance industry.

American Economic Association. Founded in 1885, this highly respected association includes members from both industry and education and pursues economic education and research. In addition to an electronic data base and several other services, it also is the publisher of the renowned *Journal of Economic Literature*, the *American Economic Review*, and the *Journal of Economic Perspectives*.

American Gas Association. This association provides services to over 4,000 companies ranging from individual operators to distributors, transporters to manufacturers. Some of the services include safety and awareness programs, research and marketing studies, operating procedures and standards, lobbying, as well as testing and certification. They produce publications spanning journals, newsletters, directories, reports, services, and data bases. Chief among these is the very useful annual guide *Gas Facts*.

American Hospital Association. Including both institutional and individual members, this association provides lobbying for its members and conducts many educational and public awareness programs. It also for collects and disseminates statistics on the industry and annually publishes *Hospital Statistics*. Another very important and invaluable publication is the annual *Guide to the Health Care Field*, the best source for obtaining operational data on hospitals and their executive staff.

American Hotel and Motel Association. This association provides research, public relations, and training for its members, who represent lodging chains and individual hotels and motels. Among its leading publications are *Directory of Hotel and Motel Systems* and the magazine *Lodging*.

American Institute of Certified Public Accountants. With over 280,000 members, this professional association of certified public accountants is the leading organization in its field. Heavily involved with licensing and certification, this group is instrumental in shaping the accounting profession. They publish many sources dealing with standards, taxation, examinations, etc. Among their more popular publications are *CPA Examinations, Journal of Accountancy*, and *Accountants' Index*. They feature publication catalogs, telephone hot lines, ordering services, and technical assistance.

American Management Association. With over 70,000 members, the AMA links the educational and business sectors through programs, publications, and conferences. It publishes several important journals, including *Compensation and Benefits Review, Management Review, Personnel,* and *Supervisory*

Management. The AMA has gained a considerable reputation for its extensive catalog of management books and monographs.

American Marketing Association. Supporting a broad mixture of marketing executives and educators, this industry group is a leader in promoting marketing education. With over 50,000 members, the association is involved with conferences, workshops, and student clubs. They also publish the leading journals in the field, including: *Journal of Health Care Marketing, Journal of Marketing, Journal of Marketing Research, Journal of Public Policy and Marketing,* and *Marketing Research.*

American Meat Institute. This trade association includes meat packers, wholesalers, and other meat processors. The group provides research, training, and legislative assistance for its members. Chief among its publications is the annual *Meat Facts.*

American National Standards Institute (ANSI). This association is important because it serves as the clearinghouse for other trade associations in the dissemination of standards. The institute provides ANSI certification for U.S. standards and represents the U.S. in foreign standards issues. Publications produced include the annual *Catalog of American National Standards.*

American Petroleum Institute. With many large multi-national companies as members, this trade group is responsible for influencing governmental decision making and providing public information about the oil industry. They publish many excellent information sources that are extremely useful for research in this area. Among their publications are catalogs, newsletters, journals, databases, fact books, and other statistical reports.

American Stock Exchange. The ASE is a securities market which includes several divisions and committees involved with day-to-day activities. Available publications include an annual report, a newsletter, and the annual *AMEX Fact Book.* The latter is invaluable for securities data analysis.

Association for Computing Machinery. One of the larger groups to study the development of information science, this association includes scientists, scholars, and lay people. In addition to providing awards and recognition of leaders in the field, ACM also publishes several journals, conference proceedings, and the annual *Guide to Computing Literature* (an index to books, reports and journal articles from many different computing information sources).

Association for University Business and Economic Research (AUBER). AUBER, as this association is more commonly known, is geared towards university economic research centers. In addition to functioning as a clearinghouse for economic ideas and information they publish directories, newsletters and bibliographies including *AUBER Bibliography.*

Chamber of Commerce of the United States. Publishers of the well-known magazine *Nation's Business*, this highly respected business group provides a voice for business across the nation through governmental relations and public information. It produces several television shows, has important committees charged with international business affairs, and provides other avenues of business advocacy.

Conference Board. This leading independent, nonprofit research institution has been active for decades in providing economic information to libraries and other centers of research around the world. It is famous for its *Economic Road Maps* and other monographs, newsletters, and statistical bulletins. Publications include *Across the Board, Consumer Attitudes and Buying Plans, Consumer Confidence Survey,* and the *International Economic Scoreboard.*

Direct Marketing Association. This is an important association because of its involvement with promoting this technique of sales. It provides assistance to its members in the form of research, training, and governmental relations. Publications include the *Direct Marketing Manual* and the *Fact Book on Direct Marketing.*

Distilled Spirits Council of the U.S., Inc. This trade association is instrumental in providing data to its members, governmental policy makers, and the general public.

Footwear Industries of America. FIA coordinates the collection and dissemination of statistics and facts for its members of footwear manufacturers, wholesalers, and retailers. Publications available include *Footwear Manual* and the *U.S. Footwear Industry Directory.*

Foundation Center. The Foundation Center is a national service organization supported primarily by foundations. It disseminates information to the public on philanthropic giving and provides valuable assistance to researchers in determining where to appropriately apply for funding. In addition to maintaining a national office and library, the center assists in developing satellite foundation and grantsmanship libraries around the country. It is known for numerous publications outlining the distribution of foundation funds, recipient profiles and geographical areas.

International Monetary Fund. The IMF was formed at the end of World War II by the leading countries who recognized that the destructive competition in trade and exchange rates of the 1930's had worsened the Depression throughout the world. International in scope, the IMF of today works to achieve monetary cooperation and to facilitate economic policies among all countries. The IMF also publishes several important international digests, including *Balance of Payments Statistics, Direction of Trade Statistics, International Financial Statistics Yearbook,* and *World Economic Outlook.*

Mail Advertising Service Association International. This trade association provides research for its members topics such as wage and salary surveys, financial ratios analysis, computer usage reports, and availability of mailing lists.

Manufacturers' Agents National Association. This trade association offers membership to manufacturer's representatives across a broad range of industries. It is well known for its *Agency Sales Magazine* and the heavily used *Membership Directory of Manufacturers' Sales Agencies.*

National Association of Home Builders of the U.S. The major responsibilities of this industry group are to collect and disseminate information, hold educational seminars, conduct research, provide public relations, and coordinate standards among its many members. Chief among the publications produced by the NAHB are *Builder Magazine, Housing Economics,* and *Housing Market Statistics.*

National Association of Securities Dealers (NASD). A quasi-governmental agency, the NASD acts on behalf of the U.S. Securities and Exchange Commission in regulating and enforcing rules that govern the nation's securities dealers. Publications include an annual report and several newsletters. They also produce the annual *NASDAQ Fact Book*, which is a good source for statistical data on the industry.

National Coal Association. This trade association operates on behalf of the business members who are involved with this market. The organization impacts legislation on behalf of its members as well as facilitating resolution of industry issues. They are responsible for producing many important industry publications, including the annuals *Coal Facts, Coal Transportation Statistics, Electric Utility Coal Stockpiles*, and *International Coal*. Journals produced by this group include *Coal News, International Coal Review*, and *Weekly Statistical Summary.*

National Restaurant Association. This association, with over 20,000 members, links together distributors, educators, manufacturers, and operators. It also provides key industry information sources such as *Foodservice Information Abstracts, Washington Weekly, Restaurant Industry Operations Report*, and *Restaurants USA.*

New York Stock Exchange. The NYSE is the world's oldest existing stock exchange. The exchange's reputation is unsurpassed, as the NYSE trades the elite, or blue-chip stocks as well as others that meet very strict entrance requirements. The exchange publishes numerous brochures and pamphlets that are useful for securities research. Chief among their publications is the *Fact Book*, an annual compilation since 1956.

Radio Advertising Bureau. The Bureau is an industry leader in the promotion of radio advertising for its member stations and others, such as schools and independent consultants. They publish many industry guides, including the annual *Radio Facts,* an excellent statistical guide to industry performance.

Robert Morris and Associates. This is the national association of bank loan and credit officers. Their reputation rests on their excellent service to members through research, educational programs, and mentoring. The association is also the publisher of the leading composite financial ratio source book, *Annual Statement Studies.* They also publish the *Journal of Commercial Bank Lending.*

Satellite Broadcasting and Communications Association. This trade group represents all segments of the home satellite television industry. The association is committed to expanding the usage of satellite technology.

Satellite Dealers Association. This non-profit trade group represents satellite dealers, servicers, and installers only. The intent of this group is to attain enough members from across the country to effectively present the views of its members to other segments of the industry.

United States League of Savings Institutions. This trade association is important to the savings industry for its sponsorship of a full array of membership services, including educational programs, advertising, governmental advising, research, operating procedures, and so on. Chief among their publications is the *Savings Institutions Sourcebook,* a key annual fact book of the industry's performance, and the monthly journal *Savings Institutions.*

OTHER SOURCES

Encyclopedia of Associations. (Detroit: Gale Research Inc., published annually). This is the standard bearer of association directories. The set covers international, national, regional, state, and local organizations. Entries typically include address, phone number, date association was founded, name of executive director, number of members, budget size, and a description of the association's activities. Information on publications, electronic data bases, and conventions is available where appropriate.

World Chamber of Commerce Directory. (Loveland, CO: World Chamber of Commerce Directory). This directory is very useful for making contacts with boards of trade throughout the world. Arranged alphabetically by geographical area, each entry includes president or manager, address, and phone number.

SECTION FOUR

USING WHAT YOU'VE LEARNED

16

Business Research and Reports

OBJECTIVES: This chapter will introduce you to the final product of much business research: the report. Specifically, you will be introduced to the following information.

Research and Business
Getting Started
- Developing Your Outline
- Organizing Your Sources

Two Common Types of Reports
- Informal Reports
- Formal Reports

Citations and Documentation
- Footnotes
- Endnotes
- In-Text Citations
- Choosing a Style
- An Explanation of Key Styles

Works Cited
Finishing the Report
Tips for Successful Report Writing
Research, Writing, and Style Resources

After reading this section, you should be able to:

*Organize and write a report on a business topic for either an academic or professional audience.

RESEARCH AND BUSINESS

Time and money spent on research in business are of little value unless the findings are properly communicated to the executives responsible for policy decisions. The research report must convey the research process; the research findings, the conclusions reached, and recommendations for applying these conclusions.

Often, such research is presented in report form. This chapter introduces the major elements of a business report.

Business people make decisions every day that require research. Take, for example, a manufacturer who must counter the advances of a competitor. To compete effectively, this manufacturer must know the history, makeup, uses, and limitations of the product of the rival firm. This information is gleaned through research.

Once a research topic has been defined, your job as a researcher is to get the facts. To do this, you must select a research strategy. The following chapter will assist you in evaluating the available sources.

GETTING STARTED

The best way to begin your research is by developing an outline that lists the major topics and subtopics within each section of a report. A well-planned outline contributes to the continuity of your discussion and demonstrates a logical sequence of the points covered. Good organization ensures a continued interest on the part of the reader. Without the framework of an outline writers inevitably wander in the treatment of the subject, and readers then have difficulty understanding the information. The following outline illustrates good planning and organization:

Retail Cooperatives

I.   The Nature of Retail Cooperatives
   A.   Introduction
      1.   Thesis statement
      2.   Definition of retail cooperatives
      3.   Efficiency in retail cooperatives
      4.   Buying power in retail cooperatives
      5.   Cost control measures
   B.   Other Types of Cooperative Groups
      1.   Informal buying groups
      2.   Cooperative chains, wholesale-sponsored
      3.   Retail cooperative development

II.   Merchandise Practices of Retail Cooperatives
   A.   Leadership
      1.   Strong dominating personality in control
      2.   Board of Directors or committee organization
   B.   The Buying Function
      1.   Corporate buyers
      2.   Resident buying agencies
   C.   Conclusion
      1.   Impact in the short run
      2.   Impact in the long run

Developing Your Outline

Business school students often wonder how they can possibly write an outline before they start their research. You may choose to start your library research before you have developed a full outline.

Consider using a database search [discussed in Chapters 6 and 7] to find ten to twenty periodical articles on the general topic you have selected. After you have read these articles, ask your professor for assistance if you still need help developing your complete outline. It is perfectly proper to modify the outline as you proceed with your research.

Organizing Your Sources

After preparing the outline, methodically check your business library for the materials available. Some research guides and style manuals suggest you prepare summary notes of library sources on index cards to use when writing your report. With the low cost of photocopies, we suggest that you copy the key information in the source so that any quotation you use as well as the citation can be developed from the photocopy. You might also make a copy of the publication and table of contents page so you have the volume number and other data clearly recorded. The database printout and a photocopy of the article provide all the data generally needed for your citation. Records of interviews with business people and observations to be used as supporting data must also be documented. In each case you should include the names, titles, places, and dates of the interviews and site visits.

Having gathered your sources and documentation, you can begin to analyze the information and write your report. Remember, you must interpret the findings in light of the purpose of the study, and your conclusions should avoid any bias. The limitations as well as the contributions of the research should be made clear so specific lines of action can be recommended.

TWO COMMON TYPES OF REPORTS

You should write your report with both the topic and the reader in mind. Either the informal or the formal report style are acceptable.

Informal Reports

An informal report is usually prepared for the general business executive who likes information with little detail. This report format de-emphasizes the research methods and emphasizes the results obtained and their relationship to the executive's specific concern. Complete accuracy is vital, and the practical implications of the findings must be made obvious. This format includes the following elements:

1. Title page, including credit to the authors and a date line.
2. Purpose - why the study was made.
3. Method - how the study was made, perhaps including the research techniques employed.

4. Chief findings of the research, in some detail, with well-organized page layouts, charts and graphs, and brief explanations.
5. Summary, conclusions, and recommendations.
6. Appendix, if needed, as a record and a reference for the reader.
7. Citations and documentation of sources and interviews.

Formal Reports

Sometimes research is used by executives to make decisions that will impact many people and cost many thousands of dollars. You will want to use a formal report style to describe this type of research. A more detailed outline of a comprehensive, formal report is as follows:

I. Introduction
    A. Title Page
        1. Subject of the paper
        2. For whom prepared
        3. By whom prepared
        4. Date of the work
    B. Letter of Transmittal
        1. Authority for the report
        2. Purposes and scope of the study
        3. Methods employed
        4. Acknowledgments
    C. Table of Contents
    D. Executive Summary

II. Body of the Report
    A. Purposes stated in detail
    B. Methods explained in detail
    C. Findings described and explained
    D. Summary of findings and conclusions
    E. Recommendations

III. Supporting Material and Appendices
    A. Statistical tables showing replies to questions and breakdowns by groups
    B. Distribution of your sample and comments on your statistical procedures
    C. Appendixes, containing exhibits of forms
    D. Works Cited or Bibliography

CITATIONS AND DOCUMENTATION

A citation or footnote provides the reader with the source of a particular piece of information. It serves to document and give credit to the original author or source. In addition, it also allows the reader to investigate the specific source cited.

Footnotes

When using footnotes, place an Arabic numeral raised one-half line above the rest of the type at the end of the statement to be documented. With this style, the footnote is placed at the bottom of the page. Footnotes are usually numbered consecutively throughout the report. If you use the footnote style, the first reference to a source should give complete information including the author, title of the work, place of publication, copyright date, and page reference. In subsequent references, only the important details are repeated. The footnote style prevailed into the late 1970's.

Endnotes

Common usage has progressed from footnotes to endnotes to in-text citation over the past ten to fifteen years. Many style manuals suggest the use of end-notes rather than footnotes to simplify the keying of the report. Endnotes, as the term implies, are placed at the end of the body of the report. Like a footnote, the citation itself is identified by an Arabic numeral placed at the end of the statement to be documented. The form of the endnote is also similar to a footnote, but it is placed at the end of the report. With either the footnote form or the endnote form, a bibliography [often referred to as "Works Cited"] is included. A bibliography lists the sources used in alphabetical order by author.

In-Text Citations

Currently, "in-text citation" has become the preferred form for identifying sources. In-text citation means that the writer cites the source within the text as it is referenced. The author and page number of the reference immediately follows the corresponding material. Just as there are many variations in the types of sources that can be referenced, so there are many variations in the manners of writing in-text citations. Consult a style manual for the form that will best serve you.

Choosing a Style

Different disciplines, even within the field of "business," use different styles for citations. Ask your librarian which journal is the key journal in your field of interest, and then evaluate the style used within that journal. Consider adopting that style of documentation for your work.

An Explanation of Key Styles

Three distinct "styles" have emerged in professional writing and college research reports. The style developed by the Modern Language Association is known as the "MLA" style and is primarily used in the Humanities, including college English courses. The style developed by the American Psychological Association is known as the "APA" style and is commonly used within the general social science fields including business. The third style is known as the "Chicago" style and is presented in a book entitled the *Chicago Manual of Style*. This style was developed at the University of Chicago many years ago. Full citations for the publications which detail each of these styles are included in the "Research, Writing, and Style Resources" section of this chapter.

The business researcher should examine another book, *A Manual for Writers of Term Papers, Theses, and Dissertations*, originally written by Kate L. Turabian, and now revised and expanded by Bonnie Birtwistle Honigsblum. This well-known and widely-used book presents concise format suggestions for both footnote and endnote entries as well as bibliographic entries and information to assist in developing a works cited section.

Kate L. Turabian was a dissertation secretary at the University of Chicago and developed her book in conformity with the *Chicago Manual of Style*. In fact, the fifth edition by Turabian was developed in 1987 as a result of the thirteenth edition of the *Chicago Manual of Style* published in 1982. The *Chicago Manual of Style* is also different from the MLA, APA, and Turabian books in that it contains additional extensive sections on the physical aspects of bookmaking, production, and printing.

WORKS CITED

Works Cited is a list of the sources used in a report. Some style manuals suggest a bibliography as an alternative to a works cited listing. The bibliography may include items not cited in the report. The works cited listing is placed at the end of the report before the index, if the report includes an index. Sources are arranged alphabetically according to the surname of the author, if available, otherwise by the name of the pamphlet, newspaper, or encyclopedia article that has no author. They conclude with publication data.

Examples of entries for a works cited section follow. These references will lead you to additional sources of business information. Creative researchers may make use of many traditional and non-traditional information sources to solve their research problems. Since different types of source materials require different forms in the works cited or bibliography, check the style manuals listed later in this chapter for additional information.

Consumer's Resource Handbook, Pueblo, CO: U.S. Office of Consumer Affairs, 1984.

Daniells, Lorna M. *Business Information Sources.* 3rd ed. Berkeley, CA: University of California Press, 1993.

Freed, Melvyn, and Virgil P. Diodato. *Business Information Desk Reference: Where to Find Answers to Business Questions.* New York: Macmillan, 1992.

Hawbaker, A. Craig, and Judith M. Nixon. *Industry and Company Information: Illustrated Search Strategy and Sources.* Library Research Guide Series, No. 10. Ann Arbor, MI: The Pierian Press, 1991.

Lavin, Michael R. *Business Information: How to Find It, How to Use It.* 2nd ed. Phoenix: The Oryx Press, 1992.

Strauss, Diane Wheeler. *Handbook of Business Information: A Guide for Librarians, Students, and Researchers.* Englewood, CO: Libraries Unlimited Inc., 1988.

Untener, Deborah, ed. *Consumer Sourcebook*, 9th ed. Detroit: Gale Research Inc., 1995.

Woy, James, ed. *Encyclopedia of Business Information Sources*, 10th ed. Detroit: Gale Research Inc., 1994.

FINISHING THE REPORT

Reports are normally keyed in a double-spaced format, especially more formal ones. Some reports may be single spaced. The report should be proofread at least twice, preferably by two different people. Collate the report carefully, making sure that the pages are in the correct sequence and facing the correct direction. The report can either be bound or unbound (if it contains only a few pages). Make this decision before you key the report so you can use appropriate margins. Information on margins, spacing, page numbering, and other format concerns can be found in the style manuals listed at the end of this chapter.

The finished report should be professional looking and should present the material in a business-like manner. The appearance should lend credit to the researcher. To ensure a professional look consider having the final report printed from a laser printer.

TIPS FOR SUCCESSFUL REPORT WRITING

The quality of your report will depend largely upon your research and writing strategy. The tips that follow reflect common concerns and questions raised by people involved in library research and report writing.

1. What you see is what you get. This is true for most things, but not for libraries. What you see is only a small part of what you can get. Libraries should be seen as resource centers rather than as collections of materials. The library staff can use library technology to assist you in locating materials in your particular library and obtain copies of articles and books from other libraries. Consider the library staff a key resource in determining your research options.

2. Start early and give yourself time to do a thorough job. Procrastination is something to be aware of and something to overcome. Very few people can do quality work when they place themselves under strict time constraints. Chances are you will need some sources from library collections other than the library you are using. Allow at least three weeks to receive the items you request. In some cases you will simply have to wait for another patron to return the book you need. In other cases, you may need to phone librarians at other libraries to check for a particular source. Give yourself time to assemble the needed materials.

3. Narrow your topic. Researchers sometimes broaden their topics to ensure they can find enough information to write a paper and meet their page requirements. Too often the result is that they never quite get focused. To solve a lack of focus, narrow the topic and concentrate your efforts on one aspect of that topic. This new aspect becomes the new topic. With a narrower, more defined topic, the focus of your research will be sharp.

4. Use of brackets versus highlighting in margins. Some people highlight their sources as they read and often end up with more text highlighted than not. Some highlighting makes further copying of the source material more difficult. Try marking the margins of the text with brackets as an alternative. If you really must highlight, make a copy of some highlighted text to ensure it is legible. If you cannot read the text because of the highlighting, find a lighter color such as a yellow or light green.

5. Paper and pencil versus word processing. Some people have still not taken the plunge into computerized word processing. Word processors, particularly those which use the point-and-click mouse technology, allow you to edit material more easily than you could with paper and pencil or a typewriter. With word processing software you can highlight an area of text, and "cut and paste" it to any other place in your report. You can call on a spell checker for assistance and even use a grammar checker if you choose. Try a few different word processor software packages before making a final choice.

6. Develop a research strategy. To do good research you must precisely define what it is that you are attempting to find. Successful researchers work with a well-developed plan for doing the research. If you need help in developing

this plan, ask a librarian for assistance. See Chapters 2 and 3 for further discussion of "research strategy."

7.   Evaluate report length. Some researchers may wonder how long their report should be. The answer to this question is really, "As long as it needs to be to present your ideas, findings and results." Part of the decision on length can be related to the need to develop believability. If you expect anyone to take an action suggested in your report, evaluate your research and report in terms of believability. Ask yourself if you have told the client enough to convince her or him that your research was credible and adequate, and that your conclusions follow from the research.

8.   Just get started. Researchers often face the dilemma, "I don't know where to begin writing my report." The best answer really is, "It doesn't really matter—just start writing." If you are using a word processor, you can rearrange your text so easily that it is much more important to write something than to expect what you write to be in final form. Very simply—write and revise.

RESEARCH, WRITING, AND STYLE RESOURCES

Alward, Edward C. *Research Paper: Step-by-Step*. Westhampton: Pine Island Press, 1991.

Brock, Susan L. *Writing Business Proposals and Reports*. Menlo Park, CA: Crisp Publications, Inc., 1992.

Cash, Phyllis. *How to Develop and Write a Research Paper*, 3rd ed. New York: Macmillan Publishing Company, 1995.

Chicago Manual of Style, 14th ed. Chicago: University of Chicago Press, 1993.

Coyle, William. *The Macmillan Guide to Writing Research Papers*. New York: Macmillan Publishing Company, 1990.

Dodd, Janet S., ed. *The ACS Style Guide: A Manual for Authors & Editors*. Washington: American Chemical Society, 1986.

Emory, C. William. *Business Research Methods*, 5th ed. Burr Ridge, IL: Richard D. Irwin, Inc., 1995.

Farrell, Thomas J. *Writing Business Research Papers: A Complete Guide*. Durham: Carolina Academic Press, 1991.

Gay, Lorraine R. *Research Methods for Business and Management*. New York: Macmillan Publishing Company, 1991.

Gibaldi, Joseph, *MLA Handbook for Writers of Research Papers*, 4th ed. New York: The Modern Language Association of America, 1995.

Gill, John. *Research Methods for Managers*. Bristol, U.K.: Taylor & Francis, Inc., 1991.

Hager, Peter J., and Scheiber, H.J. *Report Writing for Management Decisions*. New York: Macmillan Publishing Company, 1992.

Jankowicz, D. *Business Research Projects*, 2nd ed. New York: Chapman & Hall, 1995.

Klein, David H. and Klein, Jean H. *Write for Success: A Guide to Effective Technical & Professional Writing*. Dubuque: Kendall/Hunt Publishing Company, 1991.

Longyear, Marie. *The McGraw-Hill Style Manual*. New York: McGraw-Hill Inc, 1989.

Maniak, Angela J. *Audit Report Writing Manual*. Chicago: Bank Administration Institute, 1990.

Mort, Simon. *Professional Report Writing*. Brookfield, U.K.: Ashgate Publishing Company, 1992.

Oliver, Marvin E. *Writing Student Papers*. Cheney: High Impact Press, 1991.

Perry, Carol R. *The Fine Art of Technical Writing: Key Points to Help You Think Your Way Through Scientific or Technical Publications, Theses, Term Papers & Business Reports*. Hillsboro: Blue Heron Publishing, Inc., 1991.

Publication Manual of the American Psychological Association, 4th ed. Washington: American Psychological Association, 1994.

Rubens, Philip, ed. *Science and Technical Writing*. New York: Holt, Henry, & Company, Inc., 1992.

Sekaran, Uma. *Research Methods for Business: A Skill-Building Approach*, 2nd ed. New York: John Wiley and Sons, Inc., 1992.

Smith, Charles B. *A Guide to Business Research: Developing, Conducting & Writing Research Projects*, 2nd ed. Chicago: Nelson-Hall, Inc., 1995.

A Style Guide for Authors & Editors, 2nd ed. Cincinnati: South-Western Publishing Co., 1986.

Truitt, K.E. and Turner, John R. *Fundamentals of Researched Writing: How to Write a Research Paper and Come Out Alive*. Dubuque: Kendall/Hunt Publishing Company, 1991.

Turabian, Kate L. *A Manual for Writers of Term Papers, Theses, and Dissertations*, 6th ed. Chicago: University of Chicago Press, 1987.

U. S. Government Printing Office Staff. *Manual of Style*. Avenal: Outlet Book Co. Inc., 1988.

Varner, Iris I. *Contemporary Business Report Writing*, 2nd. rev. ed. Fort Worth: Dryden Press, 1991.

Walker, Melissa. *Writing Research Papers: A Norton Guide*, 3rd ed. New York: W. W. Norton & Company, 1993.

Zikmund, William G. *Business Research Methods*, 4th ed. Fort Worth: Dryden Press, 1994.

Subject Index

A lower-case "n" following a page number indicates only a brief mention in the text.

Author/Title Index

A lower-case "n" following a page number indicates only a brief mention in the text.

Organization and Association Index